"Savvy, funny, and chock-full of great information, *I ♥ Female Orgasm*
is a treasure trove for all of us."
—JUDY NORSIGIAN and HEATHER STEPHENSON,
coauthors of *Our Bodies, Ourselves*

"Women should put [*I ♥ Female Orgasm*] on their 'gotta-have' list
and memorize it."
—SUE JOHANSON, RN, host of *Talk Sex with Sue*

"*I ♥ Female Orgasm* will take you from zero to O in no time flat! Reading it
feels like having a slumber party with Dorian and Marshall, the cool friends
who fill you in on everything sex ed failed to teach you."
—TASHA WALSTON, founder of VaginaPagina.com

"*I ♥ Female Orgasm* will help singles and couples learn the best way to enjoy
each other and themselves during foreplay and lovemaking."
—DR. RUTH WESTHEIMER, sex therapist and author of *Ask Dr. Ruth*

"After a lifetime of celebrating and teaching about women's sexuality and
orgasms, I'm thrilled to see Dorian and Marshall carry forward the message
of positive sexuality for the next generation of women and men!"
—BETTY DODSON, PhD, author of *Sex for One* and *Orgasms for Two*

"One of the most sex-positive, cheerful, and fun sex guides that I've seen in a
long time. An amazing book!"
—CHARLIE GLICKMAN, PhD, Education Program Manager, Good Vibrations

"Oh, yeah! Finally a book on female orgasm I can refer my clients to.
I ♥ Female Orgasm hits all the right buttons."
—CHRIS FARIELLO, PhD, LMFT, Director, Institute for Sex Therapy

"Drawing on the authors' rich knowledge of sexuality and their willingness
to learn from their audiences, *I ♥ Female Orgasm* has just the right mix of
anecdotes, tips, expert advice, candor, and humor."
—BILL TAVERNER, Cofounding Editor, *American Journal of Sexuality Education*

"While drug companies continue to try but fail to find a Viagra for women,
Dorian Solot and Marshall Miller have written a book that offers more to
help women experience sexual pleasure than any pill is ever likely to."
—AMY ALLINA, Program and Policy Director,
National Women's Health Network

DORIAN SOLOT
and
MARSHALL MILLER

are nationally known sex educators who specialize in teaching about female orgasm. Over the last eight years, they've presented over 450 funny, educational programs at colleges, conferences, and adult education centers about female orgasm, healthy sexuality, safer sex, and gay, lesbian, bisexual, transgender issues. Graduates of Brown University, Dorian and Marshall have appeared on ABC, NBC, CBS, CNN, *The O'Reilly Factor*, and National Public Radio, and in *The New York Times, USA Today, Time, Men's Health, Cosmo*, and hundreds of other newspapers, radio, and television shows. They live in Albany, NY and can be contacted at www.ilovefemaleorgasm.com.

DORIAN SOLOT & MARSHALL MILLER

ILLUSTRATIONS BY SHIRLEY CHIANG

I ♥ FEMALE ORGASM®

AN EXTRAORDINARY ORGASM GUIDE

Da Capo
∞
LIFE
LONG

A MEMBER OF THE PERSEUS BOOKS GROUP

"Absolut Impotence." Reprinted by permission of Adbusters Media Foundation.
External female anatomy illustration. © Cary Bell. Courtesy of Cary Bell.
Hitachi Magic Wand Household Electric Massager instruction booklet excerpts. Reprinted by permission of Hitachi America, Ltd.
"First National Masturbate-a-Thon" brochure excerpts. Used with permission from Good Vibrations® 2006.
"The Clitoris" photograph. © Kim Sallaway. Reprinted by permission of Kim Sallaway.
"Top Ten Safest Condoms" data. © 2005 by Consumers Union of U.S., Inc. Yonkers, NY 10703-1057, A nonprofit organization. Reprinted with permission for the February 2005 issue of Consumer Reports® for educational purposes only. No commercial use or reproduction permitted. www.consumerreports.org.

Designed by Pauline Neuwirth, Neuwirth & Associates, Inc.
Set in 10.5 point Granjon by the Perseus Books Group

Cataloging-in-Publication data for this book is available from the Library of Congress.

ISBN: 978-1-56924-276-6

Published by Da Capo Press
A Member of the Perseus Books Group
www.dacapopress.com

Da Capo Press books are available at special discounts for bulk purchases in the U.S. by corporations, institutions, and other organizations. For more information, please contact the Special Markets Department at the Perseus Books Group, 2300 Chestnut Street, Suite 200, Philadelphia, PA, 19103, or call (800) 810-4145, extension 5000, or e-mail special.markets@perseusbooks.com.

20 19 18 17 16 15 14 13

contents

I ♥
FEMALE
ORGASM®

Female Orgasms:
what's not to love?

The most common response we get from women and men who see our I ♥ Female Orgasm T-shirts, buttons, and posters is, "Me, too!"

Maybe you've picked up this book because you're a fan of female orgasms—your own, your partner's, or all women's everywhere. Perhaps you're a woman hoping to learn how to have your first orgasm, how to have multiple orgasms, how to make your G-spot sizzle, or how to come during intercourse. Or maybe you're hoping to become the kind of husband, boyfriend, or partner women brag to each other about. Whatever your gender; whether you're straight, lesbian, or bisexual; single, partnered, or married; you've come to the right place. Packed with advice, ideas, and information, this book is all about the O.

As independent, self-employed sex educators, we travel the country educating audiences about this topic. We've learned there's no such thing as a place where female orgasm isn't popular: From cheering crowds in rural Arkansas to the heart of Manhattan to the New Mexico desert, the enthusiasm is the same. Our work has brought us to the mountains of Maine a half-dozen times, and we've flown through the Indianapolis airport twice as many. We've learned how to score the best seats on an airplane, we can mend a broken suitcase wheel, and we've mastered the technique of convincing hotel clerks to bake another batch of complimentary chocolate chip cookies.

As a couple traveling together (yes, we have both professional *and* personal experience with this subject), we occasionally pique the interest of fellow travelers. We travel with as much luggage as the airlines allow, so people sometimes ask us if we're heading on an extended vacation. Little do they know that our suitcases are crammed with sex education supplies and merchandise to sell at the next speaking engagement. When the airport security screeners decide they need to search a suitcase by hand, we stand nearby, never sure what kind of reaction we'll get. When one Transportation Security Administration official cracked a smile at the contents of our bag, Dorian graciously offered him an I ♥ Female Orgasm button. "This will have to be confiscated, too," he chuckled, helping himself to a second pin. "For my girlfriend," he added. "Of course," Marshall said.

Moments like this are one of the reasons we love our jobs. But our passion about our work reaches far beyond fun buttons and cute slogans. We've seen how helping women become knowledgeable about and comfortable with their own bodies can transform their daily experience—and, as Dorian discovered, can even save their lives.

dorian's story

WHEN I WAS twenty-six years old, I was diagnosed with breast cancer. I didn't have a family history or a single risk factor for the disease (in fact, a doctor later told me my statistical risk of getting breast cancer was *below* average). My cancer wasn't diagnosed by mammogram; women in their twenties don't get routine mammograms. It wasn't discovered through breast self-exam; like many women, I knew I should do them, but generally forgot. It wasn't discovered by my gynecologist, who had examined me just a month earlier and declared all was well. Instead, I noticed the lump myself, lying in bed one night and stretching, then absent-mindedly running a hand down my arm and across my chest. I wasn't too worried, because I knew that most young women's breast lumps turn out to be nothing. I ate healthy foods, I didn't smoke, I had a great relationship with Marshall; things were going so well in my life that my little lump didn't concern me in the least.

As luck would have it, I had an appointment with my doctor a month later, and I mentioned the lump to her. After examining it, she said, "You know, Dorian, I think it's probably nothing, but I'm not 100 percent sure; let's have some tests done." Still utterly unconcerned, I met with a breast surgeon for an ultrasound and biopsy.

A few days later, the surgeon left a message asking me to call her back. I did, giving the receptionist my name, and she put me on hold for the doctor. Minutes passed as I watched the January snow fall outside my window. The receptionist came back on and said, "I'm so sorry to keep you waiting, Dorian; I know the doctor really wants to talk to you."

At this point my memory switches to slow motion, like the moments before a car accident when you can see the impact coming but can't do anything to prevent it. I knew the doctor wouldn't feel so urgently about talking to me if the news were good. When she told me my lump was breast cancer, I was flabbergasted. I called Marshall, and he left work early. I picked him up at the commuter train station near our apartment. While snow fell around the car, we put our arms around each other in our puffy winter parkas, so thick we couldn't feel the bodies beneath, and we sobbed.

It's an understatement to say that being diagnosed with cancer is terrifying. It changes your life forever. When I look back, one conclusion resurfaces over and over: Thank God I hadn't internalized the messages women are bombarded with that it's bad or dirty to touch your own body. I particularly thank my parents for raising me to be comfortable in my body. I found my cancer early because I touched my own body without even thinking about it, and because I'd done the same thing enough times before that I noticed a very small change in my breast. If I hadn't, who knows how many weeks, months, or even years might have gone by until someone noticed I had cancer in my breast—and if I'd still be alive today.

On average, young women's breast cancers are diagnosed far later than older women's—and as a result the death rate is far higher—in part because the cancers typically go unnoticed for so long. Helping women make peace with our bodies and our sexuality isn't just an incidental nicety—in some cases, it can be lifesaving. Seven years after my diagnosis, I'm in remission and I'm doing great. While no breast cancer survivor can ever know what the future holds, I feel very, very lucky.

Surviving cancer fuels my passion for educating about women's sexuality. But it was an earlier experience—learning how to have an orgasm—that first sparked my interest. That didn't happen until shortly after my twentieth birthday.

I was a kid who didn't masturbate growing up. I knew what masturbation was, and my parents were the liberal types who clearly communicated that touching yourself was okay as long as you were in private (not in the sandbox!). But my limited explorations didn't impress me enough to continue, so I led a happy little-kid existence without masturbation. Didn't do it, didn't think about it, didn't wonder if other kids were doing it.

The years went by. My mom is a regular reader of the advice column Dear Abby, and when I was a teenager, she dutifully mailed $2 and a self-addressed stamped envelope for a copy of Abby's booklet *What Every Teen Should Know*. The booklet was full of advice on subjects like dating, drinking, smoking, and other topics of interest to the teenage set, and when I read through the copy my mom gave me, it all seemed quite sensible.

One section worried me, though: the part about masturbation. On this subject, Abby said, "This will be the shortest chapter in the booklet. Why? It is normal. Every healthy, normal person masturbates."

My adult self applauds Dear Abby for sending such an unambiguously positive message about masturbation. But sitting on my bed in my pink-flowered bedroom, the teenage me read and reread that sentence, "Every healthy, normal person masturbates." I knew that Abby's advice track record was stellar. If she said that every healthy, *normal* person masturbates, and I never did, I could come to only one conclusion: There must be something very, very wrong with me.

Even with this new concern, I didn't try masturbating; my sexual urges and impulses didn't truly blossom for a few more years. Since my late-blooming self wasn't touching herself, and my high school romantic life was close to nonexistent, I certainly wasn't having orgasms.

A few years later, I went away to college. At Brown University, where Marshall and I met, there was a dean who gave an annual presentation on masturbation; it was something of a tradition. My sophomore year, I saw a poster on a bulletin board about the upcoming program and thought to myself, "I think I need to go to that." The dean's talk fascinated me, and at the end, I left with the resource sheet she had distributed.

Afterward, I walked right to the campus bookstore and plunked down $5.99 to buy the only one of the books on the dean's resource list that was on the shelf that day. Over the next few months I began to do the exercises in the book, and later that semester, I had my first orgasm. It was the best $5.99 I've ever spent!

As you might imagine, I was thrilled. Ecstatic! And amazed that I was twenty years old before I discovered that my body could do this incredible thing. I couldn't believe it had been so easy to learn. Intrigued, I set out to learn everything I could about female orgasm, whiling away hours in the university library reading every journal article on the subject that I could locate. I started writing about what I was learning—first papers for classes, then articles for a wider audience. I pursued training as a sex educator while I was a student, and when I started dating Marshall, who was also studying sexuality academically, it seemed only natural that we'd continue the learning process together. Soon we began teaching sexuality workshops.

I've since learned that my experience wasn't particularly unusual. (I've even written to Dear Abby to suggest a revision of her booklet, but the most recent edition still contains the paragraph that so worried me as a teenager.) Although most boys figure out how to bring themselves to orgasm by age thirteen, half of girls don't have their first orgasms until their late teens, twenties, or beyond. Teenage girls widely agree that they get the message loud and clear that masturbation is something boys do, but girls don't, can't, or shouldn't. The cultural focus on intercourse tells young women to expect they'll begin to experience sexual pleasure once they have sex with a man (whether or not they're even interested in sex with men). Nearly all teen boys, on the other hand, experience sexual pleasure long before they get their hands—or other body parts—into a partner's pants.

Despite the massive advances in women's equality, young women's sexuality is stuck in a surprising paradox. Young women are sold provocative clothes but aren't taught where to find their own clitoris. Many girls give their boyfriends oral sex, but are too uncomfortable with their own bodies to allow the guys to return the favor. It's still a radical act to say that women need and deserve access to information about their own *sexual pleasure*—not just about the risks and negative consequences of sex.

marshall's story

WE LEARNED ABOUT female sexuality in my junior high and high school sex education classes. What did we learn about? Fallopian tubes! I suspect that like me, nearly every American can visualize the diagram of fallopian tubes, two symmetrical little egg tubes curving downward. But you know, if we never learned about fallopian tubes—if we never knew they existed—we'd be fine. Nothing bad would happen.

Yet the clitoris, an organ far more important to most people's future lives, was always mysteriously missing from those sex ed diagrams. I can only imagine how life might be different if the image burned into our brains forevermore were not the fallopian tubes, but the location of the clitoris. Now *that* would be useful! The problems with the way sex ed is taught in most high schools really hit home for me when I saw my friends taking driver's ed. Driver's ed is an eminently practical class, complete with those cars with DANGER: STUDENT DRIVER signs on the roof. In driver's ed, they teach you how to drive.

Sometimes I'd think about what it would be like if driver's ed were taught the way sex ed is. You would show up in the classroom (there would definitely *not* be a student driver car), and the teacher would say, "Welcome to driver's ed. You need to know that driving is very, *very* dangerous. You could die! So don't drive. Just don't do it—until you're married. If you absolutely *insist* on driving, wear a seatbelt." After this, class would be dismissed and your driver's education would be considered complete. But you'd never actually learn how to drive a car: where to find the gas pedal, how to turn on the headlights, or even how to back it out of a driveway.

Even as a teenager, it was glaringly obvious to me that I wasn't the only one hungry for accurate information about sex. As a writer for my college newspaper, I volunteered to cover any event on campus relating to sexuality: workshops on body image; rallies against sexual assault; panels on gay, lesbian, bisexual, transgender (GLBT) issues. Halfway through college, the university announced a new interdisciplinary major, Sexuality and Society, and I signed right up. Soon I was hired to write an online sex column for a website run by Barnes & Noble. The more I studied and wrote about sex, the more people shared stories of their own

I ♥ FEMALE ORGASM

experiences with me and asked me questions. I was blown away by the incredible diversity of people's sexual thoughts, feelings, and experiences.

When Dorian and I started dating, learning became a joint project since she, too, had training as a sex educator. We'd attend sexuality conferences together and buy each other books to discuss. Little by little, we started writing articles together, facilitating support groups, and giving workshops at conferences and adult education centers about relationships, sex, and GLBT issues. For six years after college I managed HIV prevention programs at a busy community health center in Boston, where I founded a safer sex educator team, training volunteers to talk to people in the city's bars and clubs about reducing their sexual risks.

Before long, Dorian and I started fielding requests from college students who'd heard us at conferences and wanted to bring us to speak at their universities, both together and separately. Dorian offered an educational program on female orgasm for the first time at Vassar College in 1999. It was an instant success: a big crowd of students laughing and sharing their questions and stories, with rave reviews afterward. Wanting the program to be a safe and comfortable space for women to talk about sex, Dorian and the student organizers at Vassar advertised the event as women only. Guys were not allowed in the door. I was not invited.

That's not to say male students didn't show up. Several asked respectfully, "Would it be okay if I just sat in the back and listened?" One, Dorian reported, knocked on the door partway through the program to request special permission to come in. "You don't understand," he said to Dorian quietly. "I *really* need this information." The men were politely turned away. After the program, the Vassar women hung out to chat with Dorian. One group said it had been so great that they wished their boyfriends had been in the room. "They really need this information," one woman mused thoughtfully, not knowing that earlier, a male student had said exactly the same words.

Dorian presented the program alone a few more times with similar experiences. She'd come home afterward and fill me on what had happened, including what the female attendees and male would-be attendees had said about wanting guys to be included. Dorian was concerned about losing the warm, all-female vibe, but increasingly it didn't feel right to us to exclude the guys. We decided that as an experiment, next time we'd try teaching men and women about female orgasm together. We taught all our other sex education programs together, so why should this be any different? The co-ed program was a success from the very first: The guys were eager to learn and honored to be there, and many women were happy to see that men cared. At a typical female orgasm speaking engagement these days, whether at a conference, an adult education seminar, or a college, our audiences are at least one-third male.

My role as copilot of our female orgasm programs has evolved over the past eight years. At first, I approached the subject as if men's sexuality were simple and women's complex. My role was to help men understand the mysteries of female sexuality. Over time, as I had conversations with and answered the questions of thousands of guys who attended our programs, I developed a renewed respect for the fact that men face equally complex sexuality issues. Like women, surprising numbers of men talked about their challenges having an orgasm or coming too soon, their concerns about body image, their worries that they weren't doing a good enough job in bed. Although orgasms may come more easily to most men than to most women, guys have their challenges, too. In the chapters ahead, Dorian and I share what we've learned about what men need and want to understand about women's orgasms—and how male sexuality can fit into the picture.

this book is for you (yes, you)

WE'VE WRITTEN THIS book for female orgasm connoisseurs, beginners, and every-one in between. It's for people of diverse genders and sexual orientations—anyone with an interest in women's sexuality. We'll give tips on oral sex, anal sex, and inter-course, and you'll also get to hear from the nearly 2,000 people who answered our survey (more on that below). We've tried to cover everything women might want to know about their own orgasms, from G-spots to vibrators to learning how to have an orgasm. We've devoted a chapter to the experiences of lesbian and bisex-ual women, and another to the issues guys face. We give the skinny on everything from faking it to what women really think about penis size to advanced trou-bleshooting for when your body isn't responding the way you want it to.

These pages are relevant for readers choosing abstinence and those who haven't yet had partnered sex. Plenty of virgins and people who are abstinent still have orgasms, or want to. Learning about sex doesn't mean you'll rush right out to practice. But being well-informed means you're more likely to make safe, healthy choices, and be comfortable enough to communicate what you want and don't want, whenever the time is right for you.

Some people who hear us mention female orgasm ask, "How do you define female?" As allies to the transgender, genderqueer, and intersex communities, we understand that gender is more complex than a simple male-female dichotomy. We also know that most people are raised within this system, and that a combination of biology and socialization powerfully affects how people experience their own sexuality. Because the English language doesn't yet have widely understood words to make it easy to discuss gender diversity, this book uses words like "women" and "she." If your body or your life doesn't fit neatly into the language we use, we ask you to bear with us and make the substitutions needed so our words make sense for you.

These days, we speak about female orgasm primarily to audiences of college students, but also to twentysomethings, thirtysomethings, and above (we've even had a few audience members in their eighties). We've written this book with the same diverse audience of adults in mind. The book occasionally uses the words "girls" and "boys," since that's the language many college students and young adults use to describe themselves.

We've written a book about female sexual pleasure, not an encyclopedia of sexuality. As a result, there are plenty of sex topics we don't address: no techniques for how to give great blowjobs, no detailed discussion of male masturbation or prostate massage. When we use the word "men" in this book, we're generally referring to heterosexual and bisexual men interested in pleasing a current or future female partner. (We don't expect too many gay male readers, though we've certainly had more than a few in our audiences who wanted to learn about the subject without getting "up close and personal.") A few topics that are important to female orgasm for a small percentage of people, like tantric sex and sadomasochism, we touch on only briefly. We've chosen not to tackle academic topics like the possible evolutionary basis for female orgasm. Luckily for those of you interested in exploring these paths, there are dozens of excellent, comprehensive books on all these subjects.

where we get our information

THE FOLLOWING PAGES contain the wisdom distilled from eight years of teaching about this subject, plus many more years of learning from the sexuality trainings, workshops, conferences, and academic classes we've both attended. Our bookshelves and file cabinets are crammed with books and academic journal articles on the subject.

We didn't stop there, because we believe individual experiences are as relevant as what the "experts" say. Many times we've stood at the front of some room and taught some fact out of a book, "What happens is X, followed by Y," only to have one audience member say, "For me, it's always Y before X," while another volunteers, "Really? I love X, but it usually just ends there for me," and a third adds, "My experience is that Y only comes after ABC." We've learned an enormous amount from our audiences, and from the many informal, sometimes very personal, conversations we've had with others about this topic. It's humbling to be reminded of the sheer diversity of sexual experiences, and in turn to describe the range of possibilities to others.

This book also reaps the benefits of the insights of the 1,956 people who filled out our detailed online survey. We'd read the major U.S. sexuality surveys published in the last century, from Masters and Johnson to *The Hite Report* to the 1994 "Sex in America" study, but we wanted to update the picture to include the perspective of a new century and a new generation. Our survey asked over 125 questions, some on topics like piercings, porn, female ejaculation, and sex toys that received little, if any, attention in most past national surveys. (Alfred Kinsey's 1940s research didn't ask his subjects whether genital piercings improved their sex lives!) We're immensely grateful to each person who took the time to share his or her thoughts and experiences with us.

Our survey respondents were female, male, and transgender, representing forty-five states (plus a handful from Canada and other countries outside the United States). Because our original mailing list came from attendees of our educational programs, the majority were college-age and twentysomething, but there were plenty of older folks, as well—our oldest respondent was sixty-eight. We encouraged survey-takers to spread the word, and in the end, two-fifths of the respondents had never attended one of our programs. While our sample is certainly not demographically representative, we were struck by the diversity and often startling honesty of the participants. The survey data is reflected throughout the book in people's own words (italicized quotes), in statistics (which we checked against other research studies when these were available), and in our advice. Thanks to this rich source of information, what you'll find in the pages ahead isn't just our opinion or advice from some scientist in a research laboratory. It's reality-tested against the experiences of nearly 2,000 people like you.

beyond the big O

ALTHOUGH IT MAY sound more than a little ironic coming from the authors of this book, if you think sex is just about orgasms, you're missing out. Here's the thing: Orgasms—the female variety and every other flavor—are really, *really* fun. They feel great; in fact, they're likely to be one of the most pleasurable physical sensations you'll ever experience. For many people, they rank way up there as emotional and spiritual experiences, too.

But orgasms aren't the only point of sex. Get too obsessed with orgasms, and you can miss out on a lot of other things: The sensations of touching and being touched. The experience of riding the roller coaster of arousal with its teasing climb and unexpected surges. The quieter joy of intimacy. As the best lovers know, you can have great sex without an orgasm at all.

We've seen orgasm-obsession lead people astray. Often this happens when a couple has a single sexual experience in which an expected orgasm didn't happen: a guy lost an erection for no reason whatsoever, or a woman couldn't come through oral sex, even though that had always worked before. Some turn to us in a moment of panic. Does she still find me sexy? Does he still love me? What's wrong with me, with her, with him, with us? The greater the panic, the more tension the next time they have sex. The more tense they are, the less chance of future orgasms. The downward spiral begins.

That's why each individual orgasm isn't the point. If you have an orgasm on a given night, great! If not, laugh. Or sigh. It's not a big deal, and the journey can be as sweet as the destination. There's too much fun, pleasure, and intimacy to be had—by yourself or with someone else—to spend a lot of energy worrying about any individual orgasm.

With that in mind, read this book not only for advice about how to reach the orgasmic finish line, but also about how to enjoy good sex. Listen to your own body, relax, and have fun, and you won't be disappointed.

Last but not least, if anything we say contradicts the naked person in your bed, always believe the naked person. Each person knows his or her own body better than we possibly could.

The Lowdown on the Big O

TOP TEN REASONS TO HAVE AN ORGASM

1. It feels great.
2. It's free.
3. It's legal.
4. It reduces stress.
5. It burns calories.
6. It helps you fall asleep.
7. It releases tension.
8. It can help relieve menstrual cramps and headaches.
9. It's available to you whether you have a partner or not.
10. Why not?!?

BONUS: There's nothing else quite like it.

what is a female orgasm, anyway?

ONCE YOU STRIP away the romance and openmouthed shrieks of pleasure (or the silent, blissful tremor of a quieter orgasm), a female orgasm is just a series of involuntary muscular contractions. Unlike the contractions of a hacking cough or a series of sit-ups, orgasmic contractions feel great. You can't control how an orgasm feels, just as you can't exactly control the sensation of a sneeze. (Let us guess: You, too, had that kids' book about sexuality that describes an orgasm as being like a sneeze? If so, we bet you were pleasantly surprised when your first orgasm felt nothing like a sneeze!) During arousal, a woman's bloodstream is spiked with pleasurable hormones, and at the moment of orgasm even more flood in. It's your body's best natural high.

During an orgasm, women can often feel the muscles contract in their vagina, uterus, and anus, and sometimes in other parts of their body, like their hands and feet. Some women describe a sensation like waves of warmth washing over their genitals or over their whole body; some say it feels like lightning bolts of electricity. A woman may be quite still and quiet while she comes, or she may move her body a lot.

I feel warm. My body stiffens and, with a particularly strong orgasm, my face tingles and my legs stop working.

My breath catches, I either can't make a sound, or I'm stifling a scream (thin walls in my apartment complex). My entire body goes rigid, my toes curl, my fingers clutch at whatever happens to be handy, and I shudder. I generally can't move.

It's like this unbelievable, almost unbearable buildup of tension and almost too much pleasure till I just feel like my whole body is struggling and squirming for some sort of release. And then suddenly it's like something just breaks free and I feel tingles all over and sort of an electric buzz. Then I just feel calm and relaxed.

Although being highly sexually aroused is extremely pleasurable in its own right, an orgasm is (usually) a short period where the intensity of pleasurable sensation is much higher than in the arousal period just before. Most female orgasms last three to fifteen seconds, although it's possible for them to last a minute or more. There are big, strong, wowwowwowWOW! orgasms, barely noticeable ones, and everything in between. Orgasms vary from woman to woman and from orgasm to orgasm. Each orgasm is unique—like a snowflake!

It feels so good I forget about everything else in the world for a few seconds. It just feels like being alive, with every cell vibrating.

I used to call my orgasms mini-O's because I thought orgasms were going to be better, more body-shaking, if you know what I mean. But then I came to accept the fact that this is it. But I'm learning to enjoy it more, so it's okay.

My body starts tingling, I get a fluttering in my stomach and then I feel like I have to pee really bad. Then it's like a wave comes over me, like all my muscles become relaxed.

An orgasm can feel almost spiritual, complete, like I'm one with my partner.

First it feels like lightning shoots throughout my body, and then if stimulation is continued, all the energy is sent to my genitals and then released at the same moment.

"coming" versus "having an orgasm"

A LOT OF people wonder if there's a difference between a woman *coming* and *having an orgasm*. In fact, the terms are interchangeable. The confusion is probably because the slang word for men's semen is "come" (sometimes spelled cum), so people figure that "coming" means ejaculating. Then they're not sure if a female orgasm—the non-ejaculatory kind—is also called "coming," or if "coming" only refers to female ejaculation (more on female ejaculation in chapter 6).

Banish the confusion. When a woman cries out, "I'm coming!" it means she's having an orgasm—and if she's having an orgasm, she's coming! Female ejaculation has nothing to do with the phrase.

Not sure if you've had an orgasm? Check out "Not Sure" on page 64.

the almighty clitoris

YOU PROBABLY ALREADY know that for most women, the clitoris (pronounced KLIT-eh-rus or kli-TOR-es—either way is correct) is the primary sex organ.

hold the morphine, give me an orgasm

RESEARCHERS WHO STUDY women having orgasms in laboratories find that a woman's sensitivity to pain is dramatically reduced when she's aroused, and even lower when she's coming. Several studies have first determined how much pressure women found painful under normal circumstances (for instance, by pressing on a woman's finger). When the same women were sexually aroused, these studies found, they could comfortably experience significantly more pressure before they said it was too painful. During orgasm, the pressure could be far more intense (more than twice as much in some cases) before they found it too much to tolerate.

It's not just that orgasms distract women from pain, either, because other distracting activities don't have the same pain-relieving results. MRIs show that orgasms release endorphins and naturally-occurring steroids that temporarily numb the nerve endings that signal pain.

Many women find that this lovely feature outlasts the climax itself. Some say having an orgasm reduces the intensity of their menstrual cramps, and others have found significant headache relief from having an orgasm. One woman told us she'd discovered that orgasm was the surest way to end a migraine. She laughed that while other women might use the phrase, "Honey, I have a headache," as a way to rebuff their husbands' advances, her husband knows that if she uses the identical sentence she's initiating a night of passion.

Unlike a penis, which can be used for reproduction, urination, and pleasure, pleasure is the clitoris's only reason for existence. Research finds that although the penis and clitoris grow from the same tissue in the early development of a fetus, the female organ is even more sensitive than the male's: The head of the clit has more nerve endings per square inch than any other part of human anatomy, and two to four times more than the head of a penis.

Starting in the 1970s, researchers and groups of self-taught women began to take a closer look at the clitoris. They pointed out that rather than just being a tiny nub, the entire organ has eighteen separate parts, many of them internal and some quite large. In addition to the glans, shaft, hood, and inner lips (the clit's primary externally visible parts, which you can see on page 70), inside a woman's body there are also a pair of wishbone-shaped clitoral legs made of erectile tissue. These are 2 to 3½ inches long, point back toward a woman's tailbone, and fill with blood when a woman is aroused. These "legs" were documented in the 1600s, but then "forgotten" by later anatomists.

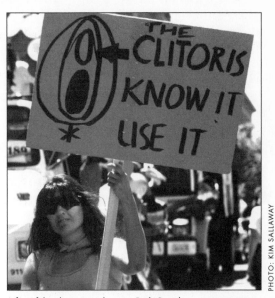

A fan of the clitoris marches in a Pride Parade.

PHOTO: KIM SALLAWAY

Bulbs of erectile tissue lie under the inner lips, and erectile tissue also surrounds the urethra (the tube you pee through). (This area, the urethral sponge, is also called the G-spot. For more on this, and a diagram of how this all fits together inside a woman's body, see chapter 6). The clitoral organ also includes a complex of nerves, blood vessels, muscles, ligaments, and glands that assist in lubrication and in some cases, ejaculation.

What does this all mean? First, it means a woman's potential for sexual pleasure is quite expansive—far more than the little "button" of a clitoris many of us learned about. Yet the clit doesn't always get the attention it deserves. Students' health textbooks sometimes neglect to include or label the clitoris in their female anatomy diagrams. (Can you imagine a diagram of male sexual anatomy omitting the penis?) In a 2005 study of heterosexual college students, 29 percent of women

does (clitoral) size matter?

WHEN IT COMES to the clitoris, size definitely does *not* matter. As far back as 1933, sex researchers found that despite considerable variation in the length and diameter of women's clits, the size and shape have no impact on a woman's orgasm. Many studies since then have come to the same conclusion: Whether your clit is dainty or voluptuous doesn't predict whether your orgasms are fast or slow, intense or gentle, challenging to coax along or easy to come by.

and 25 percent of men weren't able to locate the clitoris correctly on a diagram of female genitalia.

The word "vagina" regularly steals some of the clit's limelight. When parents try to teach their children the correct anatomical words, they often tell their son he has a penis, and tell their daughter she has a vagina. While that's true, these words are not equivalent! Many girls grow up with no idea that they have a clitoris (and rarely learn the word "vulva," the actual word for the collection of external organs they see when they look between their legs). Thanks in part to Eve Ensler's wildly successful *The Vagina Monologues*, now averaging over 2,000 performances each year, the word "vagina" has come out from the shadows. It's a major step forward, given that not long ago, the part called "hoo hoo," "coochie," or just "down there" couldn't be named in polite company, and certainly not written about in newspapers. Perhaps some day, the lusty, trusty clitoris will get her own day to shine. Women interested in getting better acquainted with their girl parts might want to check out pages 69 to 72.

female arousal: how does it work?

MASTERS AND JOHNSON, the pioneering sex researcher couple of the 1950s and '60s, studied sexual arousal in their laboratory back when hooking women up to machines and watching them masturbate or have sex was pretty radical. (Okay, so it still is!) Based on what they learned from their observations, they described what they called the "human sexual response cycle." Some contemporary experts criticize various aspects of Masters and Johnson's work, including the way it's overly simplistic, as if sex always flowed directly from arousal to orgasm without variation. Despite their shortcomings, many women find Masters and Johnson's concepts helpful in understanding their own sexual response.

what's between *your* legs?

OUR SURVEY ASKED women what words their parents used for female sexual parts while they were growing up. While most parents used words like "vagina," and many didn't ever discuss those parts of the body, some parents got pretty creative. Here are some of the words women told us their parents used instead of vulva or vagina:

area

between-the-legs

birdie

book ("Keep your book closed so no one else can read it.")

choo-choo

coochie

coochie coo

cookie

cookie jar

coolie

coos

crotch

down there

flower

fluffy

giny (rhymes with "shiny")

girl parts

hoo-hoo

hoosie

king-king

muffin

mutzie

nunu

papaya

pat-a-cake

pee pee

pee pee area

pee pee hole

pee-tu

pizza (This family called a boy's private parts a "sausage.")

pom-pom

poo

poo-poo

potty

private area

private parts

privates

putterpat

snuffleupagus

special area

thing

tinkle

tinkler

tu-tu

tulip

tweeter

twittle

wee wee

The classic Masters and Johnson cycle begins with the excitement phase (though newer theories of arousal point out that sexual desire typically comes before excitement). In the excitement phase, the fun begins! Typically, a woman's heart starts beating faster, her breathing and blood pressure increase, blood flows to her genitals, and her vagina lubricates. Her clitoris gets bigger and harder as she gets turned on, just as a man's penis gets bigger and harder during arousal. A woman may experience a "sex flush" of pink or darker skin on her neck, chest, or other parts of her body. Her nipples may become erect, and her inner and outer vaginal lips may swell. Most of the time, the woman isn't thinking about or even aware of the changes in her body. She's just thinking, "Yeah, this feels *good*!"

Then, said Masters and Johnson, there's a plateau phase. The woman is at a higher level of arousal than she normally is, but she may feel like she got stuck, like she's no longer making progress. While some later theorists of sexual response omit this phase from their models of arousal, many women we speak with say it describes their experience perfectly. Before Dorian had ever had an orgasm, she'd

tick, tick, tick, BOOM!

ON AVERAGE, IT takes a woman twenty minutes of direct clitoral stimulation to have an orgasm. The average guy takes two to five minutes. It's definitely not fair!

Keep in mind that twenty minutes is an *average*. Potentially half of women take longer than twenty minutes to have an orgasm. Thirty minutes, forty minutes, or more is not unusual.

Of course, the reverse can also be true. Some women come very quickly, and some men take a long time. People require varying amounts of stimulation, too. We can't say it any better than *The Guide to Getting It On* by Paul Joannides: "Some people have orgasms when a lover kisses them on the back of the neck; others need a stick or two of dynamite between the legs. The amount of stimulation needed to generate an orgasm has nothing to do with how much a person enjoys sex." As with everything related to sex, normal is fantastically diverse.

I ♥ FEMALE ORGASM

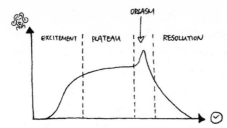

Masters and Johnson drew the plateau phase like this . . .

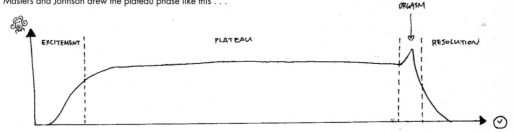

. . . but if it takes a woman a long time to have an orgasm, sometimes it can feel more like this.

get aroused, and then get frustrated when it seemed like nothing was happening. So she'd just give up trying, disappointed, and conclude, "I must be broken." Reading about the plateau phase was her number one breakthrough to having an orgasm; she was stunned to learn that *most* women experience a plateau phase. If that's the case, she concluded, it meant her going-nowhere arousal wasn't a sign she was broken—it was a sign she was *normal*. Some days a woman may slip directly from excitement to orgasm with barely a plateau phase at all, while other days she might feel like she's stuck in plateauland forever.

Most of the time, if the stimulation continues that got the woman to the plateau phase in the first place, eventually she'll have an orgasm. YAY! The woman's breathing and heart rate double. Interestingly, a woman's brain waves during an intense orgasm resemble the brain waves of a person in deep meditation. Women usually like to have the stimulation continue straight through the length of their orgasm. So if it's your finger, tongue, or penis she's riding, keep it going until she signals you to stop or moves away!

After the climax, the woman has a resolution phase, during which her body slowly returns to its nonaroused state. Unless she's having a multiple orgasm day—more on that on page 25.

clitoral troubleshooting:
what to do about a too-sensitive clit?

HERE'S ANOTHER FREQUENTLY asked question: "Sometimes my clit (or my partner's clit) gets so sensitive, it hurts to be touched. It's as if it skipped over the orgasm and reached the kind of sensitivity I'd expect *after* I have an orgasm. What can I do?" Others describe having their clitoris become numb, rather than overly sensitive. If you've had either experience, or your girlfriend or wife has, here are some things you can try:

○ Try more indirect touching. For many women, the head (glans) of the clitoris is too sensitive to touch, or may quickly become oversensitive. Try focusing stimulation only on the shaft (that's often the main part women

how do women get wet?

AS WOMEN GET turned on, their vaginas usually lubricate, creating sometimes considerable quantities (sometimes not so much) of slippery wetness that can help make touch and penetration feel great. Women's bodies have the capability to start getting wet within just seconds of the beginning of mental or physical stimulation. Where does this lovely liquid magically appear from? In early arousal, extra blood rushes to the genitals. The lubricating fluid, or transudate, is actually a colorless component of blood. It contains water, pyridine, squalene, urea, acetic acid, lactic acid, complex alcohols and glycols, ketones, and aldehydes. You can't just cook this stuff up with a chemistry set! It's squeezed through the vaginal walls, making the walls of a woman's vagina so nice and slippery.

Adding store-bought lube can also be a wonderful thing; see page 133 for more on this.

I ♥ FEMALE ORGASM

like touched), or other nearby parts of her vulva that might tug or vibrate the skin around the clitoris gently without touching it directly. For some women, the nerves in the clit are so sensitive that it's best to stimulate it through her fleshy outer lips (fingers on the outside of her outer lips, clit on the inside).

Sometimes I find it's necessary to rub to the side or above or below the clit, rather than directly on top of it. It often feels better than the painful sensation that can happen as a result of rubbing directly on the clit.

○ Take lots of mini-breaks. Some clits respond best to an approach that's a bit like, "Two steps forward, take a break, allow arousal to slide back a step, then start up again." Try lots of on-again, off-again clitoral attention, with periods of a few seconds or a few minutes without any clitoral stimulation, until you reach the orgasmic home stretch. (At that point, you'll probably want to stay with it.)
○ Keep it really wet. If you're touching your (or her) clit with your fingers, keep rewetting with saliva or lube, or "dip into the honeypot" frequently (dip your fingers into your/her vagina, if it's quite wet).
○ Partners can study what the woman does when she masturbates (if she does and is comfortable sharing the experience with you). Pay particular attention to how direct or indirect her stimulation is, what kind of motion she's using (up and down, back and forth, circles, most of the focus on one side or the other, etc.), how gentle or hard her pressure is, and how frequently she adds wetness.
○ Be gentle. This is especially true early on. If you're the partner, ask her for feedback about whether a lighter touch might help or if she'd prefer more focus on other parts of her body.

grow your O

A QUICKIE CAN be perfect sometimes, but in general, the longer the buildup, the bigger the orgasm. If you're getting too close too fast, back off the stimulation and bring yourself back up a few times for bigger fireworks.

I find that when I'm close to orgasm, if I stop and wait a minute or so and then continue, and do this over and over again as a way of teasing myself, when I finally do come, it's a lot more intense.

beyond the clitoris and the vagina

SOMETIMES PARTNERS NEED a reminder that there are other erogenous zones besides what's between a woman's legs. Here's what our survey (for more on our research see page 10) found when we asked women their favorite erogenous zones—the places they like to be kissed, licked, and caressed besides their genitals:

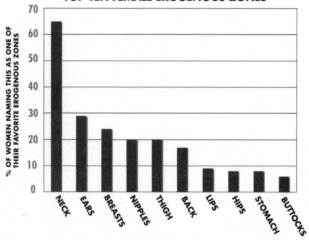

TOP TEN FEMALE EROGENOUS ZONES

And don't forget these other fave spots named by dozens of survey respondents: shoulders, collarbone, hands, feet, backs of knees, and lower torso just above the pubic hair. The truth is, *any* body part can be an erogenous zone if it's touched in the right way by the right partner at the right time. A small percentage of women can have orgasms from having their breasts or other parts of their body stroked without any below-the-waist genital stimulation. Just the same, the zone that makes one woman shiver with delight makes the next one's skin crawl, so women need to ask for what they like, and partners need to take their cues from the one they're with.

○ Recognize that some days, female orgasm is just not meant to be. Sex (including masturbation) is an imperfect art: Some days it's glorious, some days it's "good enough," some days it just doesn't work at all. That's not cause for alarm, and definitely not reason to worry that the love is over, or that you and your partner aren't meant for each other. Have a sense of humor, and remember that most women can be quite satisfied without an orgasm.

same concept, multiplied

IN JAPANESE, THE word for male masturbation is *senzuri*, which means "one thousand strokes." The word for female masturbation? *Manzuri*: "ten thousand strokes."

BIG O on the big screen: 40 Days and 40 Nights

THE LEADING MAN and woman are falling for each other fast, but he gave up sex for Lent. Since they can't touch each other, in one memorable scene they take turns caressing each other with an orchid he's brought her. He blows a flower petal across her belly and panties, getting her so aroused that she comes. Blowing flower petals across your partner's abdomen probably won't do the trick in the real world, but it's a hot scene nonetheless.

multiple orgasms:
double your pleasure, double your fun?

AFTER THEIR BIG O, some women find it easy to continue and have two or more orgasms before their arousal fades away. Others have a single orgasm and find their clitoris gets too sensitive to have any more stimulation, just as most guys don't want

sexy mamas (to be)

MANY WOMEN FIND they have higher sex drives, lubricate more, and have multiple orgasms more easily while they're pregnant, especially in the second trimester of pregnancy. Some say a particularly fun aspect of getting it on during this time (yes, it's quite safe) is not having to worry about getting pregnant! There's more on intercourse during pregnancy on page 142.

their penis touched after they come. That's perfectly fine: Orgasms aren't like coupons, where the more you collect, the better. A woman can be deeply fulfilled and sexually thrilled with only one orgasm per sexual interlude (or even fewer).

That said, if you're a woman who's curious about having multiple orgasms but hasn't been able to, try this tip from Betty Dodson, author of *Sex for One* and *Orgasms for Two*. After one orgasm, stop the clitoral stimulation for a short period of time, like ten or sixty seconds. Then try resuming clitoral stimulation. Many women find the period of hypersensitivity passes quite quickly, and that they can then start toward another orgasm (or several more, with a short break in between each one). For some women, each orgasm in a string gets bigger and bigger; for others they get smaller and smaller. Even in a series of multiple orgasms, each climax requires its own buildup (different than little "aftershocks" that are part of the original orgasm).

Although both women and men are capable of multiple orgasms (see page 29), multiples tend to come far more easily to women. This is at least in part because while both women and men have erectile tissue that swells with blood during arousal, the blood can flow in and out of women's genitals faster and more easily, so she can "re-fill" and "re-orgasm" repeatedly.

kegel your way to bigger, better orgasms

BACK IN THE 1950s, a gynecologist named Dr. Arnold Kegel invented exercises that helped his patients with urinary incontinence by strengthening the muscles surrounding the vagina and urethra. As the patients' muscle tone improved, they discovered a lovely side effect to the exercises: better orgasms! Dr. Kegel's good name would never have been remembered so fondly if his exercises had resulted only in better bladder control.

Further research has found that indeed, strengthening the pubococcygeus

I ♥ FEMALE ORGASM

muscle group (conveniently called the PC muscles, since "pubococcygeus" sounds more like an exotic disease than a sexy group of muscles) increases blood flow to the pelvic area, helps increase sensitivity, and sometimes results in stronger orgasms for both women and men. Many men say they enjoy it if a woman's PC muscles are toned enough to squeeze him while he's inside her.

Kegels are amazing!!! They make orgasms much more of an experience that you can actually FEEL.

I have been trying to do "the squeeze" more while in the act of sexual intercourse and have found it to improve both my boyfriend's and my own pleasure a lot!

FIVE REASONS WHY KEGELS ARE THE BEST EXERCISES IN THE WORLD

1. You don't have to buy any special equipment that will take up half your apartment.
2. You can do them in any position, including standing in line, sitting in front of your computer, lying in bed, and practicing headstands.
3. Because no one can tell you're doing them, you can get in shape while carrying on a conversation with your professor, boss, or Great-Aunt Sue.
4. You can multitask, transforming annoying waits at the ATM, on the phone, or at the keyboard into sexercise.
5. How many other exercises actually improve your sex life?

To do Kegel exercises, identify the muscles you're going to be working out. They're the same muscles you use if you're peeing and want to stop the flow of urine. In general, you should do the exercises when you're *not* peeing—which, lucky for you, is most of the day—but when you're just starting out, try squeezing your

dorian's kegel tip

MY FAVORITE PLACE to do Kegels is at the gas pump. The best ones for this purpose make a steady click, click, clicking sound while you fill 'er up. I discovered that since there's nothing else to do while I wait, the clicks are a great way to work out my PC muscles. I can challenge myself to hold for a full ten clicks, then do quick squeezes in rhythm with the clicks, even trying double-time squeezes. As long as you maintain the same bored expression on your face as everyone else at the gas station, no one will have any clue what you're up to. When you really get into it, you'll find you're disappointed when the pump clicks off, signaling a full gas tank and the end to your workout.

PC muscles while you pee at least once to make sure you've identified the right muscles.

There are two different kinds of exercises you can practice:

Long squeezes. Pull in as if you were squeezing a finger with equal pressure on all sides. Count to three, then relax the muscles fully. Repeat. As the muscles get stronger, hold the count to higher numbers. Can you reach ten? Twenty? Keep breathing while you squeeze. Some people like to imagine they are pulling an elevator up inside their body.

Fast little squeezes. Squeeze the muscles in short pulses, as if you were following the beat to a song. It's hard to do very fast beats at first, but as you get stronger, you'll be able to pulse faster. Remember to let the muscles relax after each beat—relaxing completely can be just as important as contracting strongly. Don't forget to keep breathing!

Try to remember to do the exercises for at least a few minutes every day, increasing the number of repetitions or the length of the holds as you feel yourself gain strength. Some people find it feels sort of "yucky" at first to work out these muscles, just as it can feel unpleasant to work any muscle that's out of shape. Keep trying to do small numbers of Kegels, and you'll find you get stronger quite quickly. Keeping these muscles in good shape throughout your life is good for vaginal and urinary health (yes, the doctor may have prescribed Kegels to your grandmother), as well as preparing for and getting back in shape after childbirth.

Because the biggest challenge to this exercise routine is remembering to do it, it helps to find some regular occurrence that's your "cue" to Kegel—ideally, something you do most days like wait for the subway, ride an elevator, or the most classic cue of all, sit in the car at a red light. (We think it would be a helpful reminder if the word "KEGEL!" were imprinted on every red light as a reminder.)

I do Kegels sometimes, when I remember to do them or when I'm nervous and fidgety and I'm trying to avoid cracking my knuckles.

multiorgasmic men?

WOMEN AREN'T THE only ones with the capacity to be multiorgasmic: Men can be, too. The capability comes naturally to some preadolescent boys and young adults, but it's also possible for other guys to learn—with a considerable amount of work. The main part of the male workout involves doing lots and lots of Kegel exercises, described on pages 26–28. A man likely already has enough strength in his PC muscle to stop himself from peeing midstream. For most men, orgasm and ejaculation happen at the same time, but Kegels can help him build up enough strength in that muscle to be able to experience orgasm without ejaculation. After a steady Kegel workout for at least several months, when he's at the point when he's about to ejaculate, he may be able to clamp down on the PC muscle and have an orgasm (the intense, pleasurable sensations) while preventing himself from ejaculating. Because he hasn't ejaculated, he can do this over and over again to be multiorgasmic. The books *The Multi-Orgasmic Man* and *Any Man Can* address in more detail how to use this and other techniques to become multiorgasmic as a man.

fantasy: imagination isn't just for kids

OUR SURVEY FOUND that 63 percent of women fantasize at least some of the time while they're being sexual with a partner, and 93 percent do so when they're masturbating, numbers that closely match other studies. Fantasizing is tapping into the power of whatever images or stories turn you on and help you reach those highest levels of arousal that launch orgasms. There's nothing shameful about allowing yourself to put these images to use: Most women do! Because the mind is the biggest sex organ, as you've probably heard, it's perfectly logical that you'd want to use yours to help you come. The movies you watch in your mind are private. No one ever has to know what they are unless you choose to share them.

> *Sexual fantasies are what keeps me in the mood most of the time. It's so easy for me to stop being aroused. If I wish to continue, it's almost pivotal for me to fantasize.*

> *The most important thing I learned that helped me have orgasms was to be unashamed of my fantasies, even if they are sometimes socially taboo, and to be honest about sharing them with my partner. That freed my mind up quite a bit to really enjoy coming.*

> *Fantasies don't help me. I've tried to use this technique, but it doesn't do it for me. I think I rely more on physical stimulation on my entire body than on images in my head or what I'm looking at in reality.*

As a young teenager, Dorian had heard about fantasizing and, lying in bed one night, decided she'd try it. She imagined a huge bed, and spent some time mentally decorating the bedroom, imagining the silky sheets and luscious comforter. She pictured herself naked in the bed. (That's how sex happens, right?) Then, she thought, I need a man. Searching her memory-banks for a sexy image of a man, what came to mind was a character who resembled all the princes in Disney movies: broad shoulders, chiseled jaw, sparkling smile. She imagined her personal Disney prince walking over to the bed, and then the fantasy stalled. She didn't know what she wanted to have happen next, and she wasn't feeling turned on *at all.* Of course not: It wasn't a real sexual fantasy, just a weird fusion of too many Disney cartoons and interior design catalogs.

Some women know exactly what fantasies turn them on, or might replay the memory of a favorite sexual interlude or a movie scene that made them wet. If you're coming up empty-handed in your search for fantasies, one easy source of ideas is erotica, stories written to arouse. For this purpose, we recommend stories rather than pictures or movies, because they engage your imagination and allow you to create your own mental images. There are fantastic books of erotica, but if you're trying to figure out what you like, nothing is faster and easier than going online to the many free erotica sites. These have thousands of stories divided into categories, including the predictable and others you wouldn't imagine in your wildest dreams. Skimming a few in each category can be fascinating, because some will summon your inner "ick!" while others intrigue you. Take note of those stories that get the blood throbbing, the ones that really absorb you. Soon, you'll get a sense of what genres you like and which details grab you. When you're being sexual later, replay them in your mind, using your own imagination to tweak the plot or improve the characters. Before long, you'll be fantasizing like a champion!

I watch or read sex stories, then fantasize about my sex partner doing those things to me. It's helped me figure out what I like and don't like.

I figured out my fantasies by hearing about different fantasies of other people, and whichever turned me on the most and sounded like something I would try became a fantasy of my own. I may have modified them a bit, because of what I already know I do and don't like.

I figured out what I liked from pornography, and I often play one particular scene in my head when I'm with or without a partner.

No one knows why specific thoughts or stories arouse specific people. Some fantasies that turn you on may be things you'd like to act out someday, especially if the situation were right and you had a partner you particularly trusted. Other fantasies that get you going may involve situations your analytic mind finds downright problematic or offensive, that you never, ever want to have happen in the real world. For example, numerous studies find it's quite common for women to fantasize about being overpowered and forced to have sex; some research even finds it's among the most common sexual fantasies for women.

Obviously, it can be disturbing to be aroused by a rape scenario, since no one wants to have sex against her will in real life. Many researchers and women themselves point out that a sexual fantasy is definitely *not* the same thing as a sexual desire. Just because a woman finds it sexy to imagine a given scene does *not* mean she ever wants this scene to come true. In fact, there are huge differences: In a fantasy (even a fantasy of being forced to do something), the woman is actually in total control. She creates the imaginary situation and decides exactly what will happen and when it will end. Exactly the opposite is true in a real-world rape, where a woman is powerless and is definitely not controlling what happens to her. Many women say understanding this difference has helped them sort out the confusing feelings that can arise if these are the fantasies that turn them on, and give themselves permission to use the fantasies that work for them. Of course, if you're concerned that you may act on a fantasy that could be dangerous to yourself or others, it may be wise to turn your imagination down a different path. You can seek professional help if that's too hard to do on your own.

According to the Kinsey and Hite reports, 1 to 2 percent of women can have an orgasm from fantasy alone, with no genital stimulation at all. Lucky girls!

The universe of sexual fantasies is limitless. Here are just a few examples that women shared on our survey:

I fantasize about being with my partner. He turns me on so much, I just think about the times we've been together. Sometimes I throw Brad Pitt in it, too.

If I fantasize about being an exotic dancer, I can dress and act accordingly, which I've found to improve my libido and hunger for sex. It may be the excitement of trying something new or putting away conventional and shameful beliefs about having sex that allows me to enjoy it more. I feel as though if I'm someone else, I can shamelessly flaunt my passion and desire for sex.

I usually think about a penis inside of me (especially my partner's) and not just during masturbation. I think about it even while the penis is inside of me. I think it just turns me on so much quicker. I don't know why; it just works for me. I don't have any other image. I just solely focus on the penis.

I ♥ FEMALE ORGASM

I consider myself straight, but I almost always fantasize about women going down on me. I just find women's bodies so hot! I want to be in a long-term relationship with a man, but women are beautiful and exciting, as well. It could also be that I've never hooked up with a girl before, which makes it even more forbidden and exciting.

One of the things that I fantasize about (which is difficult for me as a feminist, especially a sex-positive feminist) is rape. Sometimes I find it incredibly arousing. I'm almost certain it's the power thing that turns me on. In my fantasies I see the survivor/victim (which is usually me) as powerful because of my sexual prowess, and the rapist as completely unable to control himself. I know that this is nothing like rape in real life, and when I think about actually being raped I'm completely terrified.

I enjoy thinking about guys I would never have sex with, like professors, celebrities, friends, old friends, neighbors.

Many women who fantasize while they masturbate aren't sure about the etiquette of doing so while they're with a partner. We believe that doing so is fine, quite common, and another way to increase the likelihood of an orgasm. Because fantasizing happens only inside your own head, it's not cheating, as some worry, but harnessing the erotic power of your mind. (Women should remember, too, that many partners fantasize during every sexual encounter, keep their thoughts private, and never think twice about it.) The best kinds of fantasies during partnered sex are often blended, where you mentally integrate your partner's caresses or strength into the story, so the real-life sex and fantasy sex merge. It's up to you whether you choose to share the fact that you were fantasizing, or the details, with your partner. Talking about or acting out a fantasy with a partner you trust can build intimacy—not to mention being totally sexy. In fact, the powerhouse combination of fantasy and masturbation is why some people—especially those in long-distance relationships—swear by phone sex.

My boyfriend is away a lot, so I have to imagine what I would be doing with him. That usually leads to more than just imagining. Also, we'll talk about our fantasies together and that will give us ideas of what to do or even cause us to both want to jump on each other right then.

My girlfriend and I are aware that we each fantasize during sex. We talk each other through scenarios. They help me orgasm. I've always had difficulty orgasming from pure physical stimulation.

clitoral tips for partners

AS A WOMAN'S partner, just locating her clitoris and rubbing merrily away isn't going to do the trick. Whether you're using your fingers, your tongue, a vibrator, or something else, here are a few tips:

○ Don't reach for her clit too early in the sexual interaction. Many women find their clitoris likes to be touched only after they're somewhat aroused.

   Don't jump right in. Touch her somewhere else first and move in on her genitals gradually. If your hands are really dry, lick your fingers first.

   When a finger goes directly to my clitoris, I sort of jump because it hurts. Don't go straight for the clit, and once you get to the clit, don't ignore the rest of the vulva area. It feels really good to have the rest of it stroked, too.

○ Cut your nails, especially the one or two most likely to be touching her genitals. Being touched by a partner with long or dirty nails can be uncomfortable, painful, or downright gross.
○ Start gently. Touch and stroke her vaginal lips. Slowly work your way inside. Once you're touching her clitoris, remember, this is an exquisitely sensitive organ. Being "gentle" and "soft" were the most common pieces

of advice women in our survey gave partners about how to touch their genitals. You can start up at the top of the shaft, just under the bone, and move down closer to the head if she wants you to. She may want firmer pressure, but ask her about that or follow her lead. ("More, harder!" is a much better response than "Ow!")

> *I think genitals and gentle go hand in hand. Being a little rough is okay, but sometimes a partner tries too hard to stimulate you and it actually hurts. There's something to be said about passionate, gentle lovemaking. It can be just as erotic as kinky, wild, crazy, rough, hard sex.*

> *Be very gentle unless you know she likes it rough! Some men can go at it too hard, too fast, and it just hurts. Once a woman is wet and hot it's usually appropriate to go faster.*

○ She may love to be touched gently through her pants or panties before she's ready for more direct stimulation.

> *Stroking genitals firmly through clothing, especially tight jeans, can feel quite good. You want to do enough exterior stuff to make sure a woman is aroused before you move to penetration of any kind.*

> *Try touching around the area or put a clothing article between your hand and her body (silk scarves are VERY effective).*

○ Some women find it helpful to break down clitoral touching into three key components: *directness*, *pressure*, and *speed*. These can be helpful for couple communication, whether you're the one asking for feedback or the one giving directions. You can check in about whether she wants her clitoris touched right on the tip versus the shaft or farther away (directness), how hard she wants the stimulation to be (pressure), and how fast she wants the movement to be (speed).

○ Keep it wet. Once you've got skin-to-skin contact, lick your fingers, add lube, or dip into her vagina's wetness to wet and rewet her clit.

Don't just dive in for the clit; work the area around it, as well. Oh, and lubricate. Either remember to use artificial lube, or bring juices up from her vagina.

○ Invite her to move your hand where she wants it, or rest your hand over hers so you can get the hang of the movements she likes. If she'll let you watch her masturbate, that's a great way to see how she likes to be touched.

Ask your partner to use your hand to stimulate themselves for at least a few minutes. Often I need speeds or pressures to change during the entire process in order to climax. This way, you know what kind of pressure and speed to use, and you know what I'm talking about when I tell you to speed up or change pressures.

I've watched my partner masturbate—it was very helpful to me. It allowed me to see which part of her vaginal area she touched the most and how she touched it. It allowed me to see how many fingers she likes inside of her. Really watching her do it was a turn-on as well as an educational experience. And after watching, I could imitate the things she did to herself and she knew I had paid attention. (And there's nothing women like more than knowing someone is paying attention to them, right?)

○ Stimulate multiple parts at once. Many women love having other parts of their body touched simultaneously with clitoral stimulation (though actually pulling this off can be a bit like rubbing your head and patting your stomach at the same time).

The longer the foreplay and the more you communicate how much you want me, the more likely I am to have an orgasm (or two or three) and the better it will be. Playing with multiple body parts at once—pinching my nipples or touching my clit or grabbing my butt—is always great stimulation.

I enjoy multiple stimulation. I like anal with vaginal with clitoral. Or any combination of those—although clitoral with either vaginal or anal will make me have an orgasm faster and better.

○ Ask, ask, ask. What women like varies *dramatically*. Ask her to guide you and teach you, and be open to learning the nuances of her body's dance. If you don't know what to say, ask, "How's this?" or short questions like, "Up here?" "Side to side like this?" "Harder?" Women, don't expect your partner to read your mind: Appreciate his or her efforts, make adjustments, give gentle suggestions, and provide plenty of positive feedback about what works!

> **sweet dreams**
>
> BETWEEN 6 AND 37 percent of women report having had orgasms in their sleep, depending on the study.
>
> *In my sleep I get vaginal orgasms, which I can't achieve through sex, and I like those the best. My vaginal muscles start tightening and spasming, and I wake up and it just feels really good.*

Every woman is different, so ask what she likes. Some don't like it right on the clitoris, some do, but either way, don't rub it like you're trying to sandpaper something down. It hurts after a while. Penetration is good too, but don't go too deep. Realize that the canal curves. Some partners wave their fingers around in there and it just feels weird, like there is a fish out of water up your vagina. Just rub around a little and massage the inside slowly.

It's very frustrating when someone is unable to find the clitoris, so if you're unsure of whether or not you're stimulating it, ask.

Watch their reactions. I personally don't like direct clitoral stimulation some of the time. If a woman squirms around and tries to wiggle away from your hand, then it probably doesn't feel good and you should vary your technique.

- ○ Enjoy yourself. A woman can find it hard to relax and enjoy if she gets the sense that her partner is bored, uncomfortable, or disinterested. On the flip side, if her partner is clearly enjoying him/herself (or even turned on), that's fun! Don't let clit play become a chore; it'll stop working.
- ○ Once she's close to coming, don't change what you're doing. This is not the time to add variety or mix things up! Stay in the same spot, doing the same movement, until she comes or instructs you otherwise.

for those who have experienced abuse or assault

TRAUMATIC SEXUAL EXPERIENCES like sexual abuse or sexual assault can have a long-lasting impact on one's sexuality. This is true regardless of exactly what happened, whether you're male or female, whether the events were one-time or repeated, whether they happened as a child or an adult, and whether they were perpetrated by a stranger, relative, partner, doctor, teacher, or someone else. Abuse and assault survivors can face a myriad of different sexual challenges, including:

- ○ difficulty getting aroused or having orgasms
- ○ emotions, memories, or flashbacks of the traumatic event(s) related to certain kinds of touch or positions
- ○ guilt about enjoying sex
- ○ lack of interest in sex
- ○ having sex compulsively even when they know it's physically or emotionally unhealthy or unsafe
- ○ discomfort with what kind of sex they like or what fantasies turn them on
- ○ dissociating: keeping themselves mentally or emotionally separate from what they're experiencing physically during sex

Sadly, given how common sexual abuse and sexual assault are, these issues and others affect too-large a percentage of people.

I was assaulted by a boyfriend when I was seventeen, and it has definitely

I ♥ FEMALE ORGASM

affected the way I experience sexual relationships and pleasure. I sometimes don't orgasm because I flash back to the assault and freeze up.

On the subject of orgasm, some survivors are confused because they had an orgasm while they were being abused or assaulted, or found the experience physically pleasurable. This does not mean that they wanted the abuse—physical arousal, pleasure, and orgasm are the body's automatic, physiological responses to certain kinds of stimulation. Even if a survivor experienced these things, the experience was still unwanted and abusive.

I was raped when I was eleven. I'm just now able to begin to heal. As a survivor, I numbed myself from anything sexual. I dissociated my mind from my body. I still have trouble with masturbation—I have trouble not having flashbacks when I do it. I also have trouble feeling any kind of pleasure because when I was raped I did feel pleasure. I can't get past my mental blocks yet, but I WILL!

The good news: It *is* possible to have a healthy, positive sex life after experiencing sexual trauma. The journey may (or may not) involve therapy, helpful books and websites, a support group, introspection, journaling, and a supportive partner. For addressing sex-related issues, we highly recommend the book *The Survivor's Guide to Sex: How to Have an Empowered Sex Life After Child Sexual Abuse*, by Staci Haines. It's relevant even if your sexually traumatic experience happened as an adult, and it's inclusive of women of all sexual orientations. Also excellent are *Courage to Heal: A Guide for Women Survivors of Child Sexual Abuse*, by Ellen Bass and Laura Davis, and *The Sexual Healing Journey: A Guide for Survivors of Sexual Abuse*, by Wendy Maltz, which address the broader issues of healing from abuse. For male survivors, we also recommend *Victims No Longer: The Classic Guide for Men Recovering from Sexual Child Abuse*, by Mike Lew. Many people find it helpful to work with a psychologist, clinical social worker, or other therapist as part of their healing process. You can also find local support groups and phone and online hotlines through the Rape, Abuse, and Incest National Network, www.rainn.org.

I was date raped when I was eighteen years old. Sometimes I think about that when I'm having sex and start sobbing and can't continue with the sex. Now I am taking some "time off" to learn how to have healthy sexuality, starting with myself.

I was raped in high school, and for the next five years it affected both sexual experiences and the way I treated myself. The majority of my lovers were wonderful, warm, generous people, so it was time that healed my wounds, and now I respect my body and have the best sex life I could ever hope for.

If you're the partner of an abuse or assault survivor, you may find helpful *Allies in Healing: When the Person You Love Was Sexually Abused as a Child,* by Laura Davis. It's written for partners who want to better understand the impact this past experience can have on their relationship, and how they can best support their loved one through the healing process.

Partners and allies can join survivors in working to end sexual violence. Some choose to get involved as volunteers at their local rape crisis center, or to participate in a campus or community group that educates about sexual assault prevention. National groups like Men Can Stop Rape (www.mencanstoprape.org) provide trainings and educational materials.

All people have the right to reclaim their sexual lives and find healthy, fulfilling, consensual sensuality and sexuality. The essential work continues as survivors, partners of survivors, and allies of all genders join together to create a culture free of sexual violence.

2

Petting the Bunny:
masturbation & female orgasm

masturbation is the fastest and easiest way for many women to have orgasms, and the most common way for a woman to come for the first time. In our survey, women who had masturbated were far more likely to be orgasmic (by themselves or with a partner) than women who had never masturbated (88 percent compared to 48 percent). With no disease risk and no chance of accidentally getting knocked up, masturbation clearly has a lot going for it.

I knew some of my friends masturbated, but in general, I didn't have much of a sex drive and wasn't interested in sex with myself or others of any sort. It wasn't until I was twenty that I first masturbated (two years after I first had sex), and after that, I realized that I was FAR better at making myself happy than anyone else was!

Masturbating is actually the quickest way for me to have an orgasm. While I really enjoy being sexual with my partner, it's one of those things where you know your own body better than anyone else does. When I do it myself, it can happen in just a few minutes.

Some women are practically female masturbation cheerleaders; others enjoy self-loving privately but would be horrified to discuss the matter. Still others don't masturbate at all for a variety of reasons. Whatever the case, the taboo against female masturbation is powerful. Not only do girls get the message that they're not supposed to do it, they're not even supposed to acknowledge that girls *can* masturbate. Confusion is rampant. One woman told us that growing up, she heard that masturbation was "touching yourself," so she assumed she was masturbating anytime she scratched her ear or touched her arm. Another said she got the idea that masturbation required a large, expensive machine. "I was just a little kid," she said, "so I couldn't afford one of those machines. But I figured maybe I'd get one when I grew up."

People start absorbing information about this subject from the time they're babies. Parents often move babies' hands away from their genitals and don't teach them the words for that part of the body—a very different reaction than when the same baby explores his or her belly, ears, or toes. If this happens repeatedly, the baby quickly comes to the conclusion that this part of his or her body is "bad" or that touching it is "wrong." As adults, most of us don't have conscious memories of infancy. Yet feelings of shame can run deep, sometimes because they were planted so early, and sometimes because we live in a culture saturated with negative messages.

These messages often persist through childhood. One woman shared that when she was little, any time she or her siblings put their hands anywhere near their genitals, their mother would say, "That's dirty! Move your hand!" Another remembers that after a day at the beach when she was a girl, she was in the outdoor showers with her mom and sisters. When she reached down to dump out the sand that had collected in the crotch of her bathing suit, her mom slapped her hand away, saying, "Get your hand away from there!" The take-home message that many kids learn is simple: Your genitals are nasty. Don't touch them. If you take any interest in them at all, you're a bad person.

Some girls follow instructions, not getting to know much about their own body and sexuality—and often discover they have a *lot* of catching up to do as adults. Other kids look and touch in secret, sometimes overwhelmed with shame and guilt. Most women we talk to say that if the subject of masturbation came up in conversation when they were teenagers, they'd squeal, "Eeewww, disgusting!" and swear they didn't do it—whether or not it was true. As one nineteen-year-old woman wrote on our survey:

Any time my friends talk about masturbation it's followed by giggles and, "Ewwwwww—God no!" Yet in the back of my mind I'm thinking, "I LIKE IT!" I'm scared to say that out loud because it's like masturbation is looked down upon.

To make matters worse, there's a massive double standard that says masturbation is something boys do, and girls don't. Some girls heard that masturbation is bad for everyone—but that boys can't control themselves, so people make an exception for them. As a kid, one woman heard that if boys didn't masturbate, they'd explode. (We can just imagine the seventh grade girl sitting in her classroom, watching the fiery explosion as the thirteen-year-old boy at the next desk self-combusts. "Poor thing," she'd think to herself. "He really should have taken care of that.")

My father mentioned masturbation as though it was normal for boys but only "certain kinds of girls" did it.

I was told that it was for boys to do. I never did it; I wouldn't have known how to. Since I thought it was only for boys, I never really thought about trying to do it.

On average, boys and men do masturbate more than girls and women. Parents tend to be more accepting of their sons' explorations, and boys tend to hear more about masturbation from other boys. Besides, boys' genitals are *way* easier for them to discover, the way they just hang out down there, so easy to see and touch. Girls' genitals, by comparison, are tucked neatly away where they're less visible. It's a handy place to have one's genitals, but it means that it often takes girls a while longer to discover their clitoris. Boys even have to touch their penis every time they pee. If girls had to touch their clitoris every time they peed—and some women pee a lot of times in their lives!—they'd be 10,000 times more familiar with that part of their bodies. This puts women at a huge disadvantage.

These days, growing numbers of parents are teaching their kids the real words

what's a parent to do?

MANY PARENTS TELL us, "I don't want to raise my daughter the way my parents raised me, but what am I supposed to do when she's on the playground rubbing herself up and down on the swing-set pole?" (For parents with sons, the question is often, "What I am supposed to do when we have dinner guests and he's walking around with both hands down his pants?")

Experts recommend that parents tell their kids that touching oneself is something that's okay to do, but it's something to do in private, like in your bedroom or in the bathroom. Rather than yelling, "Get your hands out of there!" a parent can say to a child quietly, "I know it feels good to touch there, but that's something people do in private. You can do it in your room later if you want to." That way, parents teach their kids appropriate behavior without inadvertently sending the message that touching your own body is fundamentally wrong.

for the sex organs, communicating that these parts are healthy and normal, and in some cases, even letting their kids know that they think masturbation is perfectly okay (in private, not at the dinner table).

My mother explained to me what masturbation was when I brought it up. She told me that there was nothing wrong with it, that everyone does it at some point, and that I should enjoy the pleasure I can give myself.

When I was in about sixth grade, I told my mom about touching myself. I felt extremely guilty about it and I almost started to cry, fearing that I was doing something horribly wrong. She laughed a little bit and then told me there was nothing wrong with what I was doing, that it was perfectly natural and most people do it.

I ♥ FEMALE ORGASM

My mom always told me that the only way somebody will ever really please you sexually is if you know your body well enough to know what you like. So she encouraged masturbation. She bought me my first vibrator when I was sixteen.

Clearly, though, most women still grow up steeped in masturbation stigma. Because the subject is so forbidden, millions of women spend decades—or lifetimes—denied of basic knowledge about their own bodies and the pleasure that comes with it. Baby, it's time to kiss this taboo goodbye!

WHAT'S THE EASIEST WAY FOR WOMEN TO HAVE ORGASMS?

12% intercourse with additional clitoral stimulation (hand or vibrator)

6% intercourse alone (no added clitoral stimulation—some women said only in specific positions)

4% partner's fingers/ hand stimulating my clitoris

3% partner's fingers/ hand stimulating my G-spot or inside my vagina

13% other, or several options equally easy, or a combination of methods

34% masturbation (includes using fingers, hands, rubbing against something, and showerhead/jets of water. "Vibrator" answers were counted separately.)

14% receiving oral sex (with or without additional G-spot stimulation from partner's fingers)

14% vibrator

Source: Answers of 555 women, survey conducted by Dorian Solot and Marshall Miller.

eight lies you may have heard about masturbation

YOU'LL PROBABLY RECOGNIZE most of these as the falsehoods they are. Maybe some of them still make you nervous, though. All eight come up regularly from women in our audiences, who say they're things they've heard, and often worried about. Let's put these long-lived fictions to rest once and for all!

Lie #1

If women masturbate, they won't be able to have an orgasm with a partner.

> **Truth:** The reverse is true: Studies find that in general, women who've had orgasms through masturbation are much more likely to have orgasms during partnered sex, and that those are more likely to be frequent and multiple. There are lots of reasons: A woman who's comfortable touching her own body is more likely to know what feels good to her sexually. She's less likely to be surprised by or afraid of the sensations as she nears orgasm. And she may be better able to let her partner know what she likes. Not only does masturbation pose no danger to your partnered sex life, it just might improve it.

> *Recently, my husband and I were having some issues in the bedroom. My mother asked if I had ever orgasmed with my husband. Unfortunately, my answer was no. She basically told me that he wouldn't know how to pleasure me unless I knew what felt good. That way, I could take my educational experience and share it with him. It worked!*

Lie #2

Masturbation will change the way a woman's genitals look—and then everyone will know she's been doing it.

> **Truth:** You can't change the shape of your clitoris or labia (inner or outer vaginal lips) by masturbating with your hand, a vibrator, or anything else

(unless your technique involves sharp objects!). Think about it: If guys could lengthen their penis by pulling on it, the streets would be full of men whose pride and joy hung below their knees. It's impossible for any doctor or lover to know if you masturbate by examining you. The only exception would be if your skin temporarily got red or irritated from rubbing, but you could see and feel the tenderness if that happened.

"Don't knock masturbation. It's sex with someone I love."
—line from the movie *Annie Hall*

Where did this myth come from? Many young women take a close look at their clitoris, labia, or some other part, notice something about it ("It's big!" "It's small! "It's lopsided!") and decide that this must be the result of touching themselves too much. It's an understandable assumption, but it's incorrect. A woman who masturbates by inserting an object into her vagina may change the shape of her hymen (vaginal tissue at the entrance to her vagina), particularly if she's never had intercourse or used a tampon, but hymens start out looking so different that the state of your hymen doesn't tell a doctor anything about you. A gynecologist can't tell whether a stretched or torn hymen got that way from a tampon, finger, penis, sex toy, or just exercise—and frankly, probably doesn't care.

The shape, size, and lopsidedness of your genitals have nothing to do with whether or how you touch them. In fact, like every other part of your body, they probably look a lot like your mom's or grandma's. (Now *there's* a dinner table conversation starter!) For more on what women's genitals look like, see pages 69–72.

Lie #3
Masturbation is only for single people.

Truth: Yes, single people masturbate. So do people in relationships and people who are married. Lots of couples use their hands or fingers to stimulate each other's genitals, or take turns by having one partner masturbate themselves while the other "helps" by caressing, kissing, licking, stroking, telling sexy stories, or otherwise further arousing the one doing the masturbating. Some find masturbation is a great way for a horny partner to get off without imposing on a partner who's not in the mood. Even if they don't masturbate together, lots of partners do so when they're apart—can you say, "long distance relationship"? One college student said that the only way she's ever been able been able to come is while having phone sex with her boyfriend (and touching herself at the same time).

Lie #4

(or at least, not as clear-cut as you might think)

The Bible says masturbation is a sin.

Truth: Bible experts are in disagreement on this one. Basically, there's one Bible story that people usually point to as evidence that the Bible says masturbation is wrong, the story of Onan in Genesis 38:7–10. In the story, Onan's brother dies. The law at the time (Biblical times, remember) requires Onan to have sex with his dead brother's wife, in order to produce an heir for his brother. Onan refuses—instead, he "spills his seed on the ground." For this offense, God strikes Onan dead. Yes, Onan was punished for a big-time crime, but most modern Bible scholars say his crime wasn't masturbation, but his unwillingness to procreate with the widow. (The story even suggests that this may have been a case of "pulling out," not masturbating.) Beyond that, many scholars say, the Bible says nothing specific about masturbation at all.

Writer and poet Dorothy Parker is said to have joked that her parakeet was named Onan because he spilled his seed on the ground.

There is similar disagreement about how to interpret Buddhist, Muslim, and other Christian and Jewish scriptures and teachings about masturbation. Overall, two things are clear: First, female masturbation is rarely, if ever, mentioned in the sacred texts of any of these faiths. Second, many respected leaders within these religious traditions say masturbation is perfectly acceptable within their faith, at least in some circumstances.

Lie #5

You can hurt yourself or damage your body by masturbating.

Truth: Obviously, anything can be risky if you don't use common sense. Case in point: masturbating while driving is dangerous, no matter how much it

BIG O on the big screen: *Pleasantville*

A TEENAGE DAUGHTER explains about sex, including the concept of masturbation, to her clueless 1950s mother. The mother tries masturbating for the first time in the bathtub that night. Her orgasm is so huge it sets a tree outside the house on fire.

might liven up a boring car trip. We don't recommend it. What you do in the backseat is, of course, your own business.

As long as you're sensible about it, masturbating is harmless. It doesn't cause acne, hairy palms, blindness, or any of the gazillion other lies used to terrify children. (If blindness really were caused by masturbation, there would be an international epidemic of sight impairment.) Even the American Medical Association agrees: Their official statement declares that masturbation is "neither physically nor mentally harmful."

Because masturbation involves some degree of friction, some women find their genitals can get irritated, particularly over long periods of *ménage à moi*. If you find this happening to you, try keeping things wet with saliva or lubricant (read more on lube on page 133).

Lie #6
A woman who masturbates will no longer be a virgin.

Truth: Though people define "virginity" in different ways, one thing is certain: Losing your virginity requires a partner. Because masturbation doesn't involve a partner, a woman can't lose her virginity doing it, even if she puts fingers or a sex toy in her vagina. In fact, plenty of virgins masturbate. For some women who are choosing not to have intercourse, masturbation helps

birds do it, bees do it?

HUMANS AREN'T THE only females of the animal kingdom who masturbate. Female horses, cows, dolphins, ferrets, cats, monkeys, chimps, gibbons, orangutans, and baboons have all been seen to play with their clitorises or rub their genitals against objects, especially when they're in heat. Porcupines in estrus sometimes straddle a stick and drag it with them as they walk. Female dolphins sometimes use the muscles of their vaginas to carry and rub against small rubber balls. Rhesus macaque (a kind of monkey) females sometimes fondle and suck on their own nipples, and stumptail macaques have been seen pulling their own tail between their legs and rubbing it against their labia.

them satisfy their sexual urges. Besides, no one would ever tell a boy who masturbates that he's no longer a virgin. Eighty-seven percent of female virgins who took our survey say they've masturbated.

Lie #7:
Only lesbians/sluts/bad girls masturbate.

Truth: Let's set the record straight about what kinds of women commonly masturbate:

○ Heterosexual women. Bisexual women. Lesbian women. Women who describe themselves as "none of the above." Women who say they're "not homosexual, not heterosexual, just sexual."
○ Women who have lots of sex. Women who've never had sex with a partner. Women who wish they were having more partnered sex than they are. Women who aren't interested in partnered sex.

I ♥ FEMALE ORGASM

- Single women. Married women. Dating women. Women who aren't sure if that person they hook up with sometimes is officially a "relationship" or not.
- Doctors. Dog-walkers. Lawyers. Janitors. Students. At-home moms. Women who don't have a job.
- Women of every age, race, ethnicity, and religious denomination. Atheists and agnostics, too.

According to *The Janus Report*, a national sex survey, nine out of ten women over age eighteen have masturbated. And the tenth woman just might give it a try when she gets in the right mood!

Lie #8
Women need to be careful not to masturbate too much.

Truth: If a woman is cutting class, not showing up for work, standing up her friends, or avoiding her significant other because she's too busy self-pleasuring, then she's overdoing it. Otherwise, there's nothing to worry about! It's perfectly fine for women to masturbate every day or several times a day. It's also fine to masturbate less or not at all. Most women find they go through phases depending on their mood, menstrual cycle, stress level, relationship status, and other factors—there's no right or wrong frequency when it comes to masturbation. After all, people don't worry about getting "addicted" to other enjoyable, perfectly healthy pastimes like bowling, knitting, or Googling themselves.

how do women masturbate?

TIME AND TIME again, women have told us, "I wanted to masturbate when I was growing up—I just didn't know how to do it." One woman said that when she was little, her mom gave her a kid's book about sexuality. The book said masturbation was healthy and normal, and the girl thought to herself, "Oh, good, now I can

out with the surgeon general— and with education for girls

IN 1994, A time when AIDS and teen pregnancy were high-profile social issues, U.S. Surgeon General Joycelyn Elders made the level-headed recommendation that American children should receive comprehensive age-appropriate sex education that includes information about masturbation. Her statements came under fierce attack and ultimately led to her forced resignation. In news commentary that week, TV host David Brinkley asked why "twelve-year-old boys should be taught skills they already have." *Village Voice* columnist Richard Goldstein pointed out in response that if masturbation were discussed in school, *girls* would learn about it too. The potential to promote female sexual pleasure, he said, was exactly what made the subject so threatening to so many people.

finally learn how to do it!" She turned the page expecting to find step-by-step instructions—but the book had already moved on to a new subject.

One of my friends asked me what masturbation was freshman year. I remember being really surprised that she didn't know, but in all honesty I wasn't 100 percent clear about the details myself.

In middle school and high school I masturbated by insertion and I never achieved orgasm. It wasn't until college that I discovered my clitoris and orgasm. I think this was all due to lack of information on the subject.

I wanted to masturbate but had no idea how to. It wasn't until after I got to college and had the privacy of my own computer to find websites geared towards women who also didn't know how. I was surprised to find that I wasn't frigid and that I was quite good at it.

Anywhere from 10 to 30 percent of the women in our audiences say they didn't masturbate as kids because they had no idea how to do it. Between 80 and 90 percent say they were told *nothing* about masturbation when they were growing up. Some figure things out on their own, or with the help of a friend, big sister, or book. Others reach young adulthood before they learn how to do it.

How do women do it? A *lot* of different ways! A woman might:

○ Touch, rub, or stroke her clitoris, especially the shaft (see diagram on page 70), using one or two fingers. This is the most common way women masturbate.

○ Use a vibrator to stimulate her clitoris (more on this in chapter 7).

○ Touch, rub, stroke, or massage other parts of her genitals, like her labia, urethra, or anus.

○ Use water to stimulate her clit: a handheld showerhead or the jet of water from a Jacuzzi or bathtub faucet.

○ Squeeze her thighs together.

○ Insert a finger or fingers, sex toy, or another object in her vagina.

○ Caress, massage, or squeeze her breasts and/or nipples.

○ Build up muscular tension by tightening muscles all over her body.

○ Rub her clitoris against something, like a pillow, pile of covers, or piece of furniture.

○ Fantasize by thinking about a story that turns her on, or imagining an image or memory that's sexy to her.

Of course, women also mix and match, using different approaches in one self-lovin' session, or playing different ways on different days. And some choose not to masturbate at all, which is okay, too.

I still don't really masturbate—I've never gotten the hang of it. I do remember discovering that I could touch myself and that it felt good, but I've never been good at actually turning myself on or giving myself an orgasm.

I never took a negative stance toward masturbation because my mother encouraged exploration of one's body, as long as it was behind closed doors.

However, I also never took advantage of masturbation; it was simply some-thing I wasn't interested in.

Why is it so hard to find complete, illustrated, step-by-step "How To Mastur-bate" instructions for women? Mostly because there are so many different ways. A technique that makes one woman's toes curl with ecstasy is likely to leave the next one limp with boredom. Sex researcher Shere Hite collected 3,000 women's answers to her in-depth sex questionnaire, and women's detailed descriptions of exactly how they get themselves off fill thirty-four fascinating pages of *The Hite Report*. If you're a woman who's never had an orgasm and you're looking for tips, check out the next chapter.

The more educated a woman is, the more likely she is to masturbate.

changing your self-love technique

SOMETIMES WE HEAR from women who feel limited by their own masturbation technique. For instance, perhaps a woman first orgasmed by lying in bed on her belly, squeezing her thigh muscles tight and pressing against her mattress. That technique may have worked fine when she was eleven, but as an adult she might find it limits her ability to have orgasms from other kinds of stimulation. If she wants to be able to come from oral sex, or have an orgasm by rubbing her clit while she's having intercourse, the lying-on-your-belly-thigh-squeezing technique may present some challenges.

Good news: It's often possible for women to learn to masturbate and have orgasms in new ways. The process can be a little frustrating, because you basically have to teach your body that it can respond to other kinds of stimulation—even when you know full well you could get off fast and easily your old way.

I couldn't get myself off with my hands for years, only with a vibrator. I finally taught myself when I was eighteen, and in the beginning it took a long time to orgasm. It was so frustrating and sometimes I'd quit before I came. Now I can get myself off with my hands in about five or six minutes and enjoy it a lot.

magic of ten game

WANT TO HAVE stronger orgasms, and be able to come in a wider variety of positions and situations? Here's a fun game a woman can play all by herself that can help:

1. Wait until you have some private time.
2. Masturbate in your most common, reliable way. Get yourself almost to the brink of orgasm, but stop before you reach "the point of no return"—do *not* allow yourself to fall over that orgasmic edge. Count, "one."
3. Change to a new position. If you were lying on your back, try kneeling on your bed, or sitting up with your back against the wall. Start masturbating again. You will have lost some of your arousal, but not all. Get yourself almost to the brink of orgasm again. It'll be a little more challenging this time, because you're not accustomed to doing so in this position. Again, stop before you reach "the point of no return"—no orgasm allowed yet. That's "two."
4. Change to a new position. You might lie on your side, or crouch doggie-style, resting on your knees and one forearm, using your head for support. You might try it with your legs closer together or farther apart than is your usual preference. Again, masturbate yourself almost to orgasm, but stop just before you get there. "Three."
5. Get yourself to that brink of orgasm ten times. You may find it helps to rest for a minute or two in between positions, to allow your level of arousal to fall back a bit before nudging it up again. On the tenth time, you're allowed to go for it—*finally*!
6. Enjoy an orgasm that will probably be particularly satisfying because of all that teasing. Longer buildups tend to result in bigger

orgasms. Plus, realizing your body has the potential to come in so many different positions can be liberating!

For advanced players: Instead of just modifying your physical position, experiment with changing the type of stimulation each time. Try one finger instead of two, vertical strokes instead of horizontal, tapping instead of rubbing. Vary your typical speed or rhythm. Masturbate with various kinds of penetration, both fingers and other phallic objects. Warning: This is a lot harder, and some kinds of stimulation may not work for your body. That's okay—you can also alternate between your reliable way of touching yourself and new approaches. Make up the rules as you go. The best part of this game is that you discover a little more about how your body responds each time you play. There's no way to lose at a game that ends in orgasm!

To make this kind of change, start masturbating using your old technique. When you get pretty aroused, switch to a new technique that will allow you more orgasmic versatility. Stick with it even though it will take longer and may not feel as arousing right away—this may require some persistence. You'll probably need to experiment a bit to figure out what feels best and how to make this new technique work for you, much like a woman who's learning to have an orgasm for the first time. (Your advantage is that you're starting with the confidence that comes with *knowing* your body is capable of having orgasms.) Make sure you orgasm using the new technique. If you're having trouble staying sufficiently aroused, switch back briefly to your old technique to boost your arousal, but then bring yourself to orgasm the new way. Keep practicing even though it'll take more time and might not feel like as much fun. Remember how many years you practiced your old technique, and be patient as your body learns this new way. (The books we recommend on page 89 also have helpful suggestions on this subject.) Approach this like an experiment: If it works, great, and it's also fine if you decide to stick with your tried-and-true way of doing things.

paddling the pink canoe

WHY IS IT that guys can take their pick of about a hundred fun—if sometimes violent—slang phrases for male masturbation (jerking off, beating off, playing pocket pool, choking the chicken, spanking the monkey) but the English language leaves women so few choices? Luckily, female self-pleasuring wordsmiths have been hard at work inventing and collecting slang for the girls. Next time, women, take your pick from many options:

beating around the bush
beating the beaver
bushwhacking
buttering the muffin
buzzing off
caressing the kitty
checking the oil
churning the butter
clitorizing
coaxing the genie out of the magic
    lamp
dipping fingers in the honey pot
double-clicking the mouse
fiddling the bean
finger dancing
flicking the switch
flitting my clit
getting to know myself
going pearl diving

going on a finger ride
having sex with someone I love
jilling off
letting my fingers do the walking
ménage à moi
mistressbating
paddling the pink canoe
parting the petals
petting the bunny
petting the pussy cat
plunging the happy hole
polishing the pearl
pushing the button
rowing the little man in the boat
rowing the little lady in the boat
rubbin' the nubbin
tiptoeing through the two-lips
two-finger tango
waxing the flesh taco

diddling for donations

FED UP WITH masturbation being relegated to the shadows, a group of women who owned sex toy stores wanted a way to build masturbation pride. In 1998 they announced a National Masturbate-a-Thon. As in a charity walk-a-thon or bike-a-thon, participants invited their friends and coworkers to pledge a dollar amount for each minute they masturbated during the designated day (in May, National Masturbation Month). The money was donated to women's health and HIV-related nonprofits. The pledge sheet proclaimed merrily, "I came for a cause."

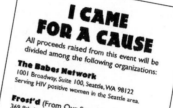

I CAME FOR A CAUSE

All proceeds raised from this event will be divided among the following organizations:

The Babes Network
1001 Broadway, Suite 100, Seattle, WA 98122
Serving HIV positive women in the Seattle area.

Frost'd (From Our Streets with Dignity)
369 8th Ave., New York, NY 10001
Health promotion and social servi...
workers on the

National Masturbate-A-Thon Pledge Form

Your name: Address: Phone:

Name of your sponsors:	Phone:	Amount per minute of masturbation:	Number of minutes:	Total Amount Collected:
Betty Dodson (Sample sponsor)	555-1212	$1	60	$60

I ♥ FEMALE ORGASM

sex tips for partners

○ If your partner masturbates, become this activity's number one fan. (Encourage her to be your solo-sex supporter, too; this should go both ways.) Let her know that you think it's great for a woman to be good friends with her clit.

> *Until I was in a relationship, I hadn't discussed masturbation, aside from dirty jokes. My boyfriend considered masturbation (mine, at any rate) to be a positive thing, and was eager to hear about what I liked. He provided me with enough encouragement to accept the practice of it, and do it more frequently.*

○ Encourage her to touch herself while you're being sexual together, if she's comfortable with this. (If she's not, she may warm up to the idea over time if you consistently let her know that *you're* comfortable with it.)
○ If your partner doesn't masturbate, buy her one of the books (see page 62) as a gift, and encourage her to read it. Or, read it together! (Of course, if she doesn't want to masturbate or share her masturbatory adventures with you, you should respect her decision about something so personal.)

some first orgasm stories

WE TREASURE THE thousands of stories women have shared with us about their first time having a big O. Here are some of our favorites.

> *I had seen those TV commercials that showed women shampooing their hair in a tropical waterfall. It looked so sexy! One day when I was ten or twelve I acted it out in the shower. I imagined the tropical fruit and the waterfall. As I soaped up my body, I imagined a man in the bushes watching me. As the water ran over me, I rubbed myself between my legs—and I had my first orgasm.*

I was a freshman in high school, and I was at a sleepover party with a bunch of friends. Someone had a magazine with an article about how to masturbate. We were all like, "Let's try it!" There were a lot of first orgasms that night.

Several women, and one mother of a toddler daughter, have told us they (or their daughter) had this experience:

When I was a little kid I was riding in the car with my parents. I was sitting in the back seat in a car seat—I don't know how old I was, but I was little enough that I still rode in a car seat. The car seat had this plastic safety bar that ran between my legs, and one day I discovered that if I squirmed against the bar it felt really good. I was a really happy little girl on long car rides.

When I was nineteen, I had my first boyfriend. After we'd been dating for a while, masturbation came up in conversation, and I told him I had never masturbated. He was totally horrified—he had trouble believing me, but I convinced him I was telling the truth. He said, "I'm going to give you a lesson." He sat me down and taught me how to masturbate. I had my first orgasm then and there!

At least three different women have separately told us experiences nearly identical to this one:

I was in high school, and this was when they had the Presidential Physical Fitness Program [which required that all public school students practice and compete at certain exercises]. I was doing that exercise where you pull yourself into a chin-up and hold it as long as you can. And while I held myself in this chin-up I had my first orgasm. At first I didn't know what was happening, but it was incredible.

Apparently when President Kennedy instituted this national physical fitness program for schoolchildren, he had no idea how many first orgasms he would facilitate. We've heard similar stories of girls having orgasms from having all their muscles tensed while holding themselves up between two bars on a jungle gym.

When I was a little kid I had a Raggedy Ann doll I used to rub against and have orgasms. I remember one day I asked my mom if what I was doing was okay, and she said, "Of course, dear, it's perfectly normal. You go right on dancing with Raggedy Ann."

The first time I got close to having an orgasm my heart was pounding so hard I was worried that I was going to have a heart attack or something, so I almost stopped. After a while I decided that maybe I didn't care and I should just go ahead. Turned out it wasn't a heart attack.

not only for the young

ACTRESS GLORIA STUART, who played 101-year-old Rose in the movie *Titanic*, wrote in her autobiography, "I am devoted to masturbation. I think it's probably one of the most pleasurable things in my life. . . . I had, and have, no guilt whatsoever when it comes to pleasuring myself."

My first orgasm happened accidentally in the pool. I moved against the jet that shoots from the side of the pool underwater, and got a really great feeling. So I stayed there until I got a rolling feeling in my stomach and my privates started throbbing. I didn't really think about what it meant, I just liked the feeling. I did that every summer.

I was doing sit-ups in gym class and I felt this sensation building in my crotch, but I got scared and stopped. The next time I was doing sit-ups it started again, and I let it come on, and I had my first orgasm. It felt really, really good, but it's sort of a problem when this happens to me because I'm in a public place and I can't let people know what's going on.

When an audience member told us this story, another woman in the same audience raised her hand to share the same exact experience. These orgasms are probably the result of muscle tension, perhaps combined with movements and breathing. Some women have told us similar stories of having orgasms while using the gym's weight machine where you repeatedly lift your legs up and swing them back. Most women aren't able to come this way, but those who can have extra incentive to stay in shape!

In college I've had a few male friends who used to constantly pester me about whether I masturbated. I would always say no, which was true, but they didn't believe me and they were always badgering me about it. It was a topic of conversation a lot. One day it was winter break and I was finally alone. There weren't a lot of people on campus and I didn't have much to do, so I thought, I'll try it. I did—and I had an orgasm. It was great. I picked up my cell phone right away and called my guy friends, and said, "I tried it, and it worked!" I was thrilled.

3

So You Want to Have an Orgasm?

You've never had an orgasm, but you want to? Not sure if you've had a big O? You've come to the right place! (If you and/or your female partner already have orgasms, and you're happy with them, you might want to skip to the next chapter.) There are more women who haven't had orgasms than you might think: About half of women have their first orgasm after age sixteen. It's *very* common for women not to learn how to come until they're in college or in their twenties. And we've met plenty of women who had their first orgasm in their thirties, forties, fifties, sixties, or beyond. This chapter may also be useful for women who find it's more challenging to reach those lightning bolts of orgasm than they'd like, and for supportive partners trying to help.

not sure

IN THE FIRST couple years that we taught about female orgasm at a center for adult education, we'd frequently distribute pre-class surveys to our students, who ranged in age from their twenties to their seventies. The first versions of our surveys asked women if they'd ever had an orgasm, and provided two options as answers: yes or no. Surprised by the number of question marks and "don't know" written in the margins, we quickly learned to add a "not sure" box whenever we asked the question.

In our online survey, 7 percent of female respondents said they didn't know if they'd had an orgasm. Some believe, "If you don't know if you've had an orgasm, you haven't"—but we disagree. Our work, and our conversations with others like Betty Dodson who have helped countless women have their first orgasms, leads us to believe there are two possible explanations for women not being sure if they've come:

1. **They've felt intense pleasure, but not an orgasm.** They feel unclear because typical arousal involves surges of pleasure, sometimes quite intense. These surges are usually shorter than orgasms, typically don't involve the same kind of repeated muscular contractions, may not have the same kind of full-body involvement as an orgasm, and while they feel good, aren't *as* good as an orgasm. But how could you know that unless you've had both?
2. **They've been having small orgasms.** Sometimes women see porn orgasms, or read descriptions of orgasms, and imagine the experience to be much bigger and more earth-shattering than the little orgasms they're experiencing. They know they're feeling *something*, but they're not convinced it's an orgasm. These women may be able to "grow" their orgasms with Kegel exercises or by building up to higher levels of arousal before they allow themselves to come. Or, they may begin to appreciate what they have, and recognize that porn-gasms are like porn breasts: bigger (and faker) than most of what you'll find in the real world.

I think I had a very definite impression of what orgasm was supposed to be and put pressure on myself to embody that image. Then I ran across an online article about female orgasm that emphasized that orgasm can take many different forms. I also finally internalized the idea that orgasm is not the end goal, and that as long as I feel satisfied by my sexual interactions (with or without orgasm), I shouldn't feel disappointed. Incidentally, since then it's been much easier to orgasm.

what if i'm one of those women who can't have orgasms?

MANY PEOPLE HAVE heard the distressing claim, "There are some women who just can't have orgasms." As a result, women who've never had one sometimes worry that they might be one of these unfortunate women. While many studies have found that 5 to 10 percent of women have never had an orgasm, this statistic is misleading. Many of these women are young and haven't learned how to have an orgasm *yet*. In *The Hite Report*, the majority of women who'd never had an orgasm were thirty or younger—which indicates that even women who didn't used to be orgasmic often figure out how to come as they get older.

I had three children before I ever had an orgasm. I was married, and we had a good sex life—I enjoyed sex a lot. It wasn't until years later that I realized just how good it could get.

Some women are too uncomfortable with sexuality to learn to masturbate (the most surefire way for a woman to have a big O, and the easiest way to learn), buy a vibrator, or seek out a sex therapist. Some may be perfectly satisfied not having orgasms, and see no reason to pursue the matter. The percentage of women who would like to have an orgasm but are truly physically unable to is minuscule. Statistically speaking, it's highly unlikely that you're one of them.

For a long period of time, I was unable to have orgasms, even though I'd been able to have them before. I think much of the problem was psychological, in that I worried something might be wrong with me. I was more anxious about having an orgasm, and so it became harder and harder to relax when I did

viagra for women?

SOME FRUSTRATED WOMEN muse about how nice it would be just to pop a pill for instant orgasms. Many find Viagra tempting. Unfortunately, research studies have conclusively found that Viagra doesn't work for women. While Viagra increases blood flow to women's genitals (as it does for men), this doesn't result in higher levels of arousal. Some women who took Viagra in clinical trials did have more orgasms—the rate was the same as for women who were being given sugar pills they believed were Viagra. (The placebo affect is powerful!) While some doctors still prescribe Viagra to women, there's no evidence that it's worth taking.

I ♥ FEMALE ORGASM

unlikely orgasms

A SMALL BODY of research finds that many women are able to have orgasms even after accidents or surgeries that might have been assumed to make this impossible. For instance, many women whose clitorises have been partly or entirely removed during female circumcision (also called female genital mutilation) still have orgasms, some reporting that their breasts are now their most sexually arousing organ. Similarly, up to half of women with spinal cord injuries, whose bodies don't transmit nerve impulses from below their injury, are able to experience and enjoy orgasms from genital stimulation, even though they can't feel the touch that brings it on. While experts once told spinal cord injury survivors that the orgasms they claimed to experience were "all in your head" and "not real," laboratory researchers have now confirmed that these women's orgasms are as physiologically real as anyone else's.

want to masturbate or have sex. It's very easy to get yourself into a self-fulfilling prophecy like, "I can't have an orgasm!" Then you try to masturbate or have sex, and don't come, which reaffirms that you can't have an orgasm. After many months of no orgasms at all, I found myself in a very low-pressure situation with a willing and eager partner, and I was able to have orgasms again.

Rather than thinking about yourself as nonorgasmic, it's helpful to think of yourself as preorgasmic—you almost certainly have the ability to have an orgasm, you just haven't had one yet. You're not allowed to declare, "I'm just one of those women who can't have an orgasm" because chances are, you haven't worked hard enough! If you read and try everything this chapter suggests, read the other books we recommend on page 89, and work with a sex therapist, and still no orgasms, well, then maybe you are one of those women. (There's information about possible medical causes of the problem on page 84.) But until you've tried it all, banish the thought!

five steps to your first orgasm

READY TO GIVE it a try? You can do these activities at your own pace, definitely not all in one day. It'll probably take at least a few weeks, and possibly a few months or longer, to work your way through them, depending on how often you work on it.

step one: start alone.

Most people in relationships have already done things that could lead to female orgasm: touching the clitoris, using fingers to stimulate the G-spot, oral sex, and possibly intercourse in various positions. If these haven't already led to orgasm, and you're ready to take on having an orgasm as an official project, it may be tempting to make it a joint one. Our best advice is to resist this temptation. That doesn't mean you can't have sex with your partner during the time you're learning how to have an orgasm—just don't make having an orgasm the focus of your time together.

If you're a partner trying to figure out how you can help a preorgasmic girlfriend or wife, see "First Orgasm Tips for Partners" on page 87.

If you're single, there's zero reason to wait until you find a skilled lover to help you have your first orgasm. Start learning now—and then when that skilled lover comes your way, you'll be ready for some incredible rock 'n' rolling together!

Why do most women find it easier to master having an orgasm themselves first, and then add orgasms into their partnered sex life? Well, if you're alone:

○ You have total control over the stimulation, so you can make the tiniest adjustments to hit your most sensitive spots exactly right (a half-millimeter to the left, a smidge more pressure, etc.) without even thinking about it, and definitely without having to ask for it.

○ You don't have to wonder what your partner thinks if it's taking a long time or worry if he or she yawns.

○ You'll be less likely to worry that your partner thinks you're a failure, or is losing interest in Project O, if there's no orgasm the first, third, or twenty-seventh time you try.

- You don't have to fret about what your partner thinks of your body, whether you should be holding in your stomach, how recently you shaved your legs, or other thoughts that steal attention away from *enjoying* your body. (Hint: It is not easy to have an orgasm while sucking in your stomach.)
- You won't be holding back out of concern about what you'll look like, what sounds you'll make, or what your partner will think when you're having an orgasm.
- There's no chance that a partner's touch or words will be distracting at the wrong moment (this is possible even with the most caring, loving partner), since having an orgasm can sometimes require intense physical and mental concentration.
- You know you won't be able to fool yourself by faking an orgasm.

When you're with a partner after you've had some orgasms on your own, you'll feel more confident and comfortable knowing exactly how it feels when you're very close to coming, and how it feels to allow yourself to "fall over the edge" into an orgasm. As you practice, you'll gain insights about what your body does and doesn't respond to, which could be handy to share with a partner later.

Okay, so you're alone. Choose times to work on this project when you won't be interrupted. Lock the door and turn off your cell phone. Make yourself as comfortable as you can—you might put on sexy music, or start by taking a bath to relax.

> ## "i deserve a treat!"
>
> HAVE YOU EVER bought yourself a sweet treat, or taken yourself shopping? Being able to give yourself an orgasm is the ultimate treat. And hey, it's free!

step two: befriend your vulva.

She's always been there with you—it's time you got to know one another.

Your vulva is your external genitalia, the parts you can see without looking inside your vagina. It helps to have a clearer sense of what's there before you start asking these parts to help you have an orgasm. Take out a mirror, sit back so you're resting on some pillows, set a light so you can see well, and take a look down there. You can prop the mirror up on a pillow, or hold it with your feet.

A lot of us got the idea that penises are beautiful, even something to be worshipped (what's with all the phallic monuments?), but that female parts are ugly, gross, disgusting, and smelly. Give us a break! Be prepared to discover something beautiful between your legs. A lot of women are surprised to find that with the lips held apart, their vulva looks like a flower, a butterfly, a seashell, a heart, or an angel spreading her wings. Female genitals are incredibly diverse: some larger or smaller, symmetrical or lopsided, in all different shapes and intricately shaded browns, purples, and pinks. Would you recognize the face of your own vulva if you saw a photo of her?

Your outer lips, also called labia majora (the ones with hair on them—or where the hair used to be if you shaved it off) are easy to find. Locate your inner lips, too (these are also called the labia minora). It's very common for some part of one or both inner lips to protrude outside the outer lips—either way (inner lips that stay hidden or friendly types that like to hang out) is totally normal. Do you have a neatly identical pair or a jaunty unmatched set? Both of those are normal, too. Your inner lips are part of the larger structure of your clitoris, and can be quite sensitive to touch.

My right labia minora is larger than my left one and I really thought this was ugly and unusual. It wasn't until college that I really started realizing my vulva was completely normal and beautiful.

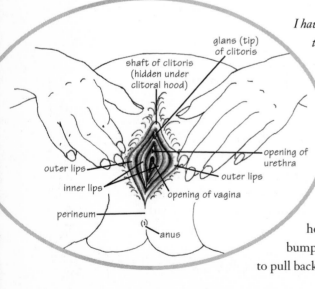

glans (tip) of clitoris

shaft of clitoris (hidden under clitoral hood)

outer lips

inner lips

perineum

opening of urethra

outer lips

opening of vagina

anus

I have a large vagina with meaty outer lips and I used to be self-conscious about it. But once my ex went down on me the first time, he loved it so much I had no shame in my game anymore!

Growing up with Barbie's genitals being a flat, labia-less crotch, it's easy to see why most girls are paranoid about their vaginas.

Up at the top, sort of where your outer and inner lips come together, find the glans (or head) of your clitoris. The part you'll see is like a bump—most are less than an inch long. You may need to pull back the hood of skin to make it visible.

I ♥ FEMALE ORGASM

porn alert

PORN IS MESSING with women's concepts of what genitals are supposed to look like. Remember: The women who act in mainstream porn films and those whose photos are online are hired because they have a specific body type—and genital type—that producers and website owners think people want to see. The same way that porn flicks nearly always show guys with big penises and women with huge, often surgically-enhanced breasts, women's vulvas in porn nearly always have the same basic "look." The look includes having inner lips that are pink, symmetrical, and smaller than the outer lips, and shaved pubic hair. If wanna-be female performers' genitals don't have the "preferred" size and shape, they either don't get the job, or they may get cosmetic surgery to change them.

Many women whose vulvas *don't* look like the ones in porn worry that their bodies are abnormal or deformed. There's even a growing industry of cosmetic surgery designed to make vulvas look more like the ones in porn, often by cutting off parts of women's inner lips.

Don't fall for it! Remember, porn may be entertaining for some people, but it's rarely an accurate source of information about sex, bodies, or what's "normal." Your inner lips are part of your clitoris—some women find they're even more sensitive than the head of their clit. Surgically altering their shape won't help you have an orgasm. It may actually work against you, due to possible scar tissue and nerve damage caused by the surgery.

In porn, female genitalia look a LOT different than mine does. But now I realize that there's nothing wrong with mine—it's theirs that are different.

Growing up, I feared that my vulva and clitoris were too big and quite deformed. I used to watch porn to see if I was the only person who looked this way and I finally found a porn star who had a similar looking vag. It wasn't until my junior year that I finally did real exploration and learned that my genitals are perfectly normal. I also learned that porn stars' bodies are not the norm. It definitely made me more accepting and freer with my body. It helped me to enjoy vaginal and oral sex, too.

See if you can feel the shaft of the clitoris (like the shaft of a penis) above the head—it feels like a small cord underneath the skin. Your clitoris continues inside your body—the entire organ is about the same size as a penis, and has sensitivity throughout, but these external parts (glans and skin-covered shaft) are usually the most sensitive.

Find your vaginal opening, the start of that incredibly elastic, muscular organ. A vagina can squeeze tightly around a finger, or, with the right rush of hormones, expand its accordion-like folds to allow a baby to be born (and afterward, with the help of Kegel exercises, become toned enough to contract tightly again). To see exactly where your vagina is, you may want to wet your finger (licking it is the easiest way) and slide it inside an inch or so.

Just above your vagina see if you can see your urethral opening, the small hole where pee comes out. The skin just below your vagina is called the perineum. The hole below that is your anus.

I used to think all girl parts down there were gross, but since seeing The Vagina Monologues *and really talking openly with friends in college, I love the vagina. It's awesome—weird looking, I guess, but in a fantastic way.*

step three: touch yourself experimentally. no goal!

Step three isn't about having an orgasm. It's a way to do an easy little science experiment on your own body. Your goal is to find out what kinds of touch feel best to you, and what places on your body are most sensitive. You're especially interested in what kind of genital touching feels good.

Again, you want to be relaxed, so turn off the phone, put on some nice music, take a bath or shower if you want. Start by running your hands all over your body in a way that feels good. Notice what areas feel nice to you. Caress your breasts and your nipples. Pay attention to the sensations.

After you've done this for a while, move your hand to your vulva (the external parts of your genitals, not inside your vagina). Touch around the different parts, noticing if there are any areas that feel particularly nice when you touch them. Many women find their inner lips and urethral opening can be very pleasurable to touch. Because the clitoris is the part that helps most women have orgasms, give it some particular attention. If you're not sure where it is, look back at page 70. See how creative you can be: How many different ways can you find to touch your clit? With each one, just notice: Does this feel more sensitive, or less? Does it feel good? Which side feels better? Would it feel better with a slightly lighter touch, or slightly firmer? Try touching:

○ Directly on the head (the tip) of your clitoris
○ On the shaft rather than the tip
○ On the left side
○ On the right side
○ Side to side
○ Up and down
○ In circles
○ The shaft of your clitoris with a rolling motion under your finger
○ With one finger
○ With two fingers
○ With tapping, massaging, stroking, and gentle pinching motions
○ Any way you can think of!

Wet your fingers by putting them in your mouth, or adding some water-based lubricant, and then try touching some more. Does it feel better if your fingers are wet?

If a partner has brought you to orgasm before using his or her fingers but you've never been able to do it yourself, definitely experiment with touching yourself the way your partner does (or did). You can even imagine that it's your partner touching you as you use your own fingers.

If you want to, try putting a finger inside your vagina and experimenting with different ways of doing that. Do you like the sensation? How does it feel if your finger moves? How about if you massage with your finger in different directions: up, down, left, right, at each different angle. Your anus also has lots of nerve endings—you can experiment with touching it, too, if you want.

Trying different speeds and pressure with my hand and moving around a lot helped me learn to have an orgasm. If one spot's not working, skip it and move on. Kind of like the SATs.

I would say exploration and experimentation are the best things to do when learning how to have an orgasm. Try everything you hear or read about. If you explore, you're bound to find something that satisfies you.

With each thing you do, just notice the sensations without judging yourself. If anything hurts or feels uncomfortable, stop doing that and try something else instead. You may feel very little at first, but pay attention to even the smallest sensations—they'll grow with practice. Try not to let any preconceived notions about what you *should* be feeling, or what you wish you were feeling, get in the way. Allow yourself to feel what you feel, and do more of the things that feel good.

I've found that turning my brain off and focusing on the pleasurable physical sensations makes a REALLY big difference. Sometimes this is easier to do than others. Being relaxed is also helpful.

step four: keep touching a few times each week. experience whatever happens. don't give up!

Now that you've spent some time observing what kind of touch your body likes best, keep doing it! Try to have a self-pleasuring/self-exploration session at least a few times a week (every day is fine if you like), for twenty minutes to an hour each time. (You probably happily shop, instant message, or watch TV for that long a few times a week, if not daily; it's a perfectly reasonable amount of time to spend on something you enjoy.) Don't worry about trying to have an orgasm—just keep touching in the ways that feel good to you. You might find that you want to touch harder or faster as you get more turned on—if so, do it! Don't stress or worry about trying to make yourself have an orgasm, and don't let yourself start analyzing or judging yourself. If an orgasm comes along, great, but if not, just enjoy the pleasurable sensations.

It's a good idea sometimes to touch yourself with full awareness, paying close attention to the process. Some women find it also helps to touch themselves almost absentmindedly (when it's appropriate—we're not recommending you start doing it in the supermarket canned goods aisle!). You could touch your clit or your whole body while you're alone watching TV or reading (whether or not what you're reading or watching is sexy). Let it be something you do sometimes for no reason at all, just because it feels nice.

Definitely don't stop doing these exercises, even if you've tried a few times and haven't had an orgasm. It can take a while for your body to "wake up" and start appreciating the sensations, and it can take a while for you to fine-tune your technique. You may notice yourself getting aroused more on some days, less on other days. That's fine. When you do get aroused, keep doing the things that got you to that place. You're on the right track: Orgasms happen at the peak of arousal.

> ### been there, tried that, didn't like it
>
> OKAY, SO YOU tried masturbating before and decided you didn't like it. Don't give up! The book *Tickle Your Fancy* wisely points out, "When you had sex for the first time, was it completely enjoyable? The first time you ate spinach or sushi, did you really like the taste?" Masturbation can be an acquired taste, and you'll get better as you practice. Don't write it off too fast.

Don't make having an orgasm a goal like trying to meet a productivity goal at work, where you work harder and harder and have less and less fun. Don't think about orgasm while you're doing these exercises—instead, think about whatever you find hot, and whatever feels good. Enjoy the journey!

Just do what feels good! I wish I had gone into it with a more "fun-oriented" mindset, rather than my systematic, goal-oriented, "something's-wrong-with-me-if-this-doesn't-work" mindset.

step five: experiment with other things that can help boost your arousal.

○ **Squeeze the muscles of your vagina.** These are the same muscles you use to do Kegel exercises (see page 26). Squeezing and relaxing them speeds up your arousal, and can help nudge you toward an orgasm. It's another thing to experiment with while you touch yourself.

○ **Move your hips.** Let them gyrate if it feels good. Move them up and back as you breathe and enjoy. Let your body move however it wants to.

○ **Relax and breathe.** You'll be able to feel more if you relax the muscles in your pelvis and genitals. Imagine breathing directly into your pelvis.

○ **Make noise.** Let yourself sigh, moan, and make whatever noises you feel moved to make.

> *For a long time I was worried I would be loud and someone would hear me, and that held me back from having an orgasm. Being confident no one can hear me helped.*

○ **Use fantasy.** In our survey, 72 percent of orgasmic women said they fantasized always or often while they masturbated. By comparison, only 45 percent of women who masturbated but hadn't yet had an orgasm said they always or often fantasized. Learning how to fantasize, or giving themselves permission to do so, is one of the most common things women say helped them learn to have an orgasm.

Use your imagination to find those images and stories that are sexy to you. Let your mind drift over them. You can replay the same moment over and over if it turns you on, or follow a whole story in your mind, making yourself one of the people in the story. You can pretend that your own hands are someone else touching you. Your fantasies are private thoughts—no one else can ever know what they are unless you tell them. Don't stress about whether your conscious, analytic mind "approves" of the stories, and don't worry about whether you'd ever want to really do these things in real life. For now, they're just thoughts that turn you on— nothing more, nothing less. Most women use fantasy when they want to have an orgasm, especially when they're alone, and often when they're with a partner, as well. For more about fantasy, and figuring out what fantasies you like, see pages 30–31.

○ If you like, use stories, pictures, or movies. If erotic stories, romance novels, sexy pictures, or X-rated movies arouse you, or the idea appeals to you, by all means, read or look at them while you touch yourself. If the idea turns you off, then don't! Some women have a strong preference for written stories with no pictures. Some aren't into stories or mainstream porn but like independent porn, porn made by feminist women, gay male porn, or European porn. Some don't like any of it at all.

Reading romance novels or something sexually stimulating is helpful prior to first touching myself. It helps me become aroused before masturbating.

○ **Try using a vibrator.** Vibrators create a different, more intense kind of sensation than your own fingers. While not all women like how they feel, many women find using one is by far the easiest way for them to have an orgasm.

My first vibrator was a liberating experience. I had masturbated for most of my life, and had had several male sexual partners, but I never reached orgasm. My vibrator helped me take masturbation "over the top" and allowed me to finally fully release. In time, I learned to orgasm other ways and with a partner.

If the idea appeals to you, get yourself a vibrator! Read more about where to get one and how to use it in chapter 7.

○ **Keep your clit wet.** A woman recently came up to Dorian *before* one of our educational programs. She was beaming. "I'm so excited to be here!" she said. "I just had my first orgasm this week, and I'd been trying to have one forever!" After congratulating her, Dorian asked what she had done that had made the difference. "I used lube," the woman said. "You've got to tell people how much of a difference it makes to get things really good and wet." So there you have it! Wet your fingers with saliva or lube at

get wet 'n' wild

JETS OF WATER can be a great way to discover your orgasmic potential. If you
have a handheld showerhead, try
pointing it at your clit. You can also
play with the jets in a Jacuzzi or the
tub faucet (finding a position that
works is the challenge there). We've heard from scores of women who owe
their first orgasm (and their 101st) to a well-aimed stream of water.

*I was taking a shower one day and pointed the water jet toward
my vagina to rinse off soap. Luckily for me, it hit my clitoris and I
discovered that I could achieve an orgasm that way. Each time I
took a shower, I placed the jet on my clitoris until I couldn't stand it
anymore; I wanted to take it off because the feelings were so overwhelming and unfamiliar, but it felt so good.*

*Running water on the clit is awesome! I like to do it lying down in
the bathtub. There are no tools and you don't have to touch yourself if you're uncomfortable with that.*

first. As you become aroused and your vagina lubricates, you may be able to dip your fingers down and bring your own wetness up to your clitoris.

In order to have an orgasm, I had to learn to stimulate my other erogenous zones to get wet before trying to stimulate my clitoris.

things that can work against you

IF YOU'RE FINDING it hard to have an orgasm, check out this assortment of things that can work against you or slow you down. Do they ring true for you?

○ **Fear.** We always ask female audience members for their tips for other women in the room who want to have an orgasm but haven't yet. "Don't be afraid!" is one of the most common answers. It's not unusual for a woman to feel apprehensive about the unknowns of orgasm, the intensity of the sensation, the sounds she'll make, what she'll look like, whether she'll feel embarrassed in front of her partner, or the possibility that she won't be able to have one. For women with a history of sexual trauma, the sensations of touch on their genitals, or of becoming aroused, may bring up powerfully negative memories or emotions. A sex therapist or the book *The Survivor's Guide to Sex* can be enormously helpful in working through these triggers.

Indeed, orgasms do involve a short loss of control and the vulnerability that comes with that. Most orgasmic women agree that an orgasm's deliciousness easily makes up for the things they used to worry about. Be bold and tap into that fearless part of yourself until your confidence comes more easily.

> ### troubleshooting:
> #### the never-ending plateau phase
>
> *Help! I've been trying to have an orgasm, and I masturbate, but my plateau phase goes on so long I get bored and eventually give up. What can I do?*
>
> IF YOUR PLATEAU phase (for a definition, see page 20) seems to stretch to Neptune and back, stop trying so hard. Don't worry about having an orgasm, but instead focus on the sensations you're feeling throughout your body. Use fantasy and get lost in the hottest storyline you can invent, or find some inspiration in great erotica. Relax and enjoy the process. Once it starts working, it won't always take so long.

○ **Negative body image.** Some women walk around all day saying to their own body, "I hate you! You're fat, you're ugly, I hate everything about you!" and then turn around and say, "Okay, body, give me an orgasm." A woman like this shouldn't be surprised when her body says, "Um, I don't think so. You hate me!" If your body hatred is intense, it can be difficult or impossible to allow yourself to experience physical pleasure. In an online Queendom.com survey of 15,000 people, 46 percent of women said self-consciousness about their body or hair was often what prevented them from having orgasms. A research study found that women and men who were anxious about their bodies tended to have lower sexual desire and enjoy sex less.

Body image is an issue facing some—though certainly not all—people with physical disabilities. The cultural assumptions that people with disabilities don't, can't, or shouldn't have sex compounds the problem. Some people living with disabilities face additional challenges, from limitations on what they're physically able to do, to the need for assistance or privacy from a care attendant, to pain or fatigue that can make sex difficult.

Whatever your relationship with your body, befriending it isn't always easy. It's possible, however, to take steps toward negotiating a peace treaty. This may involve working with a therapist, joining a body image support group, journaling, or reading positive websites or books about body image (see our suggestions on the next page).

One of the cool things about sex is that for the most part, it works fine regardless of how you look. Having thinner thighs doesn't make you a better kisser. People with zits or limp hair can orgasm just as well as anybody else. In some ways, sex (including, or perhaps especially, sex with yourself) is your chance to take a break from criticizing your body, and instead experience how great it can feel.

---

speed comes with practice

YOUR FIRST ORGASM may take a long time to work up to, but rest easy. Most women find they climax faster and more easily the more they practice. Not that the fastest orgasm is always the best, of course. But sometimes it *is* nice to be able to come before your fingertips are wrinkled prunes and you've developed a repetitive strain injury.

I ♥ **FEMALE ORGASM**

love your body

IN A WORLD obsessed with skinny, perfect bodies, loving your body isn't easy to do. Here are some juicy books and sites to help, though:

Big Big Love: A Sourcebook on Sex for People of Size and Those Who Love Them, by Hanne Blank

> A fantastic resource about sex for those with more "bounce to the ounce"—full of smart, honest attitude and down-to-earth advice. Inclusive of straight, lesbian, and bi readers.

The Body Image Workbook: An 8-Step Program for Learning to Like Your Looks, by Thomas F. Cash, PhD

> A highly interactive, well-respected book that leads readers dissatisfied with any aspect of their appearance through a process to modify their self-image.

The Ultimate Guide to Sex and Disability: For All of Us Who Live with Disabilities, Chronic Pain and Illness, by Cory Silverberg, Miriam Kaufman, Fran Odette

> By far the best book on the market about sex for people with a wide variety of disabilities. Supportive, encouraging, and loaded with resources, and inclusive of straight, lesbian, and bi readers.

About-Face
www.about-face.org

> Chock-full of facts, stories, best and worst ads, and "what you can do" ideas to tackle negative and distorted images of women's bodies.

I think the best advice I've ever heard about being self-conscious in sexual situations was, "Women are thinking, 'Oh, no, I smell weird, my thighs are huge, I should have gotten some sun last weekend, and crap, I need to do a touch-up shave.' Men are thinking, 'Woo-hoo! There's a naked lady in front of me!'"

○ The belief that someone else should give you an orgasm. Female orgasms are better and easier to come by for women who are willing to take charge of their own climax. Don't assume an orgasm should be a gift one lover gives to another; most women play an active role in seducing their own orgasm, sometimes with a lover who helps, sometimes not.

It took me a while to learn that penetration alone wouldn't induce an orgasm. Also, I couldn't expect the guy to know what he was doing— if I wanted to have an orgasm, I had to know how to position myself so I would have one. I have to take control.

○ Concern about unplanned pregnancy, HIV, and sexually transmitted infections. These are about the unsexiest things anyone could think about! Of course these aren't risks during masturbation, but these issues can easily squelch an orgasm during partnered sex. When someone else's bodily fluids are involved, there's no such thing as sex with no risk at all (heck, there are risks to crossing the street, driving your car, and eating the leftovers in your fridge). But you *can* reduce the risks of sex—and allow yourself to relax and enjoy—with well-informed decisions about contraception and safer sex. To learn more, see chapter 11.

○ Smoking, drinking, and medical conditions that affect circulation. Sexual arousal and orgasm rely on blood circulation to the genitals. You might say, "If the blood don't flow, there ain't no O." Conditions like high cholesterol, high blood pressure, and coronary heart disease can have a negative impact on blood circulation, as can smoking, because it can cause blood vessels to constrict.

Drinking heavily has a numbing effect on nerve endings throughout your body, including down below (remember how they used to use

I ♥ FEMALE ORGASM

whiskey for surgery before the invention of modern anesthesia?). While some people find that a drink reduces sexual inhibitions, going overboard reduces your ability to feel sexual sensations. Numerous studies have found that with each additional alcoholic drink a woman drinks, the longer it takes her to have an orgasm, and the less intense the orgasm is. Our advice? Get so freaking comfortable with sexuality that your sober self can be as wild and crazy as you like.

○ Some medications. Certain antidepressants (SSRIs) are the most common culprit here. One in ten women over age eighteen now takes antidepressants, and these drugs' orgasm-inhibiting side effects pose a ballooning problem. Some women say the pharmaceuticals have no negative side effects for them, but others find they reduce their sex drive, make it more difficult or impossible to come, or make their orgasms less intense or less satisfying. These issues create tough decisions for people taking the medications: It can be a painful conundrum to be forced to choose between having orgasms but being severely depressed, and feeling good about life but never having an orgasm. Several women have told us they'd been suicidal before they found the right medication—they described their stark choice as nonorgasmic living versus death.

Hormonal methods of birth control (like the pill, the patch, the ring, and Depo-Provera) can also have a negative impact on arousal and orgasm for some women, although this varies depending on the woman and the method.

If your antidepressants, contraception, or other medications you take (antihypertensive, anticonvulsant, and anti-ulcer medication, as well as sedatives, neuroleptics, and antihistamines, can all have similar side effects) are affecting your orgasms and you're frustrated by this, tell the doctor who prescribed them. Ask if there are alternative options. Some antidepressant medications and some methods of hormonal birth control are less likely to have these side effects than others (although unfortunately, some patients find that the antidepressants that work best for their depression are the ones with the negative sexual side effects).

For two years after she completed her primary cancer treatments, Dorian took a medication that reduced estrogen and testosterone production, based on evidence that this could reduce the risk of a cancer recurrence. We hope it did, because it sure didn't spice up our sex life. During this period of time and in our conversations with others on other medications, we've learned two tips for trying to have orgasms on libido-crushing medications.

First, if you have orgasms sometimes but not as reliably as you'd like, see what you learn from the pattern of times you *have* been able to come. Was it twenty-three hours after you took the last pill, when the drug load was lowest in your body? (Some people on SSRIs find it helps them to skip a dose, but this isn't safe for everyone—something to talk to your provider about.) Did it happen at a time when you were particularly aroused—maybe an especially long foreplay session, or some dirty talk that got you really hot? Was it a certain time during your menstrual cycle? (This may not apply if you're on hormonal contraception.) Finding and replicating the patterns won't make orgasms come easily, but it may help you maximize your chances of having one at all.

could it be a medical problem?

IF YOU'VE TRIED the types of techniques discussed in this chapter and you're still not having orgasms, it's possible there's a medical explanation. Ask your doctor for a pituitary function test (prolactin level) and a fasting blood sugar. These two blood tests can reveal medical issues that can impair a woman's ability to have an orgasm, according to sex therapist Judith Seifer, PhD, professor of Sexual Health at the Institute for Advanced Study of Human Sexuality.

For women who used to have orgasms but can't anymore, Dr. Seifer finds that common physical causes include multiple sclerosis, lupus, Addison's disease, adult-onset diabetes with neuropathy, and some collagen diseases. If you're living with one of these diagnoses, a doctor or a sex therapist (see page 89) may be able to help you explore your options.

The second approach involves identifying tiny increases in your sexual arousal on any given day. People's sexual thoughts and interests naturally fluctuate over the course of each day. Let's say a woman graphed her "normal" (nonmedicated) sexual interests in a twenty-four-hour period. She might wake up vaguely turned on by a sexual dream, then forget all about sex for a couple of hours, catch the eye of a cute store clerk as she buys her morning coffee and entertain a few brief seconds of sexy thoughts, go to work, have a long stretch of nothing sexy at all, until some sexual thoughts start flooding into her brain for no reason in the late afternoon and she gets quite horny. A couple of hours later she goes home, and that evening notices

I ♥ FEMALE ORGASM

mild arousal as she watches a sex scene on HBO. At the end of the day she hasn't had any sex or orgasms at all, but she could draw the lines on a graph, with small peaks (the coffee counter flirtation), high moments (that afternoon horniness with no explanation), and valleys (long morning at work).

On medication, her graph might look flatter, with fewer peaks, and the peaks of sexual interest she does have may be less intense. Still, she *will* have some mild peaks. Over the period of a few days or a week, notice when you have tiny up-ticks in sexual interest—write it down if that would help you remember. Then start looking for patterns. Do you tend to have your most sexual thoughts in the mornings, or at night? In the middle of your menstrual cycle, or just before or after your period? Is there some visual trigger during the day that creates the littlest spark? Rather than feeling sorry for the ravenous urges you know you're *not* feeling, find ways to catch your little peaks and ride them for all they're worth. Vibrators can also be particularly useful for women with decreased sensitivity.

While these approaches help some people some of the time, others choose to make peace with their lack of orgasms. Cuddling, sensual touch, massage, and other kinds of physical intimacy can be extremely pleasurable without an orgasm, and these shift the focus from what you're *not* feeling to the joy of the sensation you do feel.

troubleshooting:
wimpy orgasms

I have orgasms, but they're so little and pathetic. How can I have orgasms with "POW!"?

KEGEL EXERCISES (page 26) are the key to bigger, better orgasms—with comic book "POW!", as one woman described them. Get the muscles of your vagina in shape, and they'll be able to contract more intensely during your orgasms, resulting in more sensation for you. Avoiding quickies, and instead spending more time with long buildups (as in the game on page 55) can also give you bigger blast-offs.

orgasms with a partner

ONCE YOU'VE HAD some orgasms on your own, if you're in a relationship you may be raring to have them while you're together. Your knowledge that your body is fully capable of coming should give you a confidence boost, but that doesn't mean it's always easy to have an orgasm with a partner. It may take a while to learn how to come now that you're adding on the challenges (and sometimes fun) of:

○ having someone looking at you
○ having your body touched or stimulated in ways you're not controlling
○ having more going on in your head. Should I be pleasuring my partner? What does he/she think? Am I taking too long? Is this going to work? Not to mention the random conversations that pop up when two people are together.

Just because your body has now had orgasms doesn't mean you'll come at the drop of a hat (or the drop of a pair of boxers or a bra). You'll probably need to make sure that at some point during the interaction you get some good, sustained clitoral action, whether that's from oral sex, your own hand, your partner's hand, a vibrator, or maybe rubbing against your partner's body. Don't worry about "being greedy"—sex is about both giving and receiving, not always simultaneously. You should have plenty of time to receive sexual pleasure! Most women who have orgasms during partnered sex play find they need to be assertive and "take charge of their own orgasm" if they want to know it'll happen.

Especially while you're still learning, you may find it helps to ask your partner to cut back on "distracting" caresses to let you focus on the key sensations that may get you off. Having him or her kiss you, suck on your nipples, or thrust deep inside you may feel great, but some women find it sends them in a different direction, away from their climb toward climax. If you suspect this is the case, try saying something like, "You feel so good. . . . What you're doing with my clit is so hot, it might make me come—if I can just focus on that one sensation for a while, so I don't get distracted—yes, just like that!" There's more specifically about having orgasms during intercourse in chapter 5.

Ideally you have a supportive, patient partner who knows that this is new for you, will help you get the stimulation you need, and won't make a big deal if it takes a bunch of attempts over a period of time to get the hang of things. This is not the time to start faking—then you'll *really* confuse matters if you want to try for real the next time. Don't forget to enjoy being sexual whether or not you have

86

an orgasm. Figuring out how to have orgasms together can be a fun joint project, but it doesn't have to be your main goal; don't let it eclipse the physical and emotional pleasure of being together.

first orgasm tips for partners

YOUR PARTNER'S NEVER had an orgasm? Here are some ways you can help her:

○ Enjoy sex together without making orgasm your goal. She's much more likely to have an orgasm in your presence if she's enjoying herself. Being obsessively focused on making her come—rather than just helping her feel pleasure—can take the joy out of sex. Know that her ability to have an orgasm with you likely has nothing to do with whether or not she loves you or enjoys sex with you.

○ Spend lots of time on activities that focus on female pleasure, particularly those that stimulate the clitoris. Oral sex can work well, but only if she's comfortable with it. See "How to Make Her Very, Very Happy (Eight Tips on Being a Great Lover)" on page 197.

○ If she's never had an orgasm, encourage her to explore it on her own, and then incorporate it into sex with you once she's figured it out. Some women don't masturbate because they're worried about what their partner would think, so make sure she knows she has your support.

○ Give her this book, or the others we recommend on page 89, to give her ideas of what to do.

○ If she wants to have her first orgasm with you, or she's had orgasms through masturbation but never with a partner, be exceptionally patient. Having an orgasm with someone else in the room can be like the experience of being "pee-shy," where it's hard to urinate with another person present. Realize it will get easier and faster for her with practice. Don't add to the pressure she's probably putting on herself to make it happen. Communicate things like, "If it happens this time, great, and if not, that's fine, it'll happen some other time" and "We can take as long as you need and keep going as long as it feels good."

The first guy I had sex with couldn't please me; he wasn't patient. The guy I'm dating now has been a blessing. He's very patient, lets me try whatever positions I want, talks to me about what I like, then does it. I guess I had to learn to be comfortable with the person I'm with in order to have an orgasm.

○ If she's had orgasms before but never with a partner, do what you can to replicate her masturbatory conditions until she gets the hang of you being part of it. If she always comes while lying on her back, have her lie on her back. If she uses her fingers on her clit, have her do that. If she uses a vibrator, she should use the vibrator during sex with you. Let her get accustomed to coming in her "original way" while you touch or pleasure her; later you can expand your repertoire together so she can come in a wider variety of ways.

○ If shyness, guilt and shame about sex, a history of abuse or assault, body image issues, or a sex-negative upbringing get in the way of your partner's ability to enjoy sexual pleasure, there are no overnight cures, but you can certainly help her. With honesty and respect, compliment whatever aspects of your partner's body and genitals are attractive or sexy to you (don't lie to her—she'll be able to see right through that). She may brush aside your comments or think you couldn't possibly mean what you're saying, but over time, she may start to accept the idea that you find her attractive (even her nether regions), and rethink the way she thinks about herself.

I felt uncomfortable about the appearance of my vagina up until a few years ago because one side of my labia is bigger than the other. It wasn't until I saw pictures of sexually mature women, read educational materials, and had a loving boyfriend who adored my vagina that I came to love it. I think I look like a beautiful, sexually mature woman.

Cultivate a mutually curious, exploratory attitude toward sex in your relationship. Never push her beyond her comfort zone, but do explore anything sexual that interests her (as long as it's safe and comfortable for you). Read books about sex together—choose ones she says appeal to her—and talk about them. Attend workshops and classes about sex to learn more together—make it a fun date. Our top picks for books about healing from sexual abuse, and helping a partner heal, are on pages 39 and 40.

○ Realize that ultimately, this needs to be her own process of learning about her body. While you can help and be supportive, you can't do it for her.

for more on finding your O

LOOKING FOR MORE in-depth instruction on how to find your O? There are entire books on the subject, or you might find it helpful to work with a sex therapist. We think these are the best of the books:

- *The Elusive Orgasm: A Woman's Guide to Why She Can't and How She Can Orgasm,* by Dr. Vivienne Cass
  Written in the conversational tone of a caring therapist, this thorough book explores every possible reason why women have orgasm challenges and offers solutions. Inclusive of straight, lesbian, and bi readers.

- *Becoming Orgasmic: A Sexual and Personal Growth Program for Women,* by Julia Heiman and Joseph Lopiccolo
  An accessible, comprehensive book written for heterosexual women that leads the reader through a series of exercises to learn to have orgasms alone and with a male partner. (Skip the outdated and partially incorrect information about HIV/AIDS, though.)

- To find a sex therapist near you:
  American Association of Sexuality Educators, Counselors, and Therapists
  www.aasect.org
  804-752-0026

4

Going Down, Down, Baby:
oral sex and female orgasm

When Dorian invites groups of women to brainstorm things that could help a woman have an orgasm, tongues rank high on the list, and frequently cheering ensues when they're mentioned. Why so popular? Well, tongues are wet, soft, and warm, fast or slow, and they can make all sorts of luscious strokes. In short, they're brilliantly designed for clitoral stimulation, the heart of orgasm for most women. One research study of married women found that on average, they rated oral sex as the most enjoyable way to have an orgasm. Certainly, not all women like to receive oral sex, and not all partners want to give it, but for many, oral action is one of sex's sweetest delicacies.

Cunnilingus, oral sex on a woman, wasn't always an "everybody's doing it" sort of activity in the United States. For the generation born in the 1930s, oral sex wasn't something good husbands and wives (and certainly not girlfriends and boyfriends) did—only about 44 percent of women had received oral sex in their lifetimes (or admitted it to researchers who asked). Many Baby Boomers say that in their day, oral sex was considered far more intimate than intercourse, something some couples would do only if they felt truly comfortable with each other. Still, the numbers climbed: 75 to 80 percent of female Boomers say they've received oral attention. Today, the number of women in their early thirties who have received oral sex has reached its highest number in recorded history, topping out at 87 percent. The numbers aren't quite as high yet among today's twentysomethings, but all indicators suggest they'll catch up—some haven't yet had an opportunity to give it a try.

The first time I had an orgasm was when my boyfriend at the time gave me oral stimulation. It was amazing. I told him that if he wanted to he could do that every hour on the hour for the rest of my life.

A lot of partners are pretty enthusiastic, too:

It's lots of fun to be able to pleasure a woman while being so close to the center of pleasure. I also think there's beauty in the female genitalia. It's great to be able to not worry about yourself and focus completely on her pleasure.

At first I just wanted to try going down on her. Her reaction and mood afterward make me want me to do it over and over again. It's the only thing I can do that makes her cry out my name and use the phrase, "Oh, God."

Despite the popularity of oral sex, most of our female survey respondents reported they aren't receiving as much as they'd like. Some were too self-conscious, some had partners who didn't like or preferred not to give oral sex, some weren't sure how to ask for more.

Oral sex on men is so external, whereas on women it's so internal and much more personal. You could give a man head while he still has his pants on! But for a woman, you have to be right there, between her legs, and she has to open up (literally and figuratively) and give herself to you.

I think I'm too shy about asking for oral sex. I enjoy spontaneity, but I would be lying if I said I didn't want it more. I need to speak up and ask for it more often.

My girlfriend won't perform oral sex on me very often (she's only done it about three times) because she's sensitive to my smell and taste. I don't mind doing it to her, but it sucks for me.

While some women said they found other kinds of sex more or equally pleasurable, many more expressed a desire to make oral sex a bigger part of their lives. Since feeling self-conscious about receiving it or about asking for it was a major barrier for many women, let's dive into that issue first. If you're already an oral sex enthusiast, skip right down to the positions on page 100.

receiving lip service:
overcoming shyness and self-consciousness

cunnilingus is nothing new

ORAL SEX'S POPULARITY just keeps growing, but it's not a new invention. The Moche civilization, which existed from 300 BC to 1000 AD in what is today northern Peru, depicted on their pottery women receiving oral sex. ("Mrs. Johnson, would you like your tea in the mug with the tiger or the one with the cunnilingus?") Similar ancient erotic art exists in Japan, China, and India.

Those who refer to oral sex as an "unnatural act" might be surprised to learn that many species also perform cunnilingus on each other, including chimpanzees, gorillas, squirrel monkeys, dolphins, red deer, moose, cheetahs, black and grizzly bears, bats, and even the humble hedgehog. For some species, oral sex is primarily a "lesbian" activity done by two females; in others males are just as likely to be the lickers.

UNLESS A WOMAN is a contortionist or a superbly flexible gymnast, oral sex offers her partner a closer view of her genitals than she's ever gotten herself. And it's not just the view: Partners get to touch, smell, and taste. Some women squirm uncomfortably at the very thought of what the experience might be like "down there" for a partner. As one woman wrote on our survey, "It's dark!"

It's not surprising that many women are shy, if not profoundly uneasy, about letting a partner get too close to their private parts. Our culture doesn't offer women much support in the vulva self-esteem department. As we've discussed earlier, many girls grew up surrounded by messages that their genitals are dirty and shameful. Middle school slurs describe vulvas and vaginas as tasting "fishy," and slang like "carpet munching" makes oral sex on a woman sound about as appealing as chewing on a doormat. Douche commercials sell the idea that women need to buy their products because their genitals are frequently "not so fresh," planting more suspicion for women that their genitals must be an unpleasant place to spend time. The few places that women get to see what female genitals

I ♥ FEMALE ORGASM

look like—porn and textbook line drawings—generally fail to show the vibrant diversity of colors, shapes, and sizes that are healthy and normal for girl parts.

In reality, most women who are terrified of how they taste or smell are basing their feelings on fear rather than experience. If this describes you, you can do a reality check: Put your finger down there, bring it up to your nose and mouth, and experience it for yourself.

I tasted my own stuff, just to see what I was subjecting others to, and realized it's not bad at all!

Va-jay-jays do have their own smell that's unique to each person, just like the variation in the scents of lovers' skin, hair, mouth, and male genitals. But the smell of a woman's vulva isn't necessarily a bad one—in fact, a lot of people say it grows on them over time. The pH of a healthy vagina is about the same as a glass of red wine, and like wine, it can be an acquired taste. Many women report that their feelings about their taste or smell changed when they saw a partner unbothered by it—or totally turned on. Indeed, several recent research studies reported that most men say it's pleasurable to go down on a woman (and while we haven't found research on what lesbians have to say on the matter, we'd dare to guess most of them agree).

I was so scared the first time. And I still am now. I constantly asked—or rather bugged—my partner whether he liked what he was doing. Or if he was sure. Although I wanted him to do it very much, I was scared that I was too smelly there. I asked him if he was doing it for my pleasure alone, or if he enjoyed it as well, and he reassured me that he loved it, and, in fact, it smelled great and tasted great. I don't think I fully believe him yet!

I had concerns until my current partner assured me that he loved the way I looked, smelled, and tasted, and that he loved giving me oral sex. Then I stopped being self-conscious and just let myself feel good.

My fiancé has told me he LOVES the way I smell and taste. He said if he didn't like it down there he wouldn't want to visit it so often!

Women's juices usually taste and smell different at different times in their menstrual cycle. Partners may notice differences just before a woman's period, just after it, and, if she's not on hormonal birth control, around ovulation. You might see if there are times of the month your partner particularly enjoys your taste or would prefer to avoid, and plan your oral interludes accordingly. Also, while women do taste different from each other and frequently come up with theories about how this is affected by what they eat or drink, most women who *try* to change their taste by eating large amounts of some food (pineapple is the most famous one) haven't found much, if any, change. Many partners have commented, however, that smokers have a noticeably bitter taste.

tips for boosting your oral sex self-esteem

1. **Shower before sex.** Showering before a date or before you expect to be in a sexual situation is generally good etiquette, given that most people aren't fans of armpit odor, either. That said, many people are far more worried about the way their own body smells than they need to be, and most couples don't feel the need to run to the shower every time sex is on the horizon. Among the many benefits of having a partner you trust and have built a rapport with is that you can rely on each other to suggest a quick break for both of you to brush your teeth or hop in the shower together.

   I want to be clean and tasty for my partner, so sometimes I suggest a shower as foreplay. That way we're both clean and we get to spend time together naked before we're actually in bed. And sometimes we never make it to bed!

2. **Stay clean in vagina-friendly ways.** A normal vagina is slightly acidic on the pH scale (and you thought that chemistry class would be irrelevant to your life!), which helps it fight disease-causing bacteria and keep cervical cells healthy. Soap, on the other hand, is alkaline, so washing inside a vagina with soap throws off the balance and can even make it smell worse. Vaginas clean themselves constantly, sort of like eyes—

president goes down on intern: the headline that didn't quite happen

PRESIDENT BILL CLINTON'S affair with intern Monica Lewinsky sparked a national debate about whether oral sex counts as sex, and whether, therefore, the Commander in Chief was lying when he said, "I did not have sexual relations with that woman." The *Starr Report*, the most scintillating government-produced document in history, revealed that although their relationship involved plenty of oral for the big boss, the day Bill talked about reciprocating on Monica, she turned him down because she had her period. Talk about bad timing!

they're generally better off if you let them do their own thing and only wash around the outside. All the vagina-owner needs to do is rinse the vulva (the outside parts) and entrance to the vagina gently with warm water. If you feel you absolutely must use soap, choose something very mild, without dyes or perfumes, or a soap that advertises itself as having a low pH.

Along the same lines, vaginas definitely do not like douching (spraying water or fluids into them). Unless you have a medical problem for which douching is a treatment, skip them. Douches disturb the normal pH levels and can spread infections, potentially leading to pelvic inflammatory disease or bacterial vaginosis. Your vagina wasn't designed to smell like a plug-in air freshener, and your partner isn't expecting it to.

3. **Plastic wrap isn't just for leftovers anymore.** On page 268, we write about using dental dams or plastic wrap for STI prevention. A bonus feature of plastic wrap is that it blocks out tastes and smells. If you're feeling self-conscious, your partner is having a hard time coping, or you're at the beginning or end of your period and prefer to have a barrier in place, a nice, long sheet of plastic wrap may be just what you need to receive the

benefits of an enthusiastic tongue while sidestepping the issue of taste and smell. For added sensation, add a few drops of lube on the vulva side of a dental dam or sheet of plastic wrap.

4. Get beyond the awkwardness. Do you identify with these women's comments?

> *For a while I wouldn't let my partner give me oral sex. I felt all vulnerable lying there naked alone while he was off exploring part of me that I wasn't comfortable with yet myself.*

> *I've felt nervous and uncomfortable to the point of pushing guys away and saying, "Oh, you don't have to do that." They take what I say to mean that I don't want them to, or probably that they're doing a bad job. Then everyone just gets humiliated and uncomfortable. Really, I guess I'm probably hoping they'll say, "No, I really want to," and keep at it. Maybe it's all just a process of looking for confirmation that in fact I'm not gross, smelly, taking too long, etc.*

> *I don't like partners to give me oral sex with bright lights on, and sometimes I put my hands on my stomach, because I feel chubby.*

If you recognize these thoughts and emotions, you're definitely not alone. Here are some things to try:

○ Think about how early sexual experiences may have affected you. How your first few partners treated you and reacted to your body can have a huge impact, particularly if they said negative or disparaging things, since you had no basis for comparison yet. Experiences like sexual abuse or assault can add to the challenges.

> *The first person who ever went down on me told me that I smelled funny and tasted funny. It took me a long time to get over feeling self-conscious as a result of that experience. Luckily I had another partner*

who told me how much he loved how I tasted and smelled and was so enthusiastic about giving me oral sex that I was able to start feeling sexy about receiving it.

If a past partner has been critical of your body, remind yourself that his or her comments were rude, and that many partners are likely to feel very differently!

○ Don't expect perfection. One woman passed along to us the advice she gave to a friend who'd given her boyfriend oral sex but was too self-conscious to receive it: "Think about the male genitals—they're not exactly pretty, either." Remember that sex in the real world will never be the picture-perfect acts and bodies you see on TV. In television sex, romance novels, movies, and porn, no one ever farts or queefs (that's when air "farts" out the vagina—charming!), people never accidentally elbow their partners in the head while changing positions, and no one ever has to pause to extract a pubic hair from his or her teeth. In real life these things happen. No biggie. You're not expected to be Ms. or Mr. Perfect in bed.

when to call the doc

GET YOUR VAGINA checked out by your doctor or a local health clinic if it has:

- a distinctly bad odor that doesn't go away,
- an unusual vaginal discharge (all vaginas have normal vaginal secretions that change through-out the menstrual cycle—you want to pay attention to some-thing that's different or smells particularly bad),
- or an itching or burning sensation.

These could be the symptoms of a yeast infection, a sexually transmitted infection (STI), or something else that requires med-ical attention. Some clinics, including many Planned Parenthood centers, provide serv-ices on a sliding scale based on income. For information on preventing STIs, see chapter 11.

I've learned to be more confident and proud of my body. I've realized that a lot of the concerns I had aren't shared by my partners! Sex can be fun, great, fantastic, mind-blowing even. It can also be messy, smelly, sweaty, and awkward. Relax and go with it! It's worth it in the end, right?

○ Read the body image and "Befriend Your Vulva" sections in chapter 3. Figure out what it would take you for you to feel more comfortable with yourself. The book *Femalia* is a cool way to see how many different ways vulvas can look, and will give you a clear picture of how yours fits in with the diversity.

5. **It's okay to say no.** You don't have to like oral sex. If you're just not that into it, it's fine to say, "No, thanks." Your feelings may change over time, as you become more experienced sexually or have different partners with different attitudes or techniques. Or they may not, and that's perfectly fine, too. Oral sex is one option among many, and there are plenty of people who prefer other activities instead.

6. **Ask for it.** The flip side of "It's okay to say no" is "It's okay to ask for what you want!" Asking for something sexual can take courage, but it usually works to your advantage (this goes for every sexual act under the sun, not just oral sex). Think about it:

○ The worst case scenario is that you ask, and your partner says he or she would rather not. While that would be disappointing, you haven't lost any ground; you ended up just where you started out.
○ Think about times your partner has asked you for something he or she wanted sexually and you agreed. There's a good chance you enjoyed getting your partner off or intensifying his or her pleasure. There's a chance he or she shares your interest in oral sex but is too shy to go for it, too insecure about his or her skills, or unsure about how to bring it up.
○ Partners aren't mind-readers. Unless you've discussed the issue before, it's unfair to assume that your partner doesn't go down on you because he or she doesn't like it. It's possible that he forgot about it because he's doing things "the usual way," or she doesn't realize how much you enjoy it.
○ Just as you have the right to ask, your partner has the right to say no, or make a modified proposal ("How about we do that this

weekend when we both have time to shower first?"). Asking isn't forcing your partner to do something he or she doesn't want to do.

I know my girlfriend won't go down on me unless she wants to. And if she's not enjoying it, she'll stop and use her hands—which is fine with me. It's good to know she doesn't feel like she has to.

If you're trying to find the right words to ask, here are some to try on for size:

○ *How about we trade? I'll do you, you do me.*
○ *How do you feel about going down on women? It's one of my favorite things.*
○ *We haven't done oral sex on me in a while—would you be up for it?*
○ *I was just thinking about that other time when you ate me out—that orgasm was incredible. Would you be in the mood to do it again?*
○ *I'd love it if you'd go down on me.*

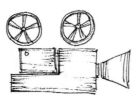

BIG O on the big screen: *American Pie*

IN THIS POPULAR coming-of-age flick about a group of high school guys hoping to lose their virginity, one guy goes down on his girlfriend in her bedroom. He secretly refers to a "Sex Bible," a compendium of handwritten sex advice passed down from high school classmates. As the girl's father approaches her bedroom door to tell her dinner is ready—nearly unknowingly walking in on the couple—he hears his daughter say, "I'm coming, I'm coming!" as she has her first orgasm. Her dad shrugs and heads back toward the kitchen, assuming she's "coming" to dinner.

positions for going lips to lips

POSITION	HOW IT WORKS	BENEFITS
Classic R & R (Rest and Recline)	Woman lies on her back or reclines against pillows. Partner lies or kneels between her legs.	■ Woman can relax, close her eyes, and focus on the pleasure radiating from below. ■ Easy access to vulva, clit, and vagina for partner.
Edge-o'-the-Bed	Woman sits or lies on bed, slides her crotch to the edge. Partner kneels on the floor or sits on a low stool beside the bed.	■ Less neck strain for the partner than the Classic R & R position. ■ Easy access for partner. Great for using fingers or toys.
Throne (aka Her Royal Highness)	Woman slouches in an armchair, couch, or seat with padded back. Partner sits on floor or footstool.	■ Easier for partners to see each other because both are partly upright. ■ Easy access for partner.
Sitting on Face (variation: Cooler Sex)	Partner lies flat on back. Woman kneels over partner, positioning vulva over mouth.	■ Woman has some control over pressure and location of stimulation by moving her hips and raising/lowering herself slightly. ■ Some partners find this position particularly sexy and like the view up at her. ■ Partner can lie back and relax.

I ♥ FEMALE ORGASM

DRAWBACKS	TIPS
■ Can lead to stiff neck and back pain for partner, especially if he/she stays put a while. ■ Not much body contact between partners—can feel far away from each other.	■ Use pillows under her butt and/or under partner's chest to improve the angle. ■ Don't make her spread her legs too wide unless she wants to (that's a porn technique designed to maximize visibility, not usually preferred in real life).
■ Where do her legs go? Dangling them off the bed isn't comfortable for long.	■ Try having the woman rest her feet on her partner's back or shoulders, on the mattress, or on other things (chairs or boxes) you set up.
■ Might require a trip to Ikea to find the perfect chair. ■ Some women find it comfortable to rest their feet on the floor or on the chair; others experience the leg-dangling problem.	■ Use pillows to adjust both partners' heights. ■ If you push the chair up to the bed, she can put her feet on the bed. ■ If you don't want a wet spot on your nicest armchair, put down a sheet or towel before she settles in.
■ Some women get tired supporting their weight up there, find it difficult to relax enough for arousal to build. ■ Position makes some women feel self-conscious. ■ Some partners feel uncomfortable about having less control and reduced ability to "come up for air."	■ Use pillows under partner's head to raise it, so woman's legs don't have to be spread so wide. ■ Major improvement: Give woman something to lean on, like a headboard or sofa. A big sturdy cooler (the kind you use to keep the drinks cold for a picnic) is even better—put it on the bed, cover it with a sheet or towel and pillows.

POSITION	HOW IT WORKS	BENEFITS
Thigh Pillow	Both people lie on their sides. Woman lifts her top leg, partner rests head on the inner thigh of lower leg.	■ Relaxing for both partners. ■ Nice body contact. ■ Face at a different angle to vulva allows for somewhat different angle stimulation than most other positions
On Your Knees	Woman stands, partner kneels in front of her.	■ A classic position for guys to receive head (some blowjob givers think it's hot, others find it degrading). Guys aren't the only ones who can enjoy this position, though, and some women like it precisely because it's often a "guy's position." ■ Can be done spontaneously in small spaces and "naughty" places.
Specialty Furniture	Several companies sell trademarked furniture with names like The Liberator and The LuvSeat, designed to expand on sex position options.	■ Who isn't intrigued by the idea of furniture designed specifically for sex? ■ Can be used for intercourse, anal sex, and other sexual activities, too. ■ Invaluable for some people whose back, knee, or hip problems or other disabilities limit their sex position options.

DRAWBACKS	**TIPS**
■ Can be trickier to get the right stimulation. Fewer options because neither partner can move much. ■ What to do with her top leg?	■ Experiment with facing the same direction or facing opposite directions.
■ Many women get tired of standing after a while and want to sit or lie down to fully appreciate the sensations. ■ Hard on the knees of the kneeler.	■ She'll probably feel more stable if she stands with her back against a wall. ■ Use a pillow under the partner's knees if he/she wants to go at it for a while but still walk later. ■ Consider starting out this way, then moving to another position to finish.
■ Expensive! ■ You can't return it if you try it out and decide you don't like it. ■ Where to store it when it's not in use?	■ If you're willing to be creative, you can probably find cheaper alternatives with firm pillows and furniture around the house. Plus, flea markets and garage sales have never been so much fun as when you're shopping for a footstool of just the right height.

69:
the fantasy (usually) exceeds the reality

SIXTY-NINE IS one of the most famous numbers on earth, because it's the slang name for the act of two people simultaneously performing oral sex on each other. The numbers sort of represent the shapes of the two bodies facing each other side by side, one right-side up, one upside down. The appeal, of course, is the potential to receive pleasure at the same time, not usually possible with oral sex. Plus, 69 keeps you close together, making it perhaps a more intimate position than most approaches to oral sex.

We'd never heard of anyone doing a 69 survey before, but we figured the time was long overdue. Our findings confirmed our suspicions:

○ Most people have tried it (or want to).
○ Most people (though certainly not all) conclude that it's better in theory than in practice.

Sixty-nine is the ultimate in multitasking. Em and Lo, the authors of *Nerve's Guide to Sex Etiquette,* put it best when they wrote, "Developing a rhythm [during 69] requires the coordination of a Cirque du Soleil performer, the patience of a Buddhist monk, and the motor skills of a bonobo ape. To say nothing of the concentration skills required." Here's what typical 69 critics had to say on our survey:

I'm afraid if he does something that feels particularly good, I'll accidentally bite him.

I hate 69. It's physically awkward (I'm very petite and my partners have generally been very tall) and I find it too distracting. I'm working too hard at what I'm doing to enjoy what I'm getting, but I can't entirely ignore what I'm getting in order to focus 100 percent on what I'm doing!

It's difficult to say, "Harder," or "Gentler," or "Up a bit" when one has a mouthful of cock.

I ♥ FEMALE ORGASM

69 is like communism. It's fair, it's equal, and it doesn't work.

But the act does have its share of fans. Men seem to be a bit more enthusiastic about 69 than women overall, perhaps because women are more likely to find they need honed concentration to be able to have an orgasm. These comments are all from women in the pro-69 camp, though:

Most of the time I like it because I like how my partner's pleasure contributes to my pleasure and vice versa. The first time I ever experienced simultaneous orgasm with a partner was in this position.

I love it! I like it because it prevents me from fully concentrating on myself and what's happening between my legs—it's distracting in a good way. I also really like giving head—it turns me on and turning on a partner is really hot. Sometimes it can be frustrating if my partner stops giving me head because it gets too distracting for him. I come more easily from this than anything except masturbation, I think.

I've tried it before with men, and with the female partner I'm currently with. With men, it's pretty awkward if the woman is ever on the bottom because she has a hard time controlling how far the penis is going into her mouth. Doing the 69 position with another woman is absolutely amazing. It allows one to grind and to sort of tease. INCREDIBLE!

If you're going to try it, keep in mind that there are two possible positions for 69-ing: side by side and top/bottom. In the top/bottom position, many women with male partners have strong opinions about whether they prefer to be on the bottom (where they can relax, possibly more like the way they usually receive oral sex) or on top (where they can control how deeply their partner's penis goes into their mouth). Side by side, both partners can relax more, and there's less of a feeling of having your partner's anus too close to your nose, but the angle of stimulation can be trickier.

Think-outside-the-box 69-ers point out there's no law that says both people have to use their mouths the whole time. Some prefer modifications where the two partners take turns, alternating their oral attentions back and forth, or where one person uses manual stimulation while the other does oral. For instance, some women find it easier to give a hand job while they receive oral sex, which gives their partners a chance to receive more genital pleasure than they normally would while going down.

oral sex tips for partners
(how to be a cunning linguist)

THE PREREQUISITES TO giving great oral sex are a positive attitude, a willingness to try and to learn, and a reasonable amount of patience. If you've got all three, you're well along the treasure trail already. Let's take a closer look:

1. *A positive attitude.* More important than whether your tongue flicks side to side, up and down, or turns backflips is whether your partner gets the sense that you enjoy—or at least are *absolutely* comfortable with—going down on her. If you get suited up with goggles and a snorkel, we guarantee she won't let you stay down there for long (and she definitely won't be having any orgasms). The number one thing that helps a woman relax, which she needs to do to be able to enjoy what you're doing down there, is knowing that you want to pleasure her this way, don't see this as punishment, and maybe even (gasp!) enjoy it yourself. If you like licking her labia, by all means let her know! If it turns you on, don't keep that a secret. If you think the color or shape of her vulva is beautiful, say so. And if you enjoy her taste or scent, or just the way you can feel or hear the pleasure run through her, tell her that, too.

   My partner assured me that he liked the taste and smell. We also explored the way it looked together with a mirror. Doing that really helped me feel at ease about myself and helped us bond.

   That doesn't mean you should lie to her if these things *aren't* true for you—most people have pretty good b.s.-meters, and if she gets the sense she's being fed falsehoods, that could backfire big time. If taste or smell is a challenge for you, check out some of the tips earlier in this chapter.

2. *A willingness to try and to learn.* This is easy enough: You let your partner know that you're willing, you initiate oral sex on her sometimes, you experiment and ask her for tips and feedback. This doesn't mean you go down on her if she doesn't want you to. But your positive attitude makes a huge difference here. On our survey, one of the most common pieces of advice women gave about oral sex was to pay closer attention to the cues the woman sends: her moans, movements, and suggestions.

> *Tell your partner before you begin, "I want you to tell me what you need. Tell me if you want faster or slower, etc." If a partner does this in a serious tone, the woman is likely to feel safe and comfortable giving instructions.*

> *Make it all about the girl, listen to her body language and you'll know what she likes. Moans and hip movements mean that she wants more. So give it to her!*

To be fair, the woman should remember to let her partner know how it feels to her, to avoid the problem this man described:

> *I usually feel very unsure about "how things are going" while I'm performing oral sex, whether the act has become monotonous or if the woman is enjoying it. I often feel like I have no idea if I'm actually producing pleasure.*

3. *A reasonable amount of patience.* As you know, on average it takes a woman longer to have an orgasm than a man. For male-female couples, intercourse leaves many men struggling against fate, doing everything in their power not to come too quickly. Cunnilingus doesn't have that same pressure—theoretically, it can last until the receiving partner is satisfied, as long as the giving partner still has the strength to lift his or her tongue.

This removes one pressure but creates a new one. The giving partner may be eager to get his or her own turn at receiving pleasure, not only giving it. (While some people find giving oral sex totally sexy, it's a rare partner who can get off this way without some added genital stimulation.) Some men are notorious for paying lip service to oral sex but ultimately not spending enough time down there. A few licks of the clit, and *BAM!*, he's back up, ready for intercourse or something else that's going to give *him* an orgasm.

Women repeatedly say that their favorite cunning linguists are the ones who make clear they're willing to spend as much time as the women need. This message can be communicated in gentle reassurances ("I'm in no rush," "We've got lots of time," "I'm happy to keep going as long as you want"). Or it can be communicated nonverbally, with enthusiastic oral sex until the woman comes (or says she's had enough), no matter how long it takes.

My partner asks, "Did you?" way too often. Just keep going and don't worry. I'll tell you when I'm done!

I've often been concerned about how long it takes me to reach orgasm, especially the first few times with a new partner. Once, after many unsuccessful attempts with a then-boyfriend, I expressed this concern. He reassured me that it doesn't matter how long it takes, that he can go for a very long time without getting tired. The next time we tried oral sex, having been relieved of that concern, I was able to have my first orgasm with him.

With that said, you'll notice we recommend "a *reasonable* amount of patience." Some partners mistakenly interpret our advice as if the goal is an entry in the *Guinness Book of World Records* for Longest Licker. For your own sake and hers, be willing to change positions and make adjustments (add pillows, etc.) so you don't end up stiff and grumpy. Also, remember that not all women can have orgasms, and not all can come from oral. If she gets the impression that you're going to keep eating at the Y until the cows come home, she may feel forced to figure out a way to wrap things up.

> *If the guy is down there for a long time, I can never figure out if he wants to come up for air or if he's enjoying himself, so I usually end up faking an orgasm.*

Okay, so some women would be happy if you stayed there all night, and others get antsy far sooner. How can you tell the difference? Ask her. If you're having trouble reading her cues about whether she's enjoying herself and just needs more time or is ready to move on to something else, you can always whisper sweetly, "Would you like me to keep going? I'd be happy to, if you want."

going down: tips for partners, continued

IF YOU FANCY dining downtown, don't take the express train straight from kissing to clit-licking. Work your way there gradually. Caress her breasts and suck on her nipples. Kiss her abdomen, her belly, her thighs, the crease where thigh becomes vulva. If she's wearing pants or underwear, breathing on her crotch or licking the fabric can be sexy. Once you're skin to skin, spend some time licking and kissing the outside of her vulva. Not only are you building her anticipation and arousal, but you're also letting her know that you like her body, not just her "hot spots."

You're aiming for her clit eventually, but even with your head between her thighs, don't jump directly to it. Explore her vulva with your mouth and tongue. Use your hands to gently open her outer lips if you need to. Lick all around slowly and appreciatively, as if her genitals were a delicious treat that you wanted to savor all over.

Once you've gotten that far, here are the compiled dos and don'ts from the 776 women who completed this section of our survey:

○ *DO focus on the external part of her clitoris, directly or indirectly.* The number one piece of advice women said they'd like to give their partners was, "Concentrate on the clitoris," "Lick the clitoris plenty," and "Stick to the outside: the clit!" In the space for oral sex advice one woman wrote simply, "Clit. Clit. Clit. Clit. Clit." Many women wrote variations of this:

I've had men try to use their tongue like they would their penis. Big mistake! The beauty of oral sex is that penetration isn't the only option. In fact, the main objective is clit stimulation.

If you're not quite sure where to find the magic button, see page 70. Women's anatomy varies quite a bit from one to the next, making some clits easier to find than others. If you're not positive, ask her! You don't have to say, "Uh, honey? Where's your clitoris?" Rather, try saying, "Show me where it feels good to you," or asking, "Is this the place where it feels best for you?" Remember that the very tip of the clit is often too sensitive—she'll likely prefer your attention to the shaft of the clitoris, or just off to one side or the other.

○ *DON'T get obsessed with the clitoris, though.* Women have somewhat conflicting preferences on this, but most say they want some attention to other parts of their vulva, not only their clit. Ask her to be sure; after you've been going at it for a while, you can say, "Do you like it better if I just focus on your clit, or if I mix it up more?"

Act like you're French kissing my clit and labia. Suck on my labia. If I'm acting like I'm into it, don't change what you're doing, just keep right on at it.

Caressing or kneading the thighs and getting the fingers involved are good ideas.

Varying strokes and tempo is important. Touching around the clitoris is just as stimulating as actually touching it, if not more so.

○ *DO be gentle, particularly at first.* Women say some partners make the mistake of diving directly for the clit and then licking ferociously. Instead of

- Add zing to your lips, and hers, by chewing on Altoids, letting a Listerine strip dissolve in your mouth, sucking on an ice cube, or sipping a warm liquid before going down. Fizzy liquids like sparkling water or champagne can be a treat, too.
- Make dining down under even tastier by adding whipped cream, strawberries, kiwi fruit, or anything else you can think of. Foods with oil in them aren't compatible with latex, but they're fine with plastic wrap. Although foods with high sugar content (like all the ones we just listed!) can increase the chance of a yeast infection, many women tolerate occasional food play just fine. If your partner is particularly prone to yeast infections, play with food on her thighs and on the outside of her labia.
- Try humming over her clitoris—the vibrations can feel great. (But we bet you can't do it long without laughing.)

jumping in hard or fast, start out tenderly, licking gently. If you're not sure, ask her, "Harder? Softer?"

> *I love when my partner acts like he's really into it and loves my pussy. That makes me feel sexy and more likely to come. And I cannot stress a gentle touch at first enough. A stronger touch should come only when the clit gets hard.*

> *Don't push too hard on my clit. That thing is sensitive. A little goes a long way!*

○ *DO incorporate your entire mouth.* This is another one of those subjects where porn is wildly misleading. In porn, the camera zooms in for a close-up of the actor or actress sticking his or her tongue out and flicking the clit. This is for the pleasure of the porn viewer, not necessarily the woman receiving the oral sex. In real life, women say that lips, mouths, and the *flat* part of the tongue (not just the tip) can provide great stimulation, too. In great oral sex in the real world (not for the cameras), the partner's face and mouth are usually too close to the woman's vulva for an observer to see the tongue movements.

○ *DO let your fingers do the walking.* Most women say they love the extra stimulation that fingers and hands can provide during oral sex. Depending on your position, while your mouth is on her vulva you may be able to use your hands to stroke or massage her thighs, caress her breasts and nipples, or insert a finger or two in her vagina for G-spot stimulation, particularly once she's turned on.

> *I don't normally get an orgasm from just oral sex. It has to be combined with fingering.*

> *Fingers are nice sometimes but sometimes they're also distracting, especially when you're trying really hard to focus.*

○ *DO experiment with a variety of tongue motions to figure out what she likes best.* If they give it no thought, many partners settle into a methodical up-down lick, lick, lick routine disturbingly similar to a cat grooming himself. This may do the trick for some women, but many prefer a bit of variety, especially early on. Try fluttering, flicking, slow steady strokes, circles and swirls, and listen for her responses. You can also add variety to simple strokes by speeding up and slowing down, and changing the amount of pressure. If you find a stroke or two she likes a lot, stick with those. If she's being too quiet to give you feedback clues, easy-to-use check-in questions are, "How's this?" and "Does this work?"

○ *DON'T go wandering once she lets you know you've hit the groove.* Many respondents had strong feelings about this, perhaps from being left in the lurch a few too many times:

> *DON'T STOP! The worst is when I'm almost "there" and the other person stops licking or moves to a different spot. I completely lose it and have to start over again. If I ask you not to stop or not to move ("Right*

there!"), then please don't, unless you really need to come up for air. Don't just decide you're going to do something else for a while.

Whenever a girl starts moaning or making noise (as long as it's pleasant noise), keep doing what you are doing. So many times, partners try something different when I start making noise and it just ruins the whole thing.

○ *DON'T suck hard or bite.* Women repeatedly say "Ouch!" to these techniques. While some women like gentle, brief sucking, many find it unpleasant. And save nibbling with your teeth for some other erogenous zone. Unless, of course, she tells you biting is what she likes.

Sucking is painful and should not be done. I think some men see it in pornography and assume that it feels good. It may to some, but it must be done VERY softly if at all.

As much as guys don't want girls using teeth, girls don't want that either! It hurts.

○ *DON'T rush or give up too soon.* You may have a mightily disappointed partner if you treat oral sex as a 40-yard dash to her orgasm, or a chore to be completed as quickly as possible to "get her ready for the ol' in-out." Instead, find a position that's going to be comfortable for you (see our suggestions above), and then take your time.

I think people assume that everything has to be so fast to be erotic. It really doesn't. Going slow and gently massaging the genital area with your tongue is very erotic.

should i lick the alphabet?

THE LICKING-THE-alphabet cunnilingus technique was popularized by a comedian, Sam Kinison, but it's no joke. Licking each letter of the alphabet keeps the licker awake (a fact which should please any lickee), and hits lots of possible tongue angles and directions. It's probably best used as an information-gathering tool, rather than a surefire orgasm technique, because most women want their partner to settle into a more consistent, repetitive motion when they're close to coming. One woman put it best when she told us on our survey, "The 'Oral Alphabet' is a good start. When your partner draws each letter on your genitals, focus on which letters feel the best and ask him/her to use those movements more frequently." Your partner might be a W girl—but don't be disappointed if you learn that a boring, repetitive set of I, I, I, I, I or a long string of hyphens is what really gets her hot.

○ *DO connect after she comes.* If you've been down below for a while, it can be nice to cuddle and have some full-body contact after her orgasm. Some women like to taste their own juices in your kisses, but others don't, so check in with her about this. If you know she's in the latter category, wipe your mouth off on a tissue or the sheets, or have a sip of water, before you snuggle up. Let her bask in her orgasmic aftershocks and catch her breath before making it obvious that you're eager for her to return the oral favor. Some women with male partners, but not all, love intercourse after oral sex.

you with your head between her thighs: you're under arrest

UNTIL JUNE 2003, oral sex was illegal in ten states (Alabama, Florida, Idaho, Louisiana, Michigan, Mississippi, North Carolina, South Carolina, Utah, and Virginia). In four more states (Kansas, Missouri, Oklahoma, and Texas), different-sex couples were free to give each other as much oral as they pleased, but the identical act was illegal for same-sex couples. A now-famous Supreme Court decision, *Lawrence v. Texas*, declared all such laws unconstitutional, concluding that what consenting adults do in the privacy of their own homes is their own business. So, lick away, and breathe easy!

5

Doin' It, and Doin' It, and Doin' It Well:
intercourse & female orgasm

not as easy as it looks on tv

In movies, TV shows, and romance novels, most female orgasms happen during intercourse. A man puts his penis inside a woman (this is mainstream, hetero pop culture we're talking about), there's some thrusting for a minute or two (which you may or may not see depending on the TV channel or the movie's rating), the couple's excited moans build to a frenzy, and they both explode in simultaneous orgasm.

Given how familiar that scene is, in the real world, women who sleep with men are often surprised and frustrated by how intercourse works—or doesn't—in their own bedrooms. The facts are stark: Only about 30 percent of women have orgasms through intercourse alone. That means 70 percent of women who have sex with men aren't having orgasms that way.

Why doesn't it work for most women? As you know, the clitoris is the organ most women need stimulated to be able to have an orgasm, and the most sensitive part of the clit is on the outside of a woman's body. While intercourse is very well designed to lead to male orgasm, it's not so good at producing the female variety. Women may find penetration pleasurable (or not, depending on the woman), but for most women it's not the right kind of stimulation in the right place to lead to a big O.

Since people's experience with intercourse varies tremendously (as with all sexual matters), in this chapter you'll find:

○ intercourse tips and positions that score extra points for female pleasure
○ lots of ideas for the majority of women who find orgasms during intercourse tough or impossible to come by, strategies to tip the odds in your favor, and what to do if it just ain't happening
○ tips for guys on what women want during intercourse
○ advice for first-timers.

a note to girls who sleep with girls

YOU MAY NOTICE that the pronouns in this chapter assume that intercourse means man-and-woman, penis-in-vagina sex. However, some of the info here certainly applies to lesbian, bi, and queer women who enjoy penetration with a dildo or other penis-shaped object. In some ways, women having sex with other women are at an advantage on this subject, because when there's no penis in the bed, there are fewer assumptions that penetration is the "main part" of sex. That can make it easier to use penetration to the degree you and your partner find it hot—or not at all. We invite you to extract whatever parts of this chapter are relevant to your sex life and change the pronouns as needed. Or, you can just skip to the next chapter.

positions for intercourse

WHAT'S THE BEST sex position? We hate to be the ones to break the news, but really, there's no such thing as a single best sex position. Why? Well, for one thing, the size, height, and length of various body parts of the people involved make one couple's favorite position physically impossible for another couple. For instance, if a tall man and a short woman try to have doggie-style sex without finding a way to compensate for the height difference, he'll find himself thrusting into the air several inches above her backside—not very satisfying for either of them. If the same couple turns their doggie-style position on its side, so they're both lying on their sides, in spooning position, it can work great (see the picture on page 121). So, the best positions for you and your partner tend to be ones where your bodies fit together in ways that feel great to *you*, which may be very different than for the couple next door.

I ♥ FEMALE ORGASM

Also, what feels good sexually varies dramatically from person to person. One woman may love the sensation of her partner's penis hitting up against her cervix (that's the deepest part inside a woman's vagina). Another finds the sensation of having pressure against her cervix downright creepy. One woman loves how being on top gives her control of the depth and angle of penetration, while another feels shy about being on top, as if she's on display. Sex positions are like ice cream flavors: You get to choose your favorites, and as you travel through life it's likely you'll discover new ones that are surprisingly good (yes, even if you're married or in a long-term relationship).

Curious to know which positions are most popular? We asked the women who took our survey, and here's what they said:

most popular intercourse positions

NAME OF POSITION	HOW YOU DO IT	POPULAR MODIFICATIONS
Missionary	Woman lies on her back, man lies on top of her.	■ Legs up: Woman rests her legs against man's chest or shoulders. ■ Add a pillow or two under the woman's hips
Woman on Top ("Cowgirl")	Man lies on his back, woman straddles him and "sits on" his penis, facing the man.	■ Reverse cowgirl: Same position, but woman faces the man's feet. ■ Woman can lean forward or backward.
Doggie Style	Woman kneels on hands and knees. Man kneels or stands behind her, entering her from behind.	■ Woman lies flat on her stomach, man lies on top of her, supports self with arms, enters from behind.
Sitting on Lap	Man sits on bed or chair. Woman straddles him or sits on his lap, sitting on penis.	■ Woman can face toward or away from man.

I love girl on top. I feel empowered. I can move the way I want to and set my own pace. Plus, both of his hands are free to touch me.

what's your favorite position for intercourse?

HERE'S WHAT WOMEN told us. Each respondent could give more than one answer if she chose.

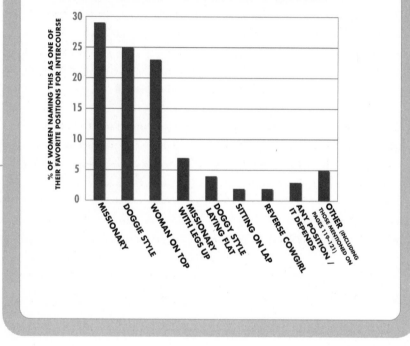

WOMEN'S FAVORITE POSITIONS FOR INTERCOURSE

% OF WOMEN NAMING THIS AS ONE OF THEIR FAVORITE POSITIONS FOR INTERCOURSE

- MISSIONARY
- DOGGIE STYLE
- WOMAN ON TOP
- MISSIONARY WITH LEGS UP
- DOGGY STYLE LAYING FLAT
- SITTING ON LAP
- REVERSE COWGIRL
- ANY POSITION / IT DEPENDS
- OTHER (INCLUDING THOSE MENTIONED ON PAGES 119–121)

I like that the missionary position allows me and my partner to be extremely close, and that we can hold each other and kiss while having sex. It also feels the best for me because positions that allow for deeper penetration often aren't comfortable for me.

I ♥ FEMALE ORGASM

I like sex on all fours from behind, with my head down. It allows for deep penetration. My partner can manually stimulate me, or I can do it myself, or he can play with my breasts. It's much easier to hit my G-spot in this position.

I actually really like being on the bottom, in missionary position. I like the security of having someone on top of me. I love being able to look up into someone's eyes and to be able to whisper into their ear that I love them or that I'm really enjoying what's happening. I like caressing their back and being able to watch what's going on down below. I also like being able to be a little rough from the bottom, either by scratching their back or by having them sort of elevate themselves above me and allowing me to thrust up to them. It can be very erotic and romantic all at once. And I love the collapse after the person on top has ejaculated. Feeling that weight on top of me just sort of completes it for me.

It depends on my mood. Sometimes I like him on top because I like to feel his weight on me; it's usually very intimate. Sometimes I like to take control and be on top. I get a better view of him, he can stimulate my genitals at the same time, I control the rhythm and the pace, and I can watch him orgasm. From behind is the best angle for the G-spot.

other positions to try out

IF YOU AND your partner haven't tested these already, here are four lesser-used positions definitely worth giving a whirl.

1. Crisscross: The woman lies on her back with her knees bent. Her partner lies on his side, with her bent knees over his buttocks area (try having one of her legs just below his butt, one leg just above). You can experiment with moving your heads closer together or farther apart to find the angle that feels best for you. Viewed from above, the couple's bodies form a "T" or an "X" with their genitals joining where the lines cross.

Many couples love this position because it's relaxing—no one has to be "on top." It's easy for either partner to reach the woman's clit. And the guy can easily control the depth and speed of his penetration.

2. Tabletop: Find a table or another flat surface that's about as high as the man's penis when he's standing up (most beds aren't nearly that high). The woman lies on her back on the table. You can use folded blankets on the table to add some padding, or use pillows under her head and/or butt to make it more comfortable or to adjust the height of her crotch. She slides her butt to the edge of the table, making it easy for the guy to insert from a standing position. Many women find this angle really comfortable because of the direct angle of penetration—there's less pulling and tugging on the skin around their vagina.

What to do with the woman's legs, other than let them dangle uncomfortably off the table? The more acrobatic among you may like to rest the woman's feet on the man's shoulders, or have her feet press against his chest. A less physically demanding solution is to pull up two chairs and have her rest her feet on the chair backs or seats. Looking up or down at your partner in this position can be a real turn-on, and either partner has easy access to the woman's clitoris.

Interestingly, sex swings, or slings, are designed specifically for the purpose of making it easy to get into this kind of position. Like a seated hammock, it hangs from the ceiling or from a stand, suspended by ropes or chains. The woman sits back in it, and her partner stands between her legs where he can easily penetrate her. Most include straps to support her legs and feet, and the swinging motion adds another dimension to intercourse. If imagining the expressions on the faces of your landlord or visiting relatives doesn't inspire you to install a sex swing in your bedroom, a table is a camouflaged, multipurpose alternative.

3. Coital Alignment Technique: There's some evidence that this modified missionary position helps some women have "look, Ma, no hands!" orgasms. To use the technique, the man is on top. Once his penis is inside, he "rides high" by moving his whole body up (toward the headboard) and to one side or the other a bit. He lays his head and shoulders down flat, rather than holding himself up on his forearms. In this position, the base of his penis rubs against the woman's clitoris as the couple moves together. The couple finds a motion where they can rock together, her rocking upward followed by him rocking downward, with the primary motion being the contact between her clit and the base of his penis. His penis doesn't go as deep as with "traditional" intercourse thrusting—the movement is more up-and-down rather than in-and-out. The research studies that find it results in high rates of female orgasm are those where couples study the technique extensively and then practice it repeatedly (conclusion: it doesn't often work on the first try).

If the man's body is positioned in a certain way during intercourse, it pushes up against an area of my body that allows me to orgasm.

I like it the best if my partner doesn't worry so much about hard thrusting. It's better if he focuses more on grinding his pubic bone against mine—it's a great source of clitoral stimulation!

4. Spooning: The spooning position is when your bodies fit together like two spoons in a drawer. (It's also a lovely way to cuddle, apart from intercourse.) Both people lie on their sides, facing the same direction, with the woman in front, and her partner entering her from behind. Spooning has many of the advantages of doggie style (easy to add clitoral stimulation, thrusting that gives G-spot stimulation, etc.) with some added bonuses. It can work better than doggie style for couples with a big height difference, and it's also less energy consuming for couples who want slow, relaxed sex.

Spooning sex is great—it's so close, expressive, tender. Plus it's possible to do manual stimulation.

invent your own position of the day!

WHY LET THOSE "Position of the Day" magazine editors have all the fun? (Admit it: You've found yourself wondering what those editorial meetings must be like where they sit around and brainstorm acrobatic sex positions, then give them zany names like "The Dangling Monkey" or "The Upside-Down Kumquat.") Here's how to play:

Start with a basic sex recipe:

○ Missionary
○ Woman on top
○ Reverse cowgirl

beginner's error

DON'T MAKE THE beginner's mistake of assuming that the more acrobatic the sex position, the faster the orgasms will fly. In fact, the reverse is often true, especially for women: Positions where they feel comfortable and relaxed are most likely to result in female orgasms.

I like all the positions I've tried, except for ones that are so complicated to get into that you lose focus and arousal by the time you've gotten into position.

For women who find it challenging to have orgasms during intercourse, simpler positions are nearly always better. Try an "is this really physically possible?" outrageous position on a day when you're in the mood to laugh or spice things up, but don't expect it to lift you to new orgasmic heights.

I 🖤 FEMALE ORGASM

- ○ Doggie style
- ○ Crisscross
- ○ Tabletop
- ○ Standing up
- ○ Sitting on lap
- ○ Parallel handstands

Add a twist:

- ○ Move your bodies closer together or farther apart (this generally changes the angle and depth of penetration)
- ○ Move one person up a little or down a little
- ○ Move your legs closer together, farther apart, or over one partner's shoulder; wrap them around one person's body, or intertwine them
- ○ Turn one of you in the other direction (like the difference between cowgirl and reverse cowgirl)
- ○ Lay the entire position on its side
- ○ Try lying flat or boosting one or both of you up off the bed

Consider a prop:

- ○ A chair
- ○ The edge of the bed
- ○ A bunch of pillows
- ○ The headboard
- ○ A tub or shower
- ○ The kitchen counter
- ○ Some other piece of furniture you own

Name it:

- ○ Almost as much fun as the position itself! Animals, machinery, occupations, playground equipment, furniture, utensils, and celebrities are all popular sources of inspiration.

what to do about an elusive intercourse O

SOME WOMEN CAN have great orgasms from intercourse, without any additional stimulation. That may be because they have a particularly sensitive G-spot or other internal area highly responsive to stimulation, because the tugging at the skin over their clit is enough to bring them to orgasm, or because they're using a position that provides stimulation just right for their body.

> *For me, the most incredible orgasms I've ever had have been from intercourse alone. I was surprised that the first time I had a really strong orgasm was my first time having intercourse!*

However, experiences like that tend to be the exception rather than the rule, and we hear lots of women and men stressing out about how to make female orgasms happen during intercourse. How do people deal with this in real-world bedrooms? Here are our top tips:

1. Have the woman take control of her own orgasms. Many girls are raised to believe that orgasms and sexual pleasure are things they'll begin to experience once they have a boyfriend or husband. As a result, once girls *do* have a partner (a boyfriend, husband, *or* a girlfriend or wife) they often believe it's this person's job to give them orgasms. By comparison, most boys figure out how to experience sexual pleasure on their own, long before they have a partner.

Of course, a great partner *does* help a woman have fabulous orgasms and lots of sexual pleasure. But many women make the mistake of thinking that their orgasm is their partner's responsibility—that they should just lie back and enjoy. If they don't have an orgasm, they blame their partner. If they have weak, inconsistent orgasms, they blame their partner. And if they don't have a partner, well, they figure they're just out of luck in the orgasm department.

We can't tell you how many women have shared with us that the time their sex life blasted to a new level was when they started taking

I ♥ **FEMALE ORGASM**

responsibility for their own orgasms. This is one area where women could stand to learn a thing or two from the guys. Guys don't lie back, waiting hopefully for their partners to give them an orgasm—they rub or thrust in just the way they like, at just the right speed for them, at just the right rhythm, at their favorite angle. Guys negotiate, ask, or set things up so they can have sex in their favorite positions, the ones that give them their favorite kind of physical or visual stimulation. Guys think the thoughts and fantasize the fantasies that turn them on while they're having intercourse. Guys make it clear that they expect to have lots of sexual pleasure, and an orgasm, and they assume the sexual interlude will continue until they do. And if guys don't have a partner, they take care of their own orgasm themselves.

> "The last time I was inside a woman was when I visited the Statue of Liberty."
> —line from *Crimes and Misdemeanors*, screenplay by Woody Allen

For most women, changing the way they think about this stuff is *huge*. When a woman takes charge of her orgasm, it means *she* takes responsibility for making sure she gets the kind of stimulation she needs to have an orgasm while she's with a partner. She moves her body in her favorite ways, thinks the thoughts, and fantasizes the fantasies that will help her come. Some women figure all of this out when they're teenagers. Some figure it out when they're in their thirties. Some have to get married three times before they figure it out. But if you ask most confident, sexy, orgasmic women what they do to have such satisfying sex lives, they'll tell you they stopped relying on the handsome prince (or princess) to have the pleasure map, and found the confidence to chart their own course.

2. Help the woman come before or after intercourse. Many couples solve the problem of the woman not having orgasms through intercourse by spending plenty of time doing things focused on her pleasure before or after intercourse. Performing oral sex on her before intercourse is particularly popular—there's even an entire book on the subject with the terrific title *She Comes First*. That way, she's highly aroused, and usually nice and wet, before penetration begins. Most women find it perfectly comfortable, or

even quite pleasurable, to have intercourse after they've already had an orgasm—they may even be able to come again now that they're warmed up. A woman could also come by masturbating or using a vibrator during foreplay, while her partner kisses and nibbles on her neck and shoulders, caresses her breasts and nipples, teases her mouth with a finger she can suck on, or adds other kinds of sensations she enjoys. If she hasn't already come, her chances increase if she's highly aroused before intercourse begins. And if the man comes first, that doesn't have to mean "game over"—the couple can continue to use fingers, hands, lips, tongues, and sex toys to let the fun continue if she wants to come, too.

3. **Get the clit in on the action.** Getting enough clitoral stimulation is the secret weapon for many women to push them over the orgasmic edge during intercourse. The easiest way for most to get that stimulation? Having either the woman or her partner touch her clit with their hand or a vibrator. Rather than feeling like this is a "second best" way to come, lots of couples recognize that it's not a big deal for a woman to need direct stimulation on the most sensitive area of her sexual parts. Some couples also make a conscious effort to seek out intercourse positions that rub against the woman's clitoris during penetration—which works for some women but not others.

Women sometimes tell us that part of the reason they settle for not coming during intercourse is because they're terrified their partner would be offended if they reached down to polish the pearl while they're having sex. We needed to find out the truth. Do guys really flip out if a woman adds external finger action to his internal thrusting? Are women right to worry? We surveyed women who've been bold enough to give it a try, and men who've been with a woman who masturbated while they had sex.

What did we find? Most of the news was great: 93 percent of women who tried it got either a positive or an "I'm comfortable with that" type of reaction from their partner. Many women said their partner found it incredibly sexy to see a woman pleasure herself. It's a turn-on for the guy, and the girl gets off. Talk about win-win sex!

During sex when I'm on top, touching my clitoris and building to an orgasm that way has been spectacular. My partner loved to watch me touch myself, especially when he could feel me clenching from inside. It also allowed us to time our climaxes together.

He's the one who wants me to! He loves to see me orgasm, and knows that I know just what to do and he doesn't even need to worry about that part.

My boyfriend LOVES it. It really turns him on—if it's been going too long and I want him to finish, I touch myself and he's done in a minute or less!

But not all the news is so rosy. Seven percent of women who tried this said they'd encountered partners who were threatened by women taking matters into their own hands. Some guys incorrectly think a woman touching herself is a sign that he's a lousy lover. Others don't want to share the fun of pleasuring a woman—they don't want her to help bring on her own orgasms because they want the glory for themselves.

Some guys seem to be more open to it. Others think you just don't enjoy sex with them. If a guy doesn't like me to do it, it kind of makes me mad. I mean, I want to have an orgasm, too, dammit!

Most of the time, partners are okay with this, but my ex-husband was totally against it. He said if he couldn't make me orgasm without me touching myself, then why was he bothering? You notice, he's my EX-husband.

So it's no wonder women worry. Even if the vast majority of men are supportive, women don't know if their boyfriend or husband is one of the small minority who will get insulted or angry. You want to let your fingers do the walking while you get it on together, but you're worried about how he'll react? Here are some tips to get you started.

how to start: tips for women

○ **Know he'll probably be fine with it.** Boost your confidence by reminding yourself that most guys think it's hot for a woman to touch herself. Here's what some guys had to say:

savvy sex tip

ALWAYS PEE AFTER you have intercourse to reduce the risk of urinary tract infections. The stream of urine pushes out any microscopic bacteria that could creep up your urethra.

It was pretty awesome. She came while I was having sex with her, which is an amazingly erotic experience.

Before we tried it, I had never thought it would make me uncomfortable, but it did initially. I wondered, am I useless? But it was a lot of fun and she liked it a lot. I started to like it too.

○ **Pick a good position.** The "traditional" missionary position is often the worst for reaching your own clit—if his body is lying flat on top of yours, that probably doesn't give you space to move your hand in the way you need to. Nearly any other position will work better: woman on top, doggie style, crisscross, spooning, etc.

○ **Boost his ego.** After he's inside you but before you touch yourself, load on the positive feedback. Use words and sounds to let him know how good he feels, how hot he looks, etc. (Don't fake or lie to him—just be honest about what's good.) That reduces the chance he'll feel threatened, because you're telling him that you're having a good time.

○ **Reach down with confidence.** Act like this is totally normal, just something women do. It is!

○ **Frame it as something fun and sexy.** If you feel like you need to say something as you first start touching yourself, try saying something like:

"Are you one of those guys who thinks it's hot if a woman touches herself while they_____ [fill in favorite slang for having sex]?"
or

"Let's see if we can both come."

or

"I'm one of those girls who needs a little extra help to be able to come—you feel *so good*, I really want to come with you."

It's unlikely he's going to say, "No, it doesn't turn me on to watch a woman touch herself," or "No, I don't want you to come." If you say things like this, you're giving him a positive (and accurate) way to look at what's going on, which reduces the chance he'll get scared and think he's doing something wrong. It's also fine to just reach down without saying anything at all.

> *My boyfriend helps me while I masturbate by fingering me and he can be a part of it. We just tried having sex while I touched myself down there and for the first time we had simultaneous orgasms.*

○ **Invite him to help.** You can just put his hand there and keep your hand over it to show him how you like it. Or try saying, "Does it work for you to touch my clit at the same time?" He'll likely need a bit of direction about what feels good once his fingers are in the right place. See the box on the next page for more on this.

○ **Ask him to slow down if needed.** Some women find the sensation of constant thrusting distracting; they need to be able to concentrate on their clitoral sensations to get over the edge. If this is the case for you, you can ask your guy temporarily to slow his thrusts way down, or just stay still inside you, moving just enough to keep himself hard. Then, as your orgasm begins to swell up inside you, you can whisper sweetly, "I'm ready for you," or use one of those great porno lines like "Oh, fuck me, fuck me!" Chances are he'll be happy to oblige.

no wonder lions have that look in their eyes

ACCORDING TO THE book *Biological Exuberance*, a female lion "may mate as often as four times an hour when she is in heat over a continuous period of three days and nights (without sleeping), and sometimes with up to five different males."

his fingers or hers?

MOST COUPLES WHO combine clitoral stimulation with intercourse find it works best if the woman takes care of providing the stimulation because she knows precisely how she likes to be touched. But lots of women enjoy or even prefer having their partner's fingers on their clit during intercourse. What works best is a matter for each pair to figure out.

She can bring herself to orgasm much better than I can usually, because she's the most familiar with her own body. Also, I tend to get distracted when doing multiple things at once, and if it's me rubbing the clitoris then often I get distracted and stop, or at the very least, do it haphazardly.

I touch the woman's clitoris as much as she directs me to, which varies by partner. The easiest positions are generally ones where I enter her from behind and can reach around in front of her to stimulate her clit.

I've touched it, he's touched it. This ought to be a regular part of sex if I'm going to get off! If he's not invested in me getting off, I won't be having sex with him again. Who's doing it changes depending on the position. It's easier for me to touch it spooning-style, while it's easier for him to touch it girl-on-top style.

Of course, not all women want or need clitoral stimulation during intercourse. Some female respondents on our survey said they found it distracting. For some couples, the answer to "his fingers or hers?" may simply be "Neither."

"but i want to come from intercourse alone!"

AFTER A TYPICAL female orgasm speaking engagement, the audience files out and a handful of people stay behind to talk with us. One question comes up without fail: "But I *really* want to come during intercourse without using my hands. Isn't there *something* I can do?"

If you haven't guessed by now, we think that if penetration doesn't lead you to O-land, you're best off enjoying penetration for itself, and pursuing orgasms in other ways. But if you insist, here are techniques that some women say have worked for them to learn how to come during intercourse without the assistance of a hand or a sex toy:

○ **Get hot and bothered.** Some women find it helps to be really, really turned on already, through oral sex, masturbation, or some other type of stimulation before intercourse begins (or even earlier in the day, before they see their partner). Starting the action at a higher level of arousal means there's less distance to travel to reach the finish line. For some, having an orgasm before intercourse makes it easier for them to come again during it.

A JOKE (At least we hope so)
QUESTION: Why do women fake orgasm?
ANSWER: Because men fake foreplay.

○ **Try the coital alignment technique,** described on page 120. CAT, as it's known, has ardent fans who swear by it as the route to female orgasm during intercourse. While it takes practice and doesn't work for everyone, it definitely holds the ticket for some couples.

○ **Be creative.** Experiment with other positions to find pleasurable ways the man's body can grind against your clit. You might rub against your partner's pelvic bone or the shaft of his penis while he's inside you, regardless of who's on top. You may find the angle of penetration makes a difference in terms of how much and what kind of clitoral contact you get. For some women it helps to move their own body in a way that stimulates them, rather than relying on the man to provide all the movement.

I like being on top at a slight angle above him. I practically lie on him. I can really grind on him this way and our heads don't get in the way.

Girl on top didn't work for me to come until I tried dangling one leg off the bed. That gives me deeper penetration and more solid clit contact.

○ **Teach your body.** A woman can try to teach herself to associate the sensations of penetration with orgasm. She starts by having intercourse with clitoral stimulation from her own hand. A second before she comes, she stops the clitoral stimulation, and allows her partner's thrusting to be the thing that pushes her over the edge to orgasm. The next time, she does the same thing, but stops the clitoral stimulation two seconds before she falls over the orgasmic edge, and lets the thrusting carry her to orgasm. Over a period of weeks or months, she continues getting herself highly aroused, most of the way to orgasm, but over time relies on intercourse to take her more and more—and maybe eventually all—of the way there. Women can also practice this using a dildo or other object for penetration.

> **The location of a woman's clitoris (higher or lower on her vulva) does not affect her ability to have an orgasm during intercourse, according to research by Masters and Johnson.**

○ **Legs together.** Experiment with closing your legs once the man is inside. Changing leg positions, and possibly squeezing your leg muscles, can increase the sensation you get. Your partner can straddle your closed legs, rather than have his legs together inside your spread legs.

The best way for me to come during sex is in the missionary position with my legs crisscrossed.

○ **Lose control.** One woman told us she was finally able to have orgasms during intercourse when she let go of the need to "control her own orgasm" and instead stayed intensely focused on the sensations she was feeling from her partner.

○ **Focus on yourself.** It helps some women to stay focused on their own pleasure and not worry so much about pleasing their partner. It's okay not to be an award-winning lover every minute. In fact, it may free you up

I ♥ FEMALE ORGASM

to stay in your own groove if you take a break from running your hands over his body, or stop worrying about moving your body the way you know he likes.

○ **Find the right rhythm.** Often the pace of intercourse is controlled by the man, but most women need their own consistent, steady rhythm to be able to have an orgasm. Try positions where you can more easily control the rhythm (like woman on top or, for some, doggie style). You can give your partner feedback about what speed feels best to you, or grasp his hips or butt to help control the motion.

○ **Use your mind.** The mind is a powerful thing in the quest for orgasms, and two-thirds of the women who answered our survey said they used fantasy at least sometimes while having sex with a partner. Find the images or stories that turn you on, and use them while you're having sex with your partner. For more about the wonders of using your own imagination, see page 29.

Does size matter? No research study has found that penis size makes a difference in terms of a woman's ability to have orgasms during intercourse. On page 214, read what we've learned from discussing the matter with thousands of women.

One or two of these tips could work for you. Or none of them may work. Keep in mind that while coming hands-free during intercourse can be fun, there's no rule that says it's the best way. If you're the kind of woman who has orgasms relatively easily, from a wide variety of kinds of stimulation, you're more likely to find these techniques may work for you. If, on the other hand, you're a woman whose body has more specific requirements—you need good, long stimulation of just the right spot with exactly the right motion and the perfect amount of lubrication—it'll probably be more difficult for you to replicate those conditions. And that's okay, too.

the wonders of lube

LUBE IS ONE of those secrets to great sex that many people wish they'd discovered much earlier in their lives. Lubricant makes things slide better—and

the myth of the vaginal orgasm

ONE HUNDRED YEARS ago, Sigmund Freud made a mistake when he declared the existence of the "vaginal orgasm," and wrote that it was far more desirable than its sorry cousin, the clitoral orgasm. Plenty of people throughout human history have been wrong about things: The early Greeks believed the world was flat. Orville and Wilbur Wright first built airplanes that didn't fly. In Colonial times many people slept propped up because they thought they'd die if they lay flat. Today, we see these other errors as quaintly misguided. But for some reason, the mistaken concept of the vaginal orgasm hasn't faded away.

It's now well established that there's only one kind of female orgasm. Certainly, different kinds of stimulation can bring on an orgasm, and various different nerves can be involved. An orgasm with or without penetration, with or without a vibrator, with or without extended tantric breathing, can *feel* very different. But what's happening in your body once the waves of sensation begin is the same, no matter what kind of stimulation brought it on. The clitoris—including the clit's internal and external structures—is responsible for all orgasms, even those that happen during intercourse. And the muscles of the vagina are involved in most orgasms once the orgasm begins.

therefore feel better—by reducing friction during sex. Women's bodies lubricate all by themselves: women get wet as they get aroused, which is a very lovely thing. But things slide better against each other if *both* surfaces are wet, rather than a wet surface sliding against a dry surface. Using lube isn't a sign that something is amiss, any more than shaving with shaving cream is a sign of weakness.

Adding lube can be a great option for days when a woman isn't quite as wet as she'd like to be (this can be affected by where she is in her menstrual cycle, stress, drugs, alcohol, age, or nothing at all), when you're having a longer sex session, when you're using condoms or sex toys (which can dry things out a little), or anytime you just want to make sure sex stays nice and slippery. We're not talking about the lube that comes on a lubricated condom, though that's a start—we mean lube like Astroglide, ID, Wet, K-Y, and many other brands that you buy in a bottle or tube at a pharmacy (near the condom section) or sex store. Some particularly cool sex stores have lube sampling stations with lots of lube brands where you can put a few drops on your fingertips and rub it around for a while to see which consistency you like best.

Lube is great for intercourse, essential for anal sex, and an excellent option for sex toys. Lots of women and men use lube (or their own saliva) for masturbation, too. For intercourse, you use lube by putting it on the guy's penis (on top of the condom, or directly on his penis if he's not wearing a condom) and/or around the entrance to and inside the woman's vagina. Adding a drop of lube inside a condom, or on the woman's clit underneath a dental dam or plastic wrap for safer oral sex on a woman, can add sensitivity for the person wearing the condom or being licked (for more on these safer sex methods, see page 263).

Because lube decreases friction, it reduces the chance that a condom will break, so adding lube when you're using condoms actually makes sex safer. The very first time you have intercourse is a fantastic time to use lube, because it makes everything slide better and can make the first time more comfortable. Too bad most people having sex for the first time don't even know lube exists!

There are three basic kinds of lubricants: water-based, oil-based, and silicone. Water-based is the most popular for most situations. It's totally safe to use with latex condoms, and if it dries out a little while you're using it you can just add some water to rejuvenate it (some couples keep a spray bottle next to the bed). Some water-based lubes contain glycerin, a sugar, which can cause yeast infections. If you find yourself prone to yeast infections, you may want seek out the glycerin-free kind. Glycerin is particularly common in flavored lubes, which are fun for oral sex but not as good for vaginal sex.

Oil-based lubes like massage oil, hand lotion, or chocolate sauce are fine for male masturbation, and for anal play if you're not using safer sex supplies, but not good for much else. Oil can lead to vaginal infections because it can trap bacteria inside the vagina. Oily lubes also aren't safe to use with latex condoms, because oil breaks down latex, so your condom could break (that means no chocolate-sauce oral sex on her followed by a romping session of condom-based intercourse).

Silicone lube is the newest on the block. It's safe with condoms, doesn't dry out as quickly as water-based lube, and can even be used underwater (ooh! ahh!). Some people find silicone lubes feel warmer, because they transmit heat better. They cost more than water-based lubes, and you need soap and water to wash them off. If you want to use silicone lube with a silicone sex toy, put a condom on it, because the silicone-silicone chemical reaction could melt your favorite toy.

Most women tell us they don't like warming gels and lubes (products that warm up with breath or rubbing). Many who tried one said that instead of feeling gently warm, it was burning hot! Some brands are milder than others, though, and a few women like the way they get their blood flowing. If you're curious, you may want to experiment with different kinds and start with a tiny dab to prevent a fiery surprise.

a sex ed party trick

HERE'S SOMETHING TO amuse you and your friends when you're hanging out late at night. Blow up two regular latex condoms like balloons and tie them off. On one condom balloon, wipe some water-based lube. On the other, wipe something oil-based (Vaseline, vegetable oil, hand lotion, etc.). Make sure you know which balloon is which.

Put them aside in a place where you can see them. Talk amongst yourselves. At some point later that night, the condom balloon with the oily lube will pop all by itself, because oil breaks down the latex over time.

And that, ladies and gentlemen, is why you should never use oil-based lube when you're using latex condoms!

simultaneous orgasms

IF MOVIES AND romance novels were your only source of information, you might conclude that simultaneous orgasms are the only kind that are physically possible. Anyone who's ever attempted this feat with a partner knows that's not quite so. While exploding at the same moment isn't impossible, it's not likely to happen without a lot of work. Often that work means that the partner who tends to come faster is going cross-eyed trying to hold back, while the partner who tends to take longer is trying every trick she or he can think of to speed up. In the end, if both people do succeed in coming simultaneously, they may just decide they were working so hard they didn't get to have very much fun.

In ancient Greece, Hippocrates believed that simultaneous orgasms were necessary for a woman to conceive, inventing the goal that many modern couples still

your body wants to get you pregnant

MANY WOMEN FIND they're horniest around the most fertile time of their cycle, the days before they ovulate. Why? A combination of high levels of estrogen and lots of slippery, wet cervical fluid (healthy vaginal secretions) combine to pump up your libido. It's nature's way of trying to seduce you into having sex—and getting you pregnant. (This effect may be different or nonexistent if you're on a hormonal form of birth control.)

Want to be able to tell with confidence when you're fertile and when you're not, even if your menstrual cycles are irregular? We recommend the book *Taking Charge of Your Fertility* by Toni Weschler—it rocks our socks. If you're having the kind of sex where a sperm could come into contact with an egg, but you don't want to get pregnant, see page 252 for an overview of birth control options.

aspire to. Now that we know that women can get pregnant regardless of the timing or existence of their orgasms, there's no reason that coming at the same time is better than any other way. (Besides, most couples having intercourse these days aren't hoping to get pregnant.) Sure, simultaneous orgasms can be fun, but they're not evidence that two people were made for each other, trophies for award-winning sex, or markers of true love.

Many couples find they actually enjoy their orgasms more if they don't even try to make them happen at the same time. With the "sequential orgasm" approach, partners alternate their focus between one person's pleasure and the other. The one being pleasured gets to luxuriate in the sensations without worrying about either racing or holding back. The one helping to provide pleasure gets the fun of the sights and sounds of his or her partner getting really turned on and having an orgasm. If their orgasms just happen to coincide, these couples certainly enjoy them, but they let go of the simultaneous goal most of the time.

If you and your partner do decide to try to come together, the best strategy for male-female couples is usually to have the guy handle the timing. It's much harder for a woman to control the speed and timing of her orgasm, but if a man has finely tuned ejaculatory control (for more on how this works, see page 210), he may be able to get himself close to orgasm and then hover around that arousal level for a while until she cues him that she's getting close. Once her orgasm starts, he can try to join in quickly.

what is tantric sex?

TANTRIC SEX IS a sexuality practice that emphasizes spirituality and energy exchange between two people. Rooted in India and various Eastern religions, tantric sexuality belief systems, approaches, and techniques are diverse. They often include slow, ritualized breathing; extended eye contact between partners; and aspects of yoga, meditation, and focused self- and partner-awareness. It's possible to spend a lifetime studying tantra, and there are countless books, websites, and workshops where you can learn more if the subject interests you.

We began with intense foreplay that involved slowly touching each other's body for a really long time. After this, we were so in tune to each other's needs that the sex was slow and passionate. We breathed in unison, finished together. It was fantastic.

Some practitioners say tantric sex revolutionizes and enhances their sex life, shifting the focus away from seeing erection, ejaculation, and orgasm as goals, and instead allowing them to make love for far longer, feel a deeper and more intimate connection with their partner, and "channel the divine energy of the universe." Others say it's just not their thing, preferring the attitude of the book called *Life's Too Short for Tantric Sex*.

My partner gets me almost there with his fingers and with his penis inside me or almost inside me, so that he is ready to come when I do. We lie side by side. We don't do this all the time, but it's a really nice treat.

intercourse tips especially for guys

○ **Slow it down.** When we asked women who took our survey what advice they would give to a partner about how to make intercourse more pleasurable for women, they overwhelmingly said things like: "Don't rush!" and "It's not a race to the end." Many men get the mistaken impression that women want hard, fast pounding because that's what they've seen in porn. On page 193 we talk more about reality versus porn.

○ **Make foreplay last.** This was the second most common tip women said they'd like to give their male partners (after "Go slow"). If she's not wet, it's too soon to start penetration. Because women's vaginas elongate as they get aroused, entering your partner before her body's ready can be uncomfortable or painful for her.

> *Foreplay is the absolute most important part of any kind of sex for me, especially intercourse.*

> *Foreplay foreplay foreplay! Get the girl super excited so that she is BEGGING you to enter her. When it finally goes in it feels AMAZING!*

○ **Bring lube.** Ask her if it's okay to put some on your penis. It may not make much difference for you, but lube often makes penetration far more comfortable for women.

○ **Enter her slowly, a bit at a time.** Many women—even those who love intercourse and have had lots of it—complain that guys push in too hard and too fast.

> *Be gentle. Give her time to adjust to you.*

○ **Experiment.** Find out what speed, depth, rhythm, angle, and strength of penetration she likes. Try slow, sensuous thrusts; lots of in and out near the entrance of her vagina; staying deep inside her while you move back and forth a shorter distance. If fast, hard thrusts are what you're used to from masturbation, you can "retrain" yourself by practicing masturbating with a slower, wetter, somewhat looser hand, more like the stimulation you'd get from a vagina.

○ **Ask for feedback.** Say to her, "Do you like it better when I move like this, or like this? Does this feel good?" Don't be silent because you think it's unromantic to talk—the third most common piece of advice women said they'd like to tell their partners was to talk to them more! This doesn't mean women want an endless stream of chatter (they don't), but checking in now and then is appreciated.

> *I think communication is the sexiest part of intercourse. Talk to me and ask me what I want. Tell me how I make you feel. All of these things make it a lot sexier and also help to make sure we're both feeling okay and getting what we want from the experience.*

> *Tell me how to pleasure YOU. Chances are, I'll be more open about what feels good for me, too.*

○ **Stay tuned in to her during intercourse.** Kiss her, caress her, whisper sweet things to her. Enjoy the emotional closeness and intimacy. Pay attention to her sounds, movements, and other nonverbal clues about what she likes and how she's doing.

> *Don't just fixate on my vagina and clitoris, but touch my breasts, my face, my neck—show me you care by being gentle and passionate.*

○ **Know that most women don't come from intercourse alone** (as you've read throughout this chapter). Don't assume there's something wrong with you, and definitely don't imply there's something wrong with her!

○ **Realize longer isn't always better.** If you have some control over how long sex lasts, don't assume she wants you to keep thrusting all night long. Some guys mistakenly think that if they can pump away for long enough, they're sure to generate an orgasm. But most women say that if their partner lasted for twenty hours of intercourse, the woman still wouldn't have an orgasm, because she's not getting the right stimulation. Women who answered our survey were more likely to complain about "marathon men" who left them sore than men who came too soon.

○ **Learn ejaculatory control**. On the other hand, if a woman *is* able to have orgasms through intercourse, the longer her partner can last, the more likely it is that she'll have enough time for the sensations to bring about her O. So if it usually takes a given woman, say, 17 minutes to have an orgasm, but her boyfriend explodes 17 *seconds* after he's inside her, she's clearly a long way from being able to have an orgasm during intercourse. Most guys find it helpful to have some degree of ejaculatory control, which is why we address this further on page 210. But just because it's handy to be able to choose when you will or won't come doesn't mean this is the critical factor that determines if your partner will come or not.

Because women can get sore and never have an orgasm when guys last *too* long, a man who's mastered ejaculatory control should check in from time to time: "Would it feel good if I kept going, or should I come now?"

○ **Be supportive of her getting the clitoral stimulation she probably needs during intercourse**, just as you're getting the stimulation you need. Experiment to see if there are positions or angles that give her clitoral stimulation she enjoys. Encourage her to touch her clit while you're going at it, or do it for her. If she uses a vibrator to masturbate, welcome it into your bed together as a fun way to rev up your sex life and amplify her pleasure. Unless your penis has its own vibrating feature, there's no reason to feel competitive with a toy.

We usually make sure one of us is touching her clit at all times. The best position for her to touch it is doggie style, the best for me is a modified missionary position where I sit upright and put more weight on my knees. This position is also good for hitting her G-spot.

○ Find a brand, size, and style of condom you like. Bring a couple with you. Take the initiative in putting it on rather than relying on her to request it. If you need to, get used to the sensations of coming with a condom on (and road test a bunch of different brands to find the one that fits you best) by wearing one to masturbate. You can get a bunch of different condoms by searching online for "condom variety pack" or "assorted condoms."

Learn to put on a condom in the dark. Girls don't really practice it, so guys need to be an expert at it.

○ Finally, don't assume that intercourse should happen every time (or even most times) you have sex. Be open to having your orgasm other ways, like oral sex, rubbing against her body, getting a hand job, or masturbating while you're together. If you're tired of hearing that she's not in the mood, this can be the perfect solution. Women tell us that when they're not in the mood for intercourse, they'd often be happy to bring their partner to orgasm some other way. But if they feel like intercourse is the only option, they'll duck out of sex altogether.

intercourse during pregnancy

IT'S PERFECTLY SAFE to have intercourse and orgasms any time while a woman is pregnant— right up until her water breaks before her baby's birth! (This assumes the woman hasn't had problems with this or past pregnancies. If she has, she should discuss the topic of sex and pregnancy with her midwife or doctor.) The man's penis can't reach or touch the baby.

When a woman is near or past her due date, intercourse with the man ejaculating inside can be an effective way to encourage labor to begin. Semen contains prostaglandins, the same substance that doctors apply to a woman's cervix to artificially induce labor. The same activity that got the baby in there can also help get the baby out!

twelve steps to making your first time a great time

ARE YOU A woman thinking about having intercourse for the first time? Here are our top twelve tips for making the first time something you'll want to remember.

1. **Do it because you want to.** Not because your friends have already done it. Not because your boyfriend wants to. Not because you think you're too old to be a virgin.

   Make sure that this is the right time and the right person. Ask yourself, if this ends today will I regret having had sex with him?

   Don't rush into it just because you think you have to. I thought I was too old to be a virgin (twenty-one) and that there was something wrong with me. So the first chance I got, I went for it. Stupidly.

2. **Be with a partner you trust.** The women who have the most positive memories of their first intercourse experience say they did so with a partner with whom they shared mutual trust, respect, and caring. Having this kind of relationship sets the stage for the rest of our advice on this subject (below).

   I think we were both nervous because we were both virgins. It actually didn't hurt as bad as I thought it would. It was a little awkward because it was our first time but it was still good because we really love each other and we were comfortable with each other.

Please, please only have sex for the first time with someone you're in a relationship with and love and feel immensely comfortable with. It's a somewhat physically uncomfortable experience, so that won't be satisfying, but the emotional experience will be.

3. **Plan for it in advance—but keep your plans flexible.** Forget the heat of the moment! You're more likely to have a good time and no regrets if you and your partner have talked things over before the day (or night) itself. Planning can also help you pick a location that's going to be comfortable for you (not squeezed into a car, or in an unlocked room where your roommate might walk in on you). Avoid the temptation to pretend you've had intercourse before— it'll work far better for you and your partner if he knows this is your first time.

If you're expecting to have intercourse for the first time on a special date like your wedding night, Valentine's Day, or your birthday, keep in mind that it's okay if things don't come together, so to speak, as you had envisioned. You or your partner may have had too much to drink, you may be exhausted, or something else may have changed your plans. Losing your virginity on the second day of your honeymoon or the day after Valentine's Day is just as sexy.

We were both virgins, and it was about 20 degrees outside, so it wasn't really "optimal." We were just two horny teenagers. He got off, but I was too uncomfortable.

I was told by everyone around me that it would hurt and be uncomfortable. Instead, it felt wonderful! My partner and I were so comfortable with each other, we just did what felt good, making sure to ask each other what we were feeling/thinking and what we enjoyed. Not bad for a first time experience for both of us.

I ♥ FEMALE ORGASM

4. Don't be drunk. We're not the preachy, finger-wagging types, but on this topic study after study find the same thing: People who say their first intercourse was pleasurable tend to be ones who didn't drink before the big event. They feel more sensation, communicate better, are more likely to use a condom correctly, and best of all, they remember what happened the next day.

> *I was drunk and it hurt a lot, even though I was drunk. I did not have an orgasm although my partner wanted me to, so we kept at it. I remember that I wanted to stop, but kept going because it was important to him that I had an orgasm. But I didn't.*

> *I was drunk at the time and don't remember too much, other than it was very rushed, and I was very disappointed.*

5. Keep your expectations down to earth. Having intercourse may or may not go smoothly the first time. It may or may not feel good from the start. Expecting first-time sex to be sparkling perfection is a recipe for a serious let-down. It's far better to be realistic—and perhaps pleasantly surprised.

> *It hurt pretty damn bad. And I was slightly disappointed. In my life, sex was something forbidden, something I wasn't supposed to do, so of course in my head I thought, if it's forbidden and worth waiting for, it must feel really good, like the best feeling in the whole world. And the first time, it definitely was not what I thought it was going to be. Although it was rather nice.*

> *From what I read in books and so on, I thought it would either hurt or be the best experience ever. It didn't hurt since I was comfortable with the guy and ready, but it was over really fast and kind of a disappointment.*

6. Be comfortable with fingers already. If you find it uncomfortable or painful to have a finger or two (your own or your partner's) inside your vagina in a sexual situation, then that's your first assignment. That can help stretch your hymen and get you used to the sensation of having something inside your vagina. (Many women's hymens have already been stretched or broken from exercise, tampon insertion, or other activities.) Get to a point where having a finger inside is comfortable for you before trying to insert a penis. Wet your finger with saliva, water, or lube before inserting it.

> *Experiment first with fingering, because it loosens the hymen and allows your partner to find places that feel good to you inside. This will also help to take away some of the mystery of sex, making it seem less intimidating. I lost my cherry during fingering over several occasions. Then, having sex for the first time felt wonderful, instead of the painful experience my friends had warned me of.*

7. Use birth control. Yes, you can get pregnant the first time. Unless you're absolutely positive neither of you could have an STI or HIV (for instance, you've both been tested, or neither of you has ever been sexually active with anyone else), you should be using condoms as birth control or in addition to another kind of birth control. Condoms plus a backup method like contraceptive film, foam, or insert—all sold near the condoms in most pharmacies and supermarkets—are a highly effective combo to prevent pregnancy.

8. Get good and turned on first. Being aroused before you try penetration isn't just a bonus—it's a requirement for making intercourse comfortable. Spend plenty of time kissing, making out, enjoying each other. Oral sex can be good if you like it. Having an orgasm before you try penetration can work well, too.

I wish I had known that it's much more enjoyable with more foreplay. I had barely any foreplay the day I lost my virginity, but that really does make a difference.

Being relaxed is the key to enjoying sex. Engage in foreplay and wait until your body signals you to move on.

9. **Use lube.** Even if you're already wet (which you should be before you start trying), and even if your partner's wearing a lubricated condom, add more water-based lube on top of the condom. Slippery is a very good thing, as you read in the last section.

It started out passionate and slow on the couch with oral sex, then we moved to the bedroom and continued to be very sweet. He was a pretty large fellow in terms of penis size, and I was terrified. But he was really gentle and took things slowly. We used lots of lubricant and good, sturdy condoms. I didn't hurt at all. We even got crazy with it and sort of did it all over the house: in the bathroom, the shower, the sink, the table. It sort of just spread everywhere. It was incredible.

It was hard because we were worried about getting caught, and I was too dry—I wish I had known about and been comfortable using lube!

10. He should definitely *not* plan to "deflower" you in one mighty, powerful thrust. Ouch! It's also okay if you don't "go all the way" in one session. If it's not feeling comfortable, get as far as you can, and try again another time.

     If your partner is on top, he should insert his penis just the smallest amount, then stop, make sure that feels okay, then push in just a teeny bit further and stop again. You'll want to kiss and breathe along the way, and let your bodies relax together. When you say it's okay, he can push in a little farther, or do an out-in motion where he pulls out and then pushes in just a little farther than last time. The woman should be in charge here: You decide when it's okay to go farther, when to rest, where to stop. You should discuss this approach in advance, using phrases like, "really slow and gentle," and "I heard it would be more comfortable for me if we . . ."

It can also work well for you to be on top—in that position, it's even easier for you to control the depth and speed of penetration.

Breathe! Have your partner go in slowwwly, maybe a half inch at a time, and make him wait until you tell him to go again. Basically play red light/green light until he's in, and then wait a few minutes before he moves again, going very slowly the whole time!

For me, it wasn't the romance you see in the movies. It was me and my boyfriend. In a dorm. Having awkward sex. And his penis didn't fit inside me for a long time. It took us a while to figure it all out.

11. **Don't expect a female orgasm through intercourse.** While it certainly isn't impossible, don't be disappointed if there's no female O the very first time. One study published in the *Journal of Sex Research* found that only seven percent of women had an orgasm their first time. Intercourse—like all sexual skills—tends to feel more pleasurable for both partners as you get better at it.

It was completely different than I expected. First of all, it didn't hurt at all. I was always told it would hurt horribly but it didn't at all, although I was really sore for the next few days.

Second, it was a serious disappointment. People don't tell you it takes practice. They make it seem like orgasms happen every time (even when you have no idea what you're doing).

12. **Have a sense of humor.** If you expect your first time to be flawless, you'll probably be disappointed. But if you're ready to enjoy each other, laugh together at unexpected glitches, and work out the fine points eventually, you'll have a memorable, stress-free experience regardless of exactly what happens.

Sex is always full of mistakes even if you've been with the same person for years. Make the best out of those funny bedroom mistakes.

I thought it would be extremely painful, and it was not, but it was not necessarily pleasurable either. I remember laughing a lot.

6

G Marks the Spot:
the g-spot and female ejaculation

A flyer in the dorm lobby caught Marshall's eye when he returned to his room late one night in his first year of college. Printed in a basic Times New Roman font, it read simply, "How to Female Ejaculate," with the next day's date, a time and location, but no other information. Marshall stared at the sign to be sure he was reading it correctly. There was no question: The topic was female ejaculation, and there was some kind of event taking place on campus the following night. By the time he came through the lobby on his way to breakfast the next morning, the flyer was gone.

Later that day, Marshall arrived at the lecture hall where the event was scheduled to take place, and was surprised to discover it packed with people. The lights dimmed, and a sexily dressed curly-haired blonde woman, Deborah Sundahl, stepped onto the stage. "I'm going to show you something that will *blow your mind*," she announced. Sundahl pointed her remote at the LCD projector to start a video, and a larger-than-life image of a woman's thighs and crotch appeared on the screen behind her. Suddenly, a clear stream of liquid shot out from between the woman's legs. The crowd of students gasped and then erupted into amazed murmurs.

Female ejaculation, Sundahl explained, is perfectly normal. Some women already ejaculate, she said, some haven't learned how, and some hold back to prevent

I ♥ FEMALE ORGASM

themselves from doing so. Because female ejaculate comes out of the body from the urethra, the same hole women pee out of, many women confuse ejaculating with urination.

In our own experience teaching about women's sexuality, we've watched light-bulbs go on over some women's heads as we've talked about female ejaculation. Many tell us afterward that this has long been part of their experience of sexuality: They were really aroused, and then all of a sudden liquid came out of their body from the same place that pee comes out. Many were horrified, assuming they'd lost control of their bladder during sex. One woman told us she was so ter-rified of this sensation of needing to pee that she literally leapt from the bed every time she could feel herself nearing this arousal peak and dashed down the hall to the bathroom. She described it as a highly unsatisfying way to end every sexual encounter!

In reality, this woman who thought she was about to wet the bed, and the oth-ers who did let loose, weren't peeing. It was the urge to ejaculate they were feel-ing, and the liquid that came out was its own unique fluid, female ejaculate, not urine. Most importantly, female ejaculation isn't a sign of something going wrong, like wetting the bed, but rather a sign of sexual pleasure and release. Once it's understood, it's an experience that many women and their partners celebrate rather than fear.

I actually discovered female ejaculation when I was a teenager. I was talking on the phone with this boy that I had been attracted to for years. One thing led to another and we both began talking dirty to each other. I will never forget it. I had my first female ejaculation in a tie-dye beanbag! And I remember freak-ing out and telling him I had to get off the phone because I had no idea what had just happened! I thought I had peed everywhere! But then it happened after that—a lot. I found out that I'm a regular "squirter" and that I can do it over and over again. While I was really insecure about it at first, I actually came to enjoy it a lot because it really turned my partners on. Now I absolutely love it. It's like I get this really hot sensation all over my body. My legs start to tingle, my toes curl, my back arches, and then it just bursts out and I shake all over. Sounds almost like a seizure, huh? But then afterwards is the best part: I'm so incredibly relaxed and I feel weightless. AMAZING.

first things first:
the g-spot

TO UNDERSTAND FEMALE ejaculation, you need a working knowledge of the G-spot, because G-spot stimulation is the most likely to produce female ejaculation. Plus, G-spot stroking feels great to some women regardless of whether they ejaculate.

Unlike the sensitive parts of the clitoris on the outside of a woman's body, the G-spot is entirely inside her vagina. It's about two to three inches inside, toward the front wall of the vagina, and it feels like ridgy tissue.

A woman can insert her own finger to feel her own G-spot, or she may like using a sex toy designed for "G-spotting." Many women find their lover's fingers to be just the ticket to G-spot bliss. G-spots tend to swell up and get more sensitive as a woman gets aroused, so she may want to try feeling it when she's turned on.

G-spots usually respond most to firm, massaging pressure, which is why it was long believed that vaginas lacked nerve endings. In the 1950s, when pioneering sex researcher Alfred Kinsey and his colleagues tested the sensitivity of different areas of women's genitals, they used an instrument similar to a Q-tip to touch gently. Not surprisingly, they found women's vaginas, including their G-spots, generally not responsive to such gentle touch. If they'd tried deeper pressure, many women likely would have responded quite differently.

Most women who enjoy having their G-spot touched say the sensation is quite different than clitoral stimulation. For the person touching it, what the G-spot feels like varies tremendously from woman to woman, and this is probably a major source of the confusion about whether or not it really exists. For some women, the G-spot feels like a little bump: a raised part of their vaginal wall that's very pleasurable to the touch. For other women, it's more of an

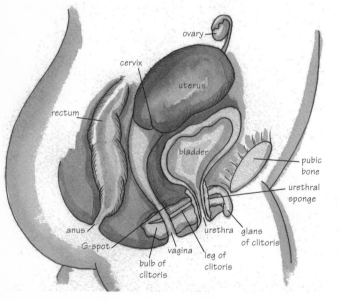

ovary
cervix
uterus
rectum
bladder
pubic bone
urethral sponge
anus
G-spot
urethra
glans of clitoris
vagina
leg of clitoris
bulb of clitoris

area that they find sensitive, particularly when pressed, and some say the sensitive area seems to be in somewhat different places on different days. Others spend hours or weeks poking around inside their own vaginas, finally concluding, "If G-spots exist, then I don't have one!" All of these reactions are perfectly normal: It's normal to have a G-spot that's really sensitive, equally normal to have one that doesn't really

what's your relationship with your g-spot?

MOST RESEARCH STUDIES have found that about two-thirds of women find the G-spot area to be sexually sensitive for them. We asked our female survey respondents how they felt about their G-spot. Here's the breakdown of their answers.

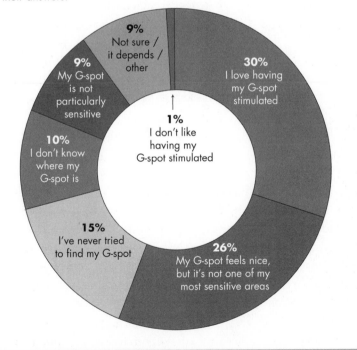

9%
Not sure /
it depends /
other

9%
My G-spot
is not
particularly
sensitive

10%
I don't know
where my
G-spot is

1%
I don't like
having my
G-spot stimulated

30%
I love having
my G-spot
stimulated

15%
I've never tried
to find my G-spot

26%
My G-spot feels nice,
but it's not one of my
most sensitive areas

who put the g in g-spot?

IN THE LATE 1970s, sex researchers Beverly Whipple and John Perry learned of a sensitive area inside the vagina that could induce female ejaculation if stimulated. Researching further, Whipple and Perry discovered that German gynecologist Ernst Gräfenberg, an immigrant living in New York City, had written about this area and about female ejaculation in a journal article in 1950, but that this anatomical fact had mostly been forgotten during the intervening years. Although the area had also been written about centuries earlier, Whipple and Perry decided to name what they were studying the "Gräfenberg spot," or the G-spot, in honor of the first modern doctor to describe it. The 1982 book *The G Spot* by Perry, Whipple, and their colleague Alice Kahn Ladas, sold over a million copies, turning "G-spot" into a household word.

feel like anything, and everywhere in between. Researchers find that the number of nerve endings and amound of arousal tissue in this part of the body varies tremendously from woman to woman.

The erectile tissue that makes up the G-spot is actually an internal part of the clitoris, part of the same network of interconnected tissue and nerve endings (see the diagram on page 152). The tissue wrapped around the urethra is called the urethral sponge, and as arousal builds, this spongy tissue becomes engorged with blood. Within the urethral sponge are thirty to forty tiny paraurethral glands, also known as the female prostate. These produce the fluid of female ejaculation, especially when they're stroked and stimulated. During ejaculation, this fluid flows from the glands through ducts into the urethra, and then out of the woman's body.

meeting ms. g

AS WITH ANY sexual exploration, a woman will have a better time finding her G-spot if she approaches it as a fun, relaxing new adventure rather than a frantic search for a lost item, as though she misplaced her cell phone or keys. This exploration works best if you're already somewhat sexually aroused. Once you're settled into a comfortable position, gently slide one or two fingers inside your vagina with your palm facing upward, toward your belly button. Push your finger inside your vagina as far as it will comfortably go, and curling it slightly, slowly pull your finger back toward the opening. Pay close attention to the sensations as you move your finger along the top of your vagina. Experiment with:

○ **The pressure:** Does it feel better if you push really hard against the wall of the vagina or just lightly touch it?

I ♥ **FEMALE ORGASM**

○ **The location:** Does it feel most sensitive when your finger is all the way inside, near the entrance to your vagina, or somewhere in the middle?

○ **The speed:** Is there more sensation when you move firmly and slowly, or do you prefer quick movement?

Also notice the curve of your finger or fingers against your vagina, which for many women is the key ingredient to making this work. You're essentially massaging your vaginal wall, and your goal is to refine your technique to zero in on the movement and touch you find most pleasurable.

Having fun? Good! Wrist getting tired? Say it ain't so! Some women find G-spot self-stimulation tiring for the hand or wrist because of the curve involved. If you have a partner, he or she can be a wonderful assistant to this project. If you recline in bed, your partner can sit or kneel between your legs, giving him or her comfortable access to your G-spot without tiring either of you out. Have your partner use the same finger techniques described in the previous paragraph. Here's your chance to practice giving him or her really clear, explicit feedback about what feels good and what doesn't. Some couples make it into a game, saying "hot" if the lover is in the perfect spot, "cold" if he or she is far from the mark, and "warmer" and "cooler" to provide encouragement and redirection along the way.

In lieu of (or in addition to) a partner, sex toys designed for G-spot stimulation can be another ingredient for a good time, and sometimes easier on the hand and wrist. Read more about these on page 180. While fingers and toys often provide the most direct G-spot stimulation, there's information about intercourse positions most likely to pleasure the G-spot in chapter 5.

the outer route to the g-spot

WOMEN CAN FEEL the back side of their own G-spot without even putting a finger inside their vagina. Here's how: First, find your pelvic bone, the hard bony area at your lower abdomen, just above the shaft of your clitoris. Inch your fingers up your pelvic bone (toward your belly button) until the bone ends, and you feel the soft flesh of your lower belly. If you push in firmly there—the soft area just above your pubic bone—you may feel a somewhat sensitive area. That's the other side of the erectile tissue that makes up your G-spot. The instructors of a Body Electric women's sexuality class taught Dorian that they called this spot "the back door to heaven." Some women enjoy pressing this area, or having their partner do so, while they're masturbating or having partnered sex. You can push on it in addition to or instead of internal G-spot stimulation.

For most women, G-spot stimulation is the sexual activity most likely to lead to ejaculation. Some women ejaculate without G-spot stimulation, though, and others find G-spot stimulation really pleasurable in its own right, but haven't found that it leads to ejaculation for them. There are plenty of women who just don't find their G-spot particularly pleasurable to massage at all, and that's perfectly fine, too.

sex tip for partners:
some pointers on "fingering"

BASED ON SNIPPETS of conversation they overheard in the schoolyard and on the backs of schoolbuses, many guys, especially, have heard that when a girl invites you to touch her below the waist, what you're supposed to do is "finger her." This unfortunate term has led generations of men astray, revealing them to be inexperienced lovers and disappointing their partners. Good fingering technique does *not* involve inserting one, two, or as-many-as-you-can-fit fingers into a woman's vagina and quickly thrusting them in and out. While some women may enjoy this practice, most will scrunch their faces in displeasure.

Should your fingers be so lucky as to have direct access to a woman's private parts, here's how most women are hoping they'll spend their time: First, locate the clitoris and spend lots of quality time there, teasing and caressing it and all around the woman's external genitalia, as described on page 34.

If your finger would like to do some further exploring, gently slide a finger into her vagina, whispering in her ear, "Is this okay?" as you do (of course, stop right away if she says no). Because women produce varying degrees of their own lubrication, if you feel slight dryness or friction at the opening, wet your finger first with saliva or lube. Once inside, casually commence G-spot stimulation, using the techniques described above. Note that some women may prefer your finger to do something else—or not move at all—rather than stimulate her G-spot. Ask her what she likes. Don't forget to cut your nails before you start!

Start at the clitoris and then work with both the clitoris and G-spot. A lot of the guys I've been with have just started right away fingering me and not even paying attention to the clitoris, which is a major letdown for me.

I ♥ FEMALE ORGASM

Unless she explicitly encourages or invites these digital behaviors, the three things to avoid are thrusting in and out with speed and force; pulling your finger all the way outside her vagina and then jamming it back in again; and trying to push in as many fingers as you can at once, as though you were trying on a glove. (If you're wondering how "the shocker" move fits in with all this, see page 246.)

Despite the confusion about the best fingering technique, don't overlook fingers' massive potential for pleasure.

I love hands! They're so versatile and sensitive. My advice would be, don't be too rough, find out whether I just want to be filled with fingers or whether I want you to move them around, touch me the way you see me touch myself, and use lube!

Gentle is key. Clean hands are a must. But mostly go really slow at first and make sure you are reading your partner like she was the instruction manual to some really cool, really expensive, really fragile gizmo. Basically, pay attention.

girls can ejaculate, too!

WITH LOTS OF G-spot stimulation, some women are able to ejaculate. (Some can ejaculate simply from clitoral stimulation, too, though this is less common.) Because female ejaculation isn't discussed much, it's a subject a lot of people are confused about. Growing numbers of female ejaculation-themed porn videos with titles like *Oh My Gush* and *See Her Squirt* are popularizing the concept of female ejaculation—but porn being porn, they don't do much to clarify or educate. In the making of a typical porn video, the female star is hired for her ability to dramatically shoot ejaculate across the room. (Some women who have appeared in these videos say they were just peeing.) In real life, ejaculation isn't the same as urinating. It *can* involve large quantities of fluid for some women, but it doesn't always involve a geyser shooting from down below. Even if it's not as dramatic, it can certainly be just as much fun.

a groaner

PERHAPS YOU'VE BEEN a target of this classic joke: Someone summons a woman across the room by insistently extending and bending his or her index finger to indicate "come here" until the woman finally walks over. Then the summoner says, "I knew if I fingered you long enough you would come!"

Ejaculating is probably the best part of sex for me. I wish it happened every time, but then I'd have a lot more laundry to do.

My partner ejaculated while I was performing oral sex on her (along with vibrator penetration), so I was really close to her vagina at the time. It was the most beautiful and sexiest thing I had ever seen.

I did it to myself [made myself ejaculate] a few months ago. It felt great and I was completely amazed that my body could do that! It was like learning I could fly—I felt incredibly alive and powerful, as cheesy as that sounds.

Q & A about female ejaculation

When a woman ejaculates, does she have an orgasm at the same time?

For most women who ejaculate, yes, orgasm and ejaculation happen at the same time. This isn't the case for all women, though—some women ejaculate some time before their orgasm, or some time after, or they ejaculate without having an orgasm at all. And, of course, lots of women have orgasms without ejaculating. As always, sexual diversity rules!

It usually happens when I have an orgasm. The stronger the orgasm, the more likely ejaculation is to happen. It is sometimes a strong quick spurt, and some-times it's a slower trickle, depending on the level of exertion I've used to get to the orgasm.

For me when I ejaculate it's a different feeling than an orgasm. It's hard to explain. My body feels great all over, intense and kind of gushy, for lack of a better word. It's not the same shuddering, vibrating feeling I feel when I have an orgasm. Ejaculating is different every time. It's sometimes well before I have an orgasm, while I'm having one, or just before.

How much comes out?

The amount a woman ejaculates can vary from a few drops to a cup or two of liquid. Some women who regularly ejaculate in large "gushes" get in the habit of preparing by putting a few layers of folded towels under themselves, or putting a plastic mattress liner under their sheets.

It seemed like my whole body got sweaty and hot. My legs started shaking, too. I thought it was weird at first, but it felt sooo good. There was so much of it, it made a huge pool around me. I didn't know that my body was holding so much fluid. I was very tired afterwards. I fall asleep almost instantly every time.

I didn't realize I was ejaculating at first, because it was always a small amount of liquid, and not as forceful as some of the female ejaculation I'd heard of before. But after learning more, I realized that I was ejaculating! For me, it's a small amount of liquid, and comes only after a large amount of sensation.

When my G-spot is stimulated, it feels like I'm about to pee.

This is a normal feeling, most common from G-spot stimulation but sometimes the result of arousal without any G-spot contact at all. As the spongy tissue surrounding the urethra swells up with blood in a woman who's sexually excited, this tissue squeezes the urethra and can press against the bladder, too, creating a sensation very similar to the urge to pee. Of course, sometimes women just have to pee while they're having sex (they never show *that* in the movies!), so if you're not sure, you can always stop what you're doing, go pee, and then return to your sexual activities. If you feel a strong urge to urinate within the first minute or two, you know you just emptied your bladder, so this time you can be reassured that the fullness you're feeling is your aroused urethral sponge and its ejaculate.

The first time I did it, I was with my boyfriend. I was terrified, I thought I peed the bed, but he laughed at me and explained what it was. Now it happens all the time when he fingers me, and we just put a towel down ahead of time for me to lie on.

The fear that they might pee holds many women back from ejaculating. If ejaculation is something you'd like to experience, but you're finding yourself fighting the urge to pee, first, be reminded that most women and men find it impossible to urinate when they're highly aroused. Once you've emptied your bladder (either before sex or by taking a quick bathroom break in the middle of it), decide not to worry about peeing. Give yourself permission to let whatever comes out of your body come out. Put a towel or two on the bed for your own peace of mind. That way, in the highly unlikely event that it's urine and not ejaculate, you can do the same thing you'd do if you had just ejaculated: Put the towels in the washing machine and call it a night!

What's the difference between pee and ejaculate?

Because female ejaculate and urine come out of the body's same orifice (the urethra), it's not surprising that many people think a woman has peed when actually, she's ejaculated. Indeed, some skeptics claim there's no such thing as female ejaculation, and that the fluid that comes out is urine from the bladder. In reality, female ejaculate is a watery liquid, either clear or somewhat milky, produced from glands inside the urethral sponge. These glands are also considered the female prostate. It doesn't smell like urine, and it's not yellow. Laboratory analysis has found that female ejaculate is an alkaline fluid that contains more prostatic acid phosphatase, prostate-specific antigen (both present in male ejaculate), and glucose than urine does. It does sometimes contain a trace amount of urine, possibly because it runs through the same "tube."

Perhaps the most compelling proof that ejaculate is not pee was done by a woman curious to figure out the source of her orgasmic expulsions. She took a medication that turns urine blue, and then proceeded to masturbate, repeating the experiment several times. She would ejaculate on her sheet, and then pee on the same sheet. The

female ejaculation on tv: *The L Word*

IN THIS LESBIAN television drama, a woman is horrified that she ejaculated while having sex with her girlfriend, but the girlfriend tells her, "It's perfectly natural." The next day when the still-mortified woman confides in her friends about what happened, a friend tells her she should be proud of her newfound ability. "Women strive for this!" she says. "You should be totally and utterly ecstatic!"

Female Orgasms on TV

I ♥ FEMALE ORGASM

pee spots were always deep blue, as expected from the medication. The ejaculation spots either had no color or a faint bluish tinge. A human sexuality professor wrote up the woman's experiments in the *Journal of Sex Research*. Who knew that masturbation could play an important role in advancing science?

What's the difference between "getting wet" (lubricating) and ejaculating?

When a woman becomes aroused, the vaginal walls sweat, so to speak, much in the same way that your skin sweats in hot weather. The liquid, or transudate, is a colorless component of blood that's secreted through the walls of the vagina. The liquid from female ejaculation, on the other hand, is produced inside the paraurethral glands inside the urethral sponge, and secreted from the urethra. Despite these differences, in some cases it can be hard for a woman to know if she ejaculated—it's common for small quantities of ejaculate to go unnoticed. As a result, no one knows what percentage of women ejaculate, because many who do may not be aware that they're doing so. If you find yourself puzzling over whether you ejaculated or just got really wet, a few key differences are that lubrication happens gradually, is produced inside the vagina, and can start quite early in the arousal process. Ejaculation, on the other hand, happens all at once, comes from the urethra, and usually (though not always) takes place around the time of an orgasm.

> ### learn more about female ejaculation
>
> IF YOU WANT more detail, including step-by-step instructions to learn how to ejaculate, get a copy of *Female Ejaculation and the G-Spot* by Deborah Sundahl. It's the most comprehensive, user-friendly book on the subject. The vast majority of the book is relevant to straight, lesbian, or bi readers, though it primarily assumes that "partners" are male.

If a woman's urethral sponge fills up with fluid but she doesn't ejaculate, what happens to the fluid?

Ejaculate that isn't ejaculated outflows into the bladder and is peed out the next time the woman urinates.

Do women like ejaculating? Is it better than just having an orgasm?

Some women love the feeling of release with ejaculation, and say it's fun to be able to see physical evidence of their orgasm coming out of their body (similar to the way many guys seem to think ejaculating is pretty cool to do). Other women say the experience is just different, neither better nor worse, than having a non-ejaculatory orgasm. There's no research evidence to suggest that women who ejaculate have better orgasms, or are more sexually satisfied, than women who don't.

Having an orgasm without ejaculating is less pleasurable for me than having one while ejaculating. It also makes for a more intense orgasm.

The feeling of ejaculating is good but not as good as a clitoral orgasm.

I like having an orgasm without ejaculating. I can concentrate on how it feels and not the mess I'm making or that I'm lying in a puddle.

Sometimes I have stronger orgasms when I'm not ejaculating and sometimes it's the opposite. I don't see a huge difference, but usually an orgasm that makes me ejaculate feels better than when I'm not ejaculating.

If you don't already ejaculate, learning to do so should definitely *not* be something you feel like you should add to your already overwhelming to-do list. Women can have fabulous, fulfilling sex lives without ever ejaculating. While we think it's important to teach about this so women who "naturally" ejaculate know what's happening, we would be depressed if "Learn to female ejaculate" started showing up on magazine lists of "Things Every Woman Should Do Before She's 30 (or 50)." Women shouldn't feel they're inadequate if they don't ejaculate.

Can all women ejaculate?

Sex experts disagree on this question. Some say that yes, all women are capable of learning to ejaculate if they don't do it already. Others say it might be more like rolling your tongue: Some people can do it; others can't. Research findings range widely, reporting anywhere from 10 to 68 percent of women saying they've ejaculated. (In our survey, 30 percent of women said they've ejaculated, 41 percent said they haven't, and 28 percent weren't sure.)

I want to ejaculate! How can I make it happen?

The best route to that goal is lots of G-spot stimulation. For most women, the most effective kind of stimulation is a "come hither" finger motion, with one or two fingers pulling against the vaginal wall where the G-spot is located. A partner or a G-spot stimulating sex toy can help, too. When you feel the urge to pee, and/or while you're having an orgasm, take the fingers, sex toy, or penis out of your vagina so the ejaculate can come out, and practice letting go and pushing out the ejaculate. As with so many other aspects of orgasms, having strong PC muscles can make a big difference, too. Be sure to do your Kegels, as described on page 26.

female ejaculation: something old or something new?

ALTHOUGH FEMALE EJACULATION is a new concept to many people alive today, it's long been known that women had the potential to ejaculate—some cultures even saw female ejaculation as healing, sacred, or essential for a woman to conceive. Ancient Chinese and Indian sexuality texts wrote about female ejaculation over 2,000 years ago. Aristotle, Galen, and other ancient Greek philosophers and scientists examined the subject in detail. Renaissance anatomists documented the existence of female glands that produced ejaculate. In sixteenth-century Japan, women used special bowls to catch their own ejaculate, which was believed to have healthy, aphrodisiacal properties. Batoro women in Uganda reportedly teach their young women how to ejaculate before they're considered eligible for marriage—their word for the custom is *kachapati*, which translates to "spray the wall."

Despite all this, the very concept of female ejaculation managed to be forgotten for most of the eighteenth and nineteenth centuries, and now is being "discovered" all over again.

Recently I got divorced, went back to college, and got a new boyfriend. In col-
lege I was taking this human sexuality class, and the textbook included some
information about female ejaculation. One night during the semester I was
taking the class, my boyfriend and I were trying some new things, and I had an
orgasm, and I squirted! I'd never done this before, but I was so excited! I was
jumping up and down naked in the bedroom, telling him, "It's just like in the
textbook! It's just like in the textbook!"

how about the a-spot?

AH, YES, THE fabled "A-spot." When an audience member first asked us about the
"A-spot," we admitted our unfamiliarity with the spot and promised a thorough
investigation. We soon discovered that entering the word "A-spot" into a search
engine doesn't produce meaningful results, because of the many other uses of the
phrase "a spot," as in "Adopt a Spot Dalmatian Rescue" or "Removing Stains: Getting a Spot Out of Your Dress." Nowadays, even an eBay advertisement on Google
promises, "A Spot: Whatever you're looking for you can get it on eBay." (If only it
were so easy!) As the question came up repeatedly from audience members, we
even asked other sex experts, but no one we asked had heard of the fabled spot.

A few years later, we heard Canadian sex educator Sue Johanson (of *Talk Sex
with Sue Johanson* fame) call a man's prostate his "A-spot," because it's inside his
anus (hence the "a" in "A-spot"). Essentially a male version of the G-spot, the male
prostate is located about three to four inches inside the rectum, toward the man's
belly, and can be stimulated using many of the same techniques as G-spot stimulation. We started sharing this fact when audience members asked about the A-
spot, but many seemed unconvinced that this was what they'd heard of
before—they thought it was an area of a woman's body.

Then, while conducting research for this book, one clue led to another, and
bingo! We found it. A-spot stands for anterior fornix spot, also known as the AFE-
zone (anterior fornix erogenous zone). It's a smooth area just below the cervix, on
the front of a woman's vagina (the same side as her G-spot) but farther up, deeper
inside her vagina. Some women find the area quite erotically sensitive, others don't.

I ♥ FEMALE ORGASM

Personally, when we follow the directions about where to find the A-spot (did you think we could write a book about female orgasm without doing any—*ahem*—hands-on research?), we think it's just another location for the G-spot. Some women's G-spots are closer to their cervix, others closer to the entrance to the vagina. But one thing is certain: the discovery of new spots and sex positions sells books and magazines. Which *Cosmo* headline would make you more likely to buy the magazine: "Don't Miss Out: Find Your A-Spot Today!" or "The G-Spot: Old Spot, Possible New Location"?

We say, if you discover a new area that feels good to touch, great, enjoy! If not, there's no need to lose sleep over it—there are plenty of good spots already.

7

Vibrators, Toys, and Piercings, Oh My!

why over a million vibrators are sold each year

Vibrators, which are essentially vibrating toys for grown-ups, come in every shape, size, and style you can imagine. They range from a little vibrating "bullet" a woman can wear in her undies to a device the size of a rolling pin that plugs into the wall. Some vibrators are cleverly disguised as a tube of lipstick, so a woman can keep one in her purse in case she has an emergency in the afternoon. Others look like bunny rabbits, rubber duckies suited for the tub, tongues, or undulating abstract sculptures. Some are designed to be worn over a penis or dildo for additional stimulation during penetration; others fit on a fingertip or over a tongue.

Why do vibrators make women so happy? It so happens that many clitorises *love* the sensation of vibration. No hand or tongue can maintain the fast, intense, consistent stimulation that a vibe provides—and a vibrator never gets a cramped neck or an aching wrist. For many women a vibrator is the fastest route to orgasm; for others it's the only way they can get there. Since it takes many women longer to come than they'd like, anything that speeds the process is a welcome enhancement. There's no stereotypical vibrator user, either. Women enjoy vibrators to make a great partnered sex life even better, and to keep them whistling when they're single. A tour of the bedside drawers of America would uncover vibrators in the bedrooms of women who are on their own, dating, partnered, and married; young, old, and in between; heterosexual, lesbian, and bi.

I had my vibrator for almost a month before I finally had the time to experiment with it. The first time, I stopped before I orgasmed; I think the pleasure kind of shocked me into stillness. It took me a few nights to figure out what I liked and what just didn't work for me. When I finally did orgasm, it was just like, whoa. My entire body was shaking and I continued to tremble for a few minutes after. This discovery was quite possibly the best thing to happen to me that year. All I could think was, Why haven't I done this before?

Vibes aren't for women only: guys play with vibrators, too, and there are vibrating toys specifically sold for men.

Vibrators have a surprisingly long history. As Rachel Mains documents in her fascinating book *The Technology of Orgasm*, from the 300s BC to the 1920s, doctors massaged women's genitals to orgasm as an accepted medical treatment for "hysteria." When a physician invented an electromechanical vibrator in the 1880s, the medical field was thrilled—finally, a faster, more reliable way to treat the "female troubles" that were then among the most frequently-diagnosed diseases. Vibratory "gynecological massage" allowed doctors to treat more patients per day, with less fatigue for the doctor and less skill required. (As many husbands and partners can attest, bringing a woman to orgasm using one's hands can sometimes be a slow and challenging process.) Offering treatment with vibrators was a major medical moneymaker for docs who offered it, since, as Mains writes, "These patients neither recovered nor died of their condition but continued to require regular treatment." You, too, might develop a case of hysteria that required the attention of a physician if the only place you could come by an orgasm were at the doctor's office!

Vibrators were among the first few electrical appliances available to the general public, appearing soon after toasters and nearly a decade before vacuum

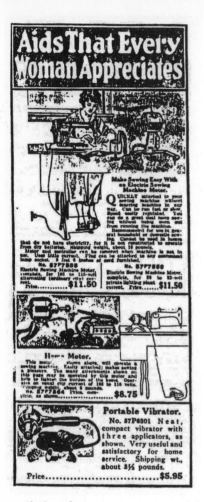

Aids That Every
Woman Appreciates

Make Sewing Easy With
an Electric Sewing
Machine Motor.

No. 57P7558   No. 57P7559
Electric Sewing Machine Motor,   Electric Sewing Machine Motor,
complete, for 101 to 115-volt   complete, for 16 to 25-volt
alternating (ordinary city) cur- private lighting plant
rent.   current.
Price.............$11.50   Price........$11.50

Home Motor.

No. 57P7564 Price, com-
plete, as shown........$8.75

Portable Vibrator.

No. 57P6301 Neat,
compact vibrator with
three applicators, as
shown. Very useful and
satisfactory for home
service. Shipping wt.,
about 3½ pounds.

Price..................$5.95

This listing from a 1918 Sears, Roebuck and Company catalog advertises vibrators right underneath the sewing machines.

cleaners and electric irons. By 1900, they were marketed openly to women for home use. Newspaper advertisements and mail-order catalogs promised women the devices would offer "thrilling, refreshing vibration" and help female buyers "realize thoroughly the joy of living."

By the 1920s, though, vibrators began to appear in the pornographic films of the time, sullying their previously healthy, innocent reputation. The advertisements vanished from public view until the 1960s, when they were marketed more openly as sex toys.

Today, we sometimes hear people say they don't want to use a vibrator (or they don't want their partners to use one) because vibrators aren't "natural." Indeed, air conditioning, hot showers, cell phones, and underwear don't occur in nature, either—but they sure improve people's lives. Also, vibrators don't just jump up and start stimulating people by themselves—there's always a human being behind the vibrator finding the right spot and directing each stroke. (Of course, whether or not to try a vibrator is up to each person to decide—they don't appeal to everybody.)

getting your hands on a vibe

CURIOUS? READY TO give it a whirl—or should we say, a buzz? Thousands of "adult stores" around the country sell vibrators, though you're particularly in luck if you live in or near a city with a woman-friendly sex toy boutique such as:

Baltimore, MD	Sugar
Berkeley, CA	Good Vibrations
Boston, MA	Good Vibrations
Chicago, IL	Early to Bed, Tulip
Denver, CO	Hysteria

Halifax, Canada	Venus Envy
Madison, WI	A Woman's Touch
Milwaukee, WI	A Woman's Touch, The Tool Shed
Minneapolis, MN	The Smitten Kitten
New York, NY	Eve's Garden, Toys in Babeland
Northampton, MA	Oh My!
Ottawa, Canada	Venus Envy
Portland, ME	Nomia Boutique
Portland, OR	It's My Pleasure
Provincetown, MA	Wild Hearts
San Francisco, CA	Good Vibrations
Seattle, WA	Toys in Babeland
Toronto, Canada	Come as You Are, Good for Her
Vancouver, Canada	Womyns' Ware

This list is definitely *not* all-inclusive. New stores pop up every year, and there are now so many great ones out there that it's hard to keep track of them all. These stores pride themselves on being welcoming to women and GLBT people (as well as to men and straight people), and on stocking high-quality merchandise. The stores listed above and others like them are typically staffed by knowledgeable women who answer questions and offer candid advice without embarrassment.

If you're not near one of these boutiques, nearly all offer online shopping (and in some cases, mail-order catalogs, too), and send products in packages that don't suggest what's inside. You can also buy a vibrator at a sex toy party, or get the "back massager" kind in a drug store or department store (just don't expect to find the word "vibrator" on the outside of the box!).

**INSTRUCTIONS
HITACHI MAGIC WAND
HOUSE HOLD
ELECTRIC MASSAGER
Model HV-250R**

POSITIONS OF MASSAGING

This is the instruction sheet that comes inside the box if you purchase the Hitachi Magic Wand "massager," one of the top-selling vibrators on the market. The folks at Hitachi helpfully suggest many body parts where buyers might want a massage. Except, it looks like they forgot one or two. . . .

Female Orgasms on TV

vibrators on tv:
Sex and the City

IN A NOW-CLASSIC episode of *Sex and the City*, Samantha tries to return her broken vibrator to the Sharper Image store where she bought it, but the salesman insists, "Sharper Image doesn't sell vibrators. It's a neck massager." Finally accepting his name for it, Samantha says, "I'd like to return my *neck massager.*" When the salesman asks her why, she says, "It failed to get me off."

Some factors to consider when buying a vibe:

Shape Because vibrators are used primarily for clitoral stimulation, you don't need something shaped like a penis—unless you want to use it for penetration, as well.

Power If you don't want to worry about having the batteries die at a crucial moment, you might want a plug-in model. Vibrators that plug into a wall outlet generally provide more intense vibration than battery-operated ones. On the other hand, battery-operated devices can be gentler and can be used anywhere. There are also vibrators that charge like a cordless phone, ones that plug into your computer's USB port (talk about multitasking!), and even solar-powered ones.

Price In general, battery-operated vibrators are less expensive, but they also break more easily. It's fine to start out with a battery-operated vibe; you can invest in a fancier model once you know you like the vibrations.

Sound If your housemate sleeps in the room next door or your dorm room has paper-thin walls, you may want to be sure your vibrator is the strong, silent type. If there's no one to hear your vibe's happy hum, then you have nothing to worry about!

Color and style What looks like fun to you? A sparkling purple cylindrical smoothie? A vibrator shaped like a well-hung penis? A waterproof curved toy perfect for some rub-a-dub-dub G-spot play? Choose one that appeals. You can always diversify down the road.

I have a small vibrator with pearly beads on the side of it. It's a pretty bubble-gum pink color. My boyfriend and I refer to it as my pink boyfriend. I got it at the sex shop near campus just as a joke. It was probably the best ten bucks I ever spent.

I use a tiny black-and-pink lipstick-shaped vibrator. I wanted one because I wasn't ready for intercourse, but I wanted to experiment to see what I would like.

Mine is blue and looks like an average-sized penis. It's tilted a quarter of the way up to enable the G-spot to be stimulated. I bought it when I was out with some friends who already had one. I wanted to become more confident with sex. I use it before going out to prevent myself from doing something stupid. I also use it before a nap when I'm really stressed out and to get my mind off things that don't allow me to relax and go to sleep.

> ### somebody tip off the energizer bunny
>
> HAVING THE BATTERIES die at a pivotal moment is one of the biggest drawbacks to using a battery-operated vibrator. Perhaps women don't need batteries that "keep going, and going, and going." Imagine if the slogan instead marketed batteries to help us "keep coming, and coming, and coming." We think the brand would be a smash hit.

I have a transparent hot pink basic vibrator. It was a gift, so I didn't pick the color, but it amuses me to no end that it is pink. It makes me feel really girly and normally I'm not a super-girly girl. My mom gave it to me when I was home from college over Thanksgiving break my freshman year, along with a book about masturbation. She wanted to make sure that I was having a good time in college, I guess.

here a vibrator, there a vibrator

AS ORGASM EDUCATORS, we never ask our audiences to turn off their cell phones. Instead, at the start of every talk, we recommend audience members set their phones to vibrate. But cell phones aren't the only devices that vibrate. We've heard plenty of stories of women having orgasms—intentionally and by surprise—from:

- back massagers
- washing machines
- subwoofer speakers playing loud, strong bass
- squiggle pens (We've heard quite a few "first orgasm" stories that involved these battery-operated pens designed to make you write wiggly.)
- electric toothbrushes
- riding lawn mowers
- motorcycles
- the gentle rumble of riding in a bus, train, car, or airplane

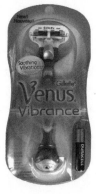

The handle of Gillette's Venus Vibrance battery-operated razor vibrates. Our advice: Just be careful which end you use for which activity.

vibrators: a user's guide

OKAY, SO YOU'VE got your vibrator in hand! Ready for a test drive? How you use it is up to you, based on what feels good, but here are a few pointers:

1. Go slow. If your vibe has multiple speeds, start out on low, then experiment to figure out what you like.

2. **Play with pressure.** Experiment with super-light touch, firm pressure, and in-between.

3. **Add a buffer.** You may want to put a piece of cloth (like a folded washcloth or some clothing) in between your clit and the vibrator, to soften the intensity.

4. **Focus on the clit.** Even if your vibrator has a shape you can insert in your vagina, most women come by using it on or near their clitoris, not by pumping it inside themselves. Of course, see what works for you!

Anything that vibrates can help me have an orgasm when it's applied directly to my clit. I don't like vibration that's too strong because I'm very sensitive and it numbs me, so my favorite toys are softer ones that vibrate gently. I prefer vibration on my clit and not inside me, so my favorite vibrators are ones that are designed specifically for clit stimulation and not for penetration.

all i want for christmas is an electric toothbrush

ONE WOMAN SHARED that as a teenager, she asked her parents to get her an electric toothbrush for Christmas. She let them believe she wanted to improve her dental hygiene, but her real plans were a *lot* more fun than cavity prevention.

5. **But don't focus on the clit *too* much.** While many women like to use their vibe directly on their clitoris (or its shaft or side), others get enough stimulation by holding it against their outer lips, or resting their fingers over their clit and using the vibrator to make their fingers vibrate. Experiment with using your vibrator to massage your whole body, and all around your genitals.

6. **Position yourself.** In addition to holding the vibrator in your hand, try resting it on some pillows and then lowering yourself down onto it in a "woman on top" position. Or, if your toy is big enough, you can lie back and squeeze it between your thighs, which frees up your hands for other pleasures.

7. **Build arousal slowly.** If you're climbing toward orgasm faster than you'd like, turn the vibrator off for a bit and then back on again. Seduce yourself: Mix up vibrations with touching your body with your hands, deep breathing, and other physical and mental turn-ons.

vibrator addiction?

THE NUMBER ONE most-asked question about vibrators is, "Can I get addicted?" For some reason, women have gotten the idea that if their body gets used to using a vibrator, they may not be able to have an orgasm any other way.

tried it, didn't like it?

THE ENTHUSIASM OF vibrator-devotees sometimes leaves women who *aren't* into vibes feeling insecure. Like all things sexual, some love 'em, some don't. If playing with a vibrator doesn't float your boat, you may decide to try another kind or another way of using it—or you may seek your thrills elsewhere. No problem!

Not to worry! Most women who use vibrators see them as way to add variety to their sexual menu, like having chocolate mousse for dessert occasionally, instead of always cookies and ice cream. Studies of vibrator users find the vast majority still come in other ways. And even if you find vibrating is your favorite (or only) way to come, that's perfectly okay! No vibrator police force will arrive at the door to confiscate your vibrator when you reach a certain age or get married. If a vibrator is what gets your O's flowing better than anything else, you can simply include your vibe in your sex life until the day you die.

If you find that a vibrator's extra-strong sensations are making it harder to tune into a hand or tongue's more subtle sensations the way you used to, no problem. Try retiring your vibrator temporarily so you can recalibrate to mellower stimulation. If you were able to come in other ways before, your body will certainly relearn. If it's never worked for you and still doesn't, that's fine, too—many women are in your situation. Of course, don't expect every orgasm to feel the same—orgasms from different kinds of stimulation feel different. For more on changing the way you come, including exploring how to come without a vibrator, see page 54.

sweetie, i'd like you to meet my vibrator

VIBRATORS LOVE THREESOMES (themselves and a loving couple). Many female vibrator aficionados like the idea but worry how their partner might respond to the idea of making love with a battery-operated "friend" taking part. Luckily, most partners think vibrator play is sexy. In a study published in the *Journal of Sex Research*, only 10 percent of female vibrator owners said their partner was negative or unenthusiastic about it. Many get the concept that if sex is about pleasure, and if vibrators provide lots of it, it's likely to be a great time all around!

He was a little wary at first, but because I use a small vibrator that doesn't get in the way, he doesn't mind, and he actually likes trying to coordinate our orgasms to happen at the same time. This wouldn't be possible without the extra stimulation from the toy.

My partner feels that a sex toy would not allow him to perform his "manly duty." He feels that he should be the only one giving me orgasms.

Part of the trick, of course, is how the woman broaches the subject (if she's the one bringing it up). If she says, "Honey, you're such a lousy lover, I got myself a machine to get the job done right," her partner's got good reason to be concerned. If, on the other hand, she says, "I think it could be really hot to play with a vibrator together sometime—do you want to try it?" or, "I have the most explosive orgasms with my vibe—want me to show you how you can use it on me?" her partner is likely to be intrigued. Going vibrator shopping together (in person, online, or with a catalog) can help make it a joint project—not to mention being an excellent conversation-starter about what sorts of bedroom fun appeal to you. Here's what some women said about using a toy with their partner:

My boyfriend actually got out my toy and used it on me. I was ecstatic! I thought it was so awesome that my boyfriend approached it before I could ask him. We still use toys, and he even has some.

vibration nation?

ACCORDING TO THE forty-one-country Durex Global Sex Survey, the United States has the second-highest percentage of people who have used a vibrator. Here's the top ten list:

1. Australia 46%
2. United States 45%
3. Canada 44%
4. Norway 44%
5. United Kingdom 44%
6. Iceland 43%
7. New Zealand 43%
8. Sweden 38%
9. South Africa 37%
10. Switzerland 30%

My girlfriend and I really enjoy using sex toys together. It allows us to be a little kinky. We're not the most kinky, sex-crazed people, so it's sort of an adventure for us.

Using a sex toy was his idea because his hands get tired (even though he plays guitar).

My partner and I both came to our relationship with a stock of sex toys and carnal knowledge, so we never had to introduce each other to the idea of sex toys. It just seemed a natural part of our sex life.

When using a vibrator with a partner, either of you can hold it, or you can get one that straps on. Some vibrators fit on a penis or dildo, or attach to a cock ring, a ring or cuff designed to be worn around the penis and testicles to constrict blood flow and hold an erection. Often a guy likes the sensation of having his penis inside his partner's vagina while the vibrator is on her clit, or of having the vibrator stimulate her clitoris and the base of his penis at the same time. Two female partners can rub against the same vibrator, take turns, or use two at once. Note that anytime two people's bodily fluids get on a sex toy, there's some risk of HIV or STI transmission, so take this into consideration when you decide whose fluids will go where. See chapter 11 for more on playing safe.

other toys

VIBRATORS MAY BE the most popular bedroom toy, but there's a vast universe of adult playthings. A few of the other top sellers:

dildos

Dildos, toys designed for vaginal or anal penetration, are popular among women who enjoy the sensation of having something inside them. Dildos generally don't vibrate, but some vibrators are phallic-shaped and can be used as dildos. While some dildos are shaped like penises (sometimes with veins, scrotum, and all),

eavesdropping on girl-talk:
do women who love vibrators still want partners?

AT ONE SPEAKING engagement, we could hear a couple of men in the audience grumbling as the women talked enthusiastically about how much they loved using vibrators. Finally, one guy raised his hand. "If girls are so into vibrators," he asked, sounding a little more miffed than he probably intended, "what do they need us for?" So we put the question to the women who answered our survey: "If you can have an orgasm from a toy, do you still want to or enjoy having sex with a partner? Why or why not?" Here's what they had to say:

Oh, please. That's like saying if I could have a metal robot cat instead of a real one, I would want it instead. One purrs, and is fluffy, soft, and warm, and the other is battery-powered.

Fret not, partners! Think of it this way: When we're using our vibrator, it's likely that we're thinking of you. When we're with you, do you really think we're fantasizing about being with our vibrator? Doubt it. . .

A plastic sex toy could never replace the warmth and feeling of my husband's hands, lips, and breath moving over my body. A sex toy might be a good thing to help stimulate a feeling or to appease a physical longing when he isn't around, but it in no way compares to the real thing.

Guys can have an orgasm any time they want by masturbating. I just find it quicker to use a vibrator. I'm a busy woman. I still enjoy sex with my boyfriend, and I usually prefer it. It's more intimate, more involved, multiple areas are stimulated, and after I masturbate I can't snuggle my vibrator.

Who wants a rubber fakey instead of human contact?! A vibrator doesn't involve another person's touch, or the excitement of not always knowing what comes next. Plus, you have to do all the work yourself.

The conclusion of the 568 women who shared their thoughts was clear: Just because something can produce an orgasm doesn't mean it meets all the needs a partner can.

how do partners really feel when women use sex toys?

ON OUR SURVEY, we also asked male and female partners how they felt when their girlfriends and wives used vibrators and dildos. Here's a sampling of what they told us:

Yay to sex toys. They're like sprinkles on ice cream.

Frankly speaking, the first time we used one I was a little put off because I felt like she was enjoying that thing rather than me, but I quickly learned to use toys as tools. I am the one using it for her, so I have a direct effect on what sensations she is experiencing. As soon as I looked at toys and props as extensions of myself, I learned to really enjoy employing them, and so we both benefit.

I really enjoyed that she was enjoying the experience, but I felt slightly emasculated at the prospect of being easily replaced by plastic. I tend to prefer if she uses sex toys smaller than me, and we don't use them very often.

I think sex toys enhance any sexual relationship that's loving and trusting. Using sex toys with my partners is always fun and some- times funny. It brings us closer and makes the sex that much more interesting.

Overall, most partners who invited a toy into their bed reported that they'd enjoyed the experience, especially if it boosted the overall levels of pleas- ure for one or both of them.

I ♥ FEMALE ORGASM

others look more like rippling magic wands in colors like magenta and periwinkle. Even women who own an army of dildos, each lovingly named, usually still need external clitoral stimulation to be able to have an orgasm. As a result, a woman will often use a dildo while something else gets her clit going: her own fingers, a vibrator, or a partner's hand or tongue.

I like my glass dildo I bought last year. It is clear and pink and very beautiful. I use it for G-spot stimulation.

Simple dildos, or items used as dildos, work best because they allow me to experience penetration while I stimulate myself.

I like using a vibrator and dildo combination. Usually one or the other can help me get there, but I have to finish with my hand. Using both I don't need to use my hands.

> ## ancient inventions:
> ### the wheel, the calendar, the dildo
>
> DILDOS AREN'T EXACTLY newfangled: Archaeologists have found 30,000-year-old specimens, and they show up in cave paintings of the time, too. Around 500 BC, the Greek port of Miletus became famed for the leather and wooden dildos it manufactured, which were designed to be used with olive oil for lube.

In the land of stereotypes, lesbians are supposedly desperate for dildos because their partners generally don't have penises. In real life, some lesbians love the feeling of penetration (and therefore might enjoy dildo play); others don't. Same thing with straight and bi women: While some women crave that feeling of fullness, others couldn't care less about it.

A woman choosing a dildo can select exactly the width and length she finds most pleasurable for penetration, an option not usually available when scoping out potential boyfriends. For a woman who's nervous about penetration, experimenting with a dildo at her own pace can help her gain confidence and comfort. Partners (male or female) can also wear a harness and "strap on" a dildo, freeing up their hands for other pleasures (more on this on page 232). If you buy a dildo with a suction-cup base, you can have hours of fun figuring out the best flat surfaces for riding (hint: the bathtub wall works well). These also make great conversation pieces when stuck to refrigerators and filing cabinets.

g-spot toys

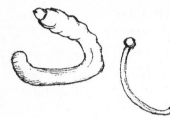

Sex toys designed for G-spot play generally have a bit of a curve, an angle, or an added bulb or ridge to help reach that sensitive area on the front wall of the vagina. Because G-spots usually respond best to firmer pressure, these toys are often made of somewhat harder, less flexible material. A woman would insert one of these toys so the curve points up toward her belly. (For more about the G-spot, see page 150)

zucchinis, carrots, and cucumbers

THE EASIEST PLACE to get a dildo? Some people start with the vegetable crisper. Once you've discovered the cheap thrills of veggie dildos, they say, you'll never look at a supermarket zucchini display the same way again.

According to many sex toy experts, a little vegetable play is recomended before springing for an expensive store-bought model. How else can you know if you prefer a dildo with a ½-inch diameter or one that's 1⅞ inches? In a sex toy catalog, the numbers can seem meaningless, but they become very real when you're inserting a crisp cuke. Buy a few different sizes, and use a vegetable peeler to shave them down until you find your favorite thickness. Then cut the veggie in half to measure its diameter (straight across, not around).

Two important tips to remember when playing with vegetables: If they come straight out of the fridge, they'll probably be too cold to insert. (And you thought diving into a cold swimming pool was shocking!) If you forgot to plan ahead by letting your toy come to room temperature, try microwaving or boiling it for a few seconds. Don't let it go limp!

Second, most vegetables are sprayed with pesticides, and you definitely do *not* want those in your nether parts. Always put a condom over your vegetable sex toy. It's yet another reason to buy organic!

I ♥ FEMALE ORGASM

butt plugs and anal toys

Anuses and rectums have lots of nerve endings, so some women enjoy anal play with toys. Butt plugs usually look like dildos with a base, and often have a narrow top and bottom to allow them to be worn inside, unmoving, rather than sliding in and out. You can use a regular dildo for anal play, too, as long as it has a base (see below). Some people enjoy anal toys that vibrate. Others like anal beads, a collection of beads on a string, because they enjoy the sensation of feeling each bead enter their body. The whole string can be pulled out to intensify the moment of orgasm, or be removed slowly afterward.

When inserting toys into your anus, keep in mind:

○ They should have a flared (wider) base, or a handle. Unlike a vagina, which is a closed-off space, the rectum leads into five feet of large intestine. If you accidentally "lose" a sex toy in your vagina, you can always fish it out again with your own finger, provided you relax enough and experiment with different positions. With the rectum, it isn't so easy to "rescue" lost toys yourself. Anyone who's worked in emergency rooms has stories about mortified patients who needed some nonflared object (most commonly a vibrator without a flared base) removed from their rectum. You can avoid finding yourself in this situation by inserting only objects with ends that prevent them from slipping completely inside.

○ Use lube. The rectum doesn't lubricate itself, so lube isn't optional for anal toys—it's required.

○ Check for smooth edges. Because the rectum's tissue is more delicate than the vagina's, don't insert any objects with rough edges.

○ Don't use a toy for vaginal contact after it's been in your anus unless you've washed it or put on a fresh condom. Bacteria from the anus can make for an unhappy vagina.

Obviously, you can't use vegetables to figure out what size butt plug you'd enjoy. (Zucchinis with flared bases: *There's* an idea for those genetically-modified seed researchers!) You're better off estimating what size you like by inserting and then measuring your or your partner's fingers.

and more . . .

While this chapter touches on the most popular toys, there's no end to the creative potential of adult-toy designers or the creativity of people who like sex. New toys make their way into stores every week, and people make homemade ones with objects they find around the house.

There's an entire world of toys related to BDSM (bondage, discipline/domination, and sadomasochism, which involve playing with pain and/or power). This kind

safewords: the sexual pause button

PEOPLE WHO CHOOSE sex play that involves pain or power generally agree on a "safeword" with their partner. (This kind of sex obviously also requires that both people consent and not be drunk or high.) If either partner says the safeword, it means both people promise to stop right away and check in. A safeword is a word no one would ordinarily use in a sexual situation, like "armadillo," "mashed potatoes," or simply "safeword" itself. Once you've agreed on a safeword, you can struggle against the silk scarves you asked your partner to tie you up with, or play out a dominant/submissive fantasy where one of you bosses the other around sexually, or enjoy the intense sensation of being flogged just the way you wanted to be, knowing that if you say your safeword, the action will stop immediately. The person who says the safeword might just need a small adjustment ("Can you re-tie that scarf on my left wrist? It's pinching a little") before the scene can continue. Or he or she might need a change of plan ("This is getting pretty intense for me—let's cuddle for a little so I can catch my breath"). People who enjoy BDSM say that having a safeword and a trustworthy partner helps them feel safe, relax, and even lets them thrash around and say, "No, stop!" if that's part of their fantasy, knowing there's a surefire way to actually stop the action if they want to.

I ♥ FEMALE ORGASM

of sex can be seemingly mild, like having your partner blindfold and then arouse you, passionately running your fingernails down your partner's back, or asking a partner to hold your wrists down while you have sex. Or it can involve more intense play and sensations, like using a whip, handcuffs, or candle wax. The most important thing is that both partners agree about what they want to do—like every kind of sex, what's highly arousing to one person may be a total turnoff to another.

Japanese nipple clamps! When I figured out my nipples added to my enjoyment, I figured I'd order a nipple toy. Best investment ever.

I really love bandanas. They can be used as blindfolds, gags, and to bind hands or feet. Also you can knot them up and use the knots as pressure points for certain locations. They're colorful and very cheap.

I like cock rings: They keep my boyfriend harder longer and some of them have little bumps on them that stimulate my clitoris. We got ours from a local sex shop—it glows in the dark. We got it to try to add some variety to the game.

Regardless of whether you're inventing your own toy at home or buying the latest gizmo that can tie your genitals into a vibrating knot, use common sense. As long as your sex play is safe and consensual, and your toys have no sharp, jagged edges or parts that could splinter or shatter, the sky's the limit.

keep 'em clean

Sex toys should be cleaned after each use. Putting a condom or plastic wrap on your sex toy makes it easy: just throw away the covering and put on a fresh one next time you're going to use it. If your friend wants to take your vibrator for a spin, make sure he or she condomizes it, too. If you're not covering your toy with a condom, read the manufacturer's instructions to find out how to clean it, or check out websites on how to clean sex toys. Most materials can be washed with soap and water, or soaked or wiped down with a bleach solution (10 percent bleach, 90 percent water). Silicone toys can be boiled or run through a dishwasher. Just don't forget to empty the dishwasher before your mom comes over, in case she gets inspired to help out!

piercing

WE GET LOTS of questions about whether female nipple and genital piercing improve women's orgasms. The answer depends on the woman's body, the kind of piercing, and the type of jewelry she wears in her piercing. Unfortunately, there's no way to know in advance whether you'll love the sensation or be eager to get the metal out of your pants.

Along with nipple piercing, there are eight basic locations for female genital piercings, plus many creative variations:

1. outer labia
2. inner labia
3. clitoral hood (the flap of skin on top of the clitoris, can be pierced either horizontally or vertically)
4. under the clitoral shaft (called a triangle piercing)
5. where the outer labia meet at the top, higher than a hood piercing (called a Christina piercing)
6. perineum (called a fourchette)
7. urethral wall (called a Princess Albertina piercing)
8. the clitoris itself (the glans)

For all these kinds of piercings, some women find they enjoy the sensations of rubbing or tugging against the metal jewelry during masturbation or partnered sex, and some find the pierced body part becomes more sensitive (at least partly because they're more aware of it). Vertical clitoral hood, triangle, and Christina piercings seem to be the most likely to increase orgasm-related sensations, because they can add pressure along the shaft of the clitoris, the area most women find most responsive.

My labia piercing is fun because it reminds partners to play with my labia, which I really like.

I've experienced climax-like feelings when just rubbing my pierced clit on my (female) partner's thigh.

I had a mini-nipplegasm once by myself when I had nipple rings. It was defi-
nitely different from my normal rush—it was more of an all-over orgasm. I
haven't been able to do it again.

Piercing the clitoris itself is rare and considered potentially dangerous because of the risk of nerve damage. Most "clitoral piercings" actually run either above or below the glans.

Many people love their own or their partner's piercings—especially labial and horizontal clitoral hood ones—for the aesthetics more than any enhancement in

flying high on harry potter's broom

WHEN THE HARRY Potter craze was first heating up, the toy company Mattel manufactured an electronic Nimbus 2000, a toy version of the flying broomstick that young wizard Harry rides while playing the sport quidditch in the popular book series. In addition to making "magical swooshing sounds," the battery-operated broomstick vibrated. What were kids supposed to do if they wanted to be just like Harry Potter in the book? Turn the broom on, put it between their legs, and pretend to fly around!

The toy got rave reviews online from parents astonished at how much time their adolescent daughters spent with it in their bedrooms ("I kind of wondered if she was too old for it, but she seems to LOVE it!"). Some moms reported riding the broom on "a very magical journey" themselves. As the collection of ecstatic reviews grew, Mattel's higher-ups finally got in on the joke—and took the electronic broom off the market.

is your suitcase buzzing?

TRAVELING WITH YOUR vibrator? Depending on its on-off switch, you might want to remove the batteries before stowing the toy in your bag, as one woman we met discovered. After checking into a posh hotel, she accompanied the porter taking her bags to her room. As the elegant elevator began its smooth ride, it became clear that her suitcase was emitting a steady, audible hum. It only took a moment for the woman to figure out why her bag was buzzing. Blushing, she wracked her brain to figure out whether to say something to the porter who stood next to her, beside her obviously vibrating suitcase. She decided to follow his lead, keep her eyes fixed on the ascending floor numbers, and pretend to hear nothing. When they arrived at her room and the porter set the woman's suitcase down, she gave him a generous tip. Before shutting the door behind himself, he smiled broadly and said, "Enjoy your stay!"

sexual pleasure. We've heard women say a sparkling ring changed their entire perception of their genitals, transforming parts they had found displeasing into art.

I feel like I'm sitting on a little silver secret.

When I first got my nipples pierced, they became way more sensitive than before. I could get close to coming just from having my nipples played with (which I hadn't experienced before). Now, after five years, they don't feel any more sensitive than before they were pierced. I still love having my nipples played with, but the piercings are more for decoration than for sexual pleasure.

While some pierced women adore their metallic sensations, others find the sensations downright unpleasant or irritating, or are disappointed to find the jeweled addition doesn't affect their responsiveness. You can't know how a piercing will feel until it's in place and healed. We *don't* recommend piercing as a way to solve orgasm difficulties. If piercing doesn't appeal to you, don't be talked into a piercing by a partner who promises it'll change your sex life—there are no guarantees, and the unpierced can have perfectly mind-blowing sex lives. Given that you can't count on a piercing to add zing to your sex life, proceed with piercing only if you know you'll like the look.

I had my nipples and clitoral hood pierced. I was surprised that they didn't significantly change the way I experienced sexual pleasure. I ended up removing them because I noticed they made my partner less comfortable and less likely to contact those areas.

I ♥ FEMALE ORGASM

My vertical hood piercing gets in the way. I find that I have to take it out a lot during sex in order to get adequate clitoral stimulation.

Neither of my piercings enhance sensation that much, but they make me feel sexier. When my partner enjoys them, it relaxes me more and makes me get more into the mood.

Piercing carries real risks of infection and disease transmission, which can be particularly nasty when it's your nipple or clit at stake. If you decide to get pierced, choose your piercer carefully. Visit the shop first, and check the piercer's credentials—www.safepiercing.org lists members of the Association of Professional Piercers. Ask about their safety and hygiene practices, and how many piercings they've done of the kind you want. You can set up a consultation appointment to get more information and let the piercer examine you to see if your anatomy is compatible with the kind of piercing you want (not all kinds are compatible with all bodies), before you do the deed.

Concerned about the pain? That's also hard to predict: The same piercing can make one person almost pass out from the pain and be easier for another than having her ears pierced. As with ear piercing, those who are happy with their piercings typically say the short-lived pain was well worth it.

toy and piercing tips for partners

○ Be open to the idea that toys may enhance your shared sex life. Don't be threatened by a piece of plastic. Remember that even women who have great orgasms with vibrators crave the human connection of a partner— and frequently say that combining the two is the loveliest of all.

○ It can be easier to feel her reactions when you're using your own fingers, tongue, or penis. When touching your partner with a toy, be extra-attentive to her reactions and facial expressions to be sure you've got the right angle or the right amount of pressure.

○ Don't pressure a partner to use a sex toy. It's great to be supportive of her toy use or even to go shopping for a toy together, but remember that not every woman is into sex toys. It's like having your parents pressure you to play soccer if playing trombone is really your thing. If *you* like toys, maybe it's time to do a little shopping for yourself!

○ Along the same lines, don't pressure her to get pierced if she's not into it. The risk, potential pain, and body modification aspects of piercing need to be freely chosen.

spicing it up:
a game for people in long-term relationships

HERE'S ANOTHER QUESTION that's all too common among those who've logged many hours together between the sheets: "My partner and I have good sex, but we always do basically the same things. How can we spice it up?" Figuring out how to shatter the monotony or expand your sexual horizons is one part of the challenge; the other is how to start the conversation.

Here's a creative, nonthreatening way to dip a toe (or some other body parts) into the pool of possibilities. Do this when you both have some free time, like during a long walk, a long drive, or while lazing around together in bed.

Step one: Together, brainstorm sexual activities that you haven't done together (or haven't done much). You can write things down if you want to, but you don't have to. Think as broadly as you can, large and small, meek and wild. There are no wrong answers—just because you name an activity doesn't mean you want to do it. In fact, the game is more fun if you name things that don't interest you as well as things that do.

   Step one, the shy version: If you or your partner are the kind who blush easily, each of you take your own piece of paper, and individually brainstorm as many sexual things you can think of. Afterward, share your lists with each other.

Step two: As you brainstorm, for each activity that either of you names, you each say whether it's in your personal "Yes," "No," or "Maybe" category. "Yes" means it's something you'd like to try. "No" means you wouldn't do it under any circumstances. "Maybe" means you might be open to it if all the conditions were right, or willing to try it if your partner were excited about it. Here's a snippet of a sample conversation between two people:

Person #1: *How about toe-sucking. Would you want to try toe-sucking?*

Person #2: *Ewww!*

#1: *What if we washed our feet first and then tried it?*

#2: *It sounds weird—but I guess I'd be willing to try it if our feet were clean. Maybe.*

#1: *I'd say yes for me.*

#2: *Okay, let's see. . . . How about having sex outdoors?*

#1: *Like that night out at the lake? That was great! Yes, definitely.*

#2: *Okay, yes for me, too. Let's do more of that.*

#1: *Ummm . . . spanking?*

#2: *No, I definitely don't like being spanked.*

#1: *I'm not really into that, either, so "no" for both of us.*

#2: *I thought of one! I always thought it would be fun to kiss for really long, just keep kissing and kissing and kissing and kissing.*

#1: *Uh, sure. I never really thought about it, but yeah, I'm willing to do that.*

#2: *What about tying each other up?*

#1: *I don't know, I don't like the idea of being tied up.*

#2: *How would you feel about tying me up? Like with silk scarves or something.*

#1: *(giggling) You'd want me to tie you up?*

#2: *I think it could be fun to try.*

#1: *Really? Okay, I'm fine tying you up—I just don't want to be tied up.*

#2: *Okay, so we both say yes to you tying me up, and you say no to me tying you up.*

#1: *All right, here's another one . . . [and the conversation continues]*

If you're having a hard time brainstorming, one way to get ideas is to get some books about sex and look through them together for ideas.

Step two, the shy version: Each of you take a new sheet of paper. Write "Yes | Maybe | No" at the top of the page and create columns for each.

I ♥ FEMALE ORGASM

Categorize each of the sexual activities you and your partner brainstormed into one of the three categories. When you're both finished, share your papers with each other.

Step three (the same for regular and shy versions): Once you have a good list—or you're running out of time—review the activities that you both said yes to. There's your list to start with—have fun! You can also review the ones that got one "Yes" and one "Maybe." For the ones that got a "Maybe," talk about why each of you put it in the category you did, and under what conditions you'd be comfortable giving it a go.

Keep in mind that no matter how long you've been together, consent is never something to take for granted. Particularly when you're venturing into new areas, be sure you're on the same page. Saying yes to something on paper doesn't mean you can't change your mind!

FOR ADVANCED PLAY

Here's a twist for the daring. Follow the advice above for the shy players, so you each end up with separate "Yes | Maybe | No" lists on paper. Compare lists, taking a good look at what's in your partner's "Yes" category that you haven't done together, or haven't done much.

Then, set a "date night" and designate one of you as the Planner. The Planner makes all the arrangements for the night, which could include dinner at the other partner's favorite restaurant or other treats. Afterward, the Planner takes the lead with sex, focusing exclusively on activities that are in his or her partner's "Yes" category. The partner's job is simply to enjoy! Next time, switch roles, with the other person taking the lead.

In a long-term relationship, this is the kind of game you can repeat from time to time as the years go by. You may be surprised to learn that things commonly shift around: One person's "No" transforms into a "Maybe," and a "Yes" becomes a "No." As you explore together, you'll get new ideas, decide to return to things you did when you were a new couple and since drifted away from, perhaps feel more adventurous in one area and clearer that you don't enjoy something else. The goal is *not* to try to prove how "kinky" you can be, and it's definitely not to push people to do things that don't appeal to them; each person's "No" category must be respected. Really, it's just a fun way to have a conversation—hopefully one that leads you to some ideas that banish bedroom boredom.

I ♥ FEMALE ORGASM

8

Let's Hear It for the Boys: men and female orgasm

Female orgasm can be a challenging subject if you're a guy. American culture says guys are supposed to know what they're doing sexually. The perfect man supposedly knows how to make any woman melt with pleasure, while having an even better time himself. Men are supposed to make the first move, lean in for the first kiss, divine the perfect moment to start removing clothing, and know all the right techniques—even from their very first sexual experience or two. The trouble is, where are they supposed to learn how? Though it's a subject many men would find valuable, "How to Help a Woman Have an Orgasm" is definitely not covered in high school sex ed.

Without much useful information from schools or parents (many of whom are terrified to discuss sex with their kids), guys are generally left to figure things out on their own—a little extracurricular activity, if you will. Besides personal experience, a lot of guys learn about sex from porn, which is easier to access now than ever before in human history. Ninety-seven percent of our male survey-takers said they've watched porn. (An additional 2 percent said they preferred not to answer the question, so maybe we should make that 99 percent?) Regardless of your opinion about the politics or morality of porn, as a source of information about sex, it leaves people wildly misinformed. If a male alien came to Earth and porn were his only source of information about human sex, he'd probably conclude something along these lines:

1. Sex is something that generally happens spontaneously between strangers.
2. Pizza delivery boys get more action than the average guy. Lucky for the pizza guys, most women answer the door naked.
3. Women scream with pleasure no matter how you touch them. No one is concerned about disturbing the neighbors.
4. Mind-reading is a standard form of communication, given that no one ever talks about what they like or don't like.

a note to female readers

THIS CHAPTER IS about men—people who have male bodies or were socialized male—who have sex with women (which is not all men, of course), because of the specific challenges facing these guys. Because of biological differences including anatomy and hormones, female bodies tend to be a more foreign territory for male partners than for female ones. Men are also socialized differently than women, and grow up with different expectations about sex, which can affect the relationship dynamics between men and women.

While we're focusing on men in this chapter, we also know that people of any gender or sexual orientation might learn a thing or two in these pages, so we welcome non-male readers. Plenty of women have female partners who may identify as lesbian, bisexual, queer, or something else. That's why we use the word "partner" throughout the book, because most of the time, the topics we're talking about could apply to a woman's partner who's either male or female. If you're interested, chapter 9 is specifically about girl-girl sex.

5. Women frequently say things like, "Oh, big boy, do me now!" Women never say, "Ow, you're on my hair."
6. People rarely, if ever, use condoms. When condoms are used they just magically "appear." No one ever pauses the action to put one on.
7. Once intercourse starts, kissing stops.
8. Men are expected to come on women's faces—women love that!
9. Humans prefer to have sex to really bad music.
10. There's no such thing as love, intimacy, sweetness, sensuality, tenderness, cuddling, or emotional connection.

We cringe to imagine the scene if this alien ever found himself alone with a human female.

Fortunately, most guys know this is a far cry from reality. It's easy to conclude that what works in porn often doesn't work in real life. The challenge is to figure out what *does* work with real, live human beings. Unlike the overly-tanned, acrobatic,

a lot of men have told us this joke:

Question: How can you tell if a woman had an orgasm?
Answer: Who cares?

So, just in case you need them:

Four Excellent Reasons a Guy Should Care if a Woman Has an Orgasm:

1. If you'd like her to sleep with you again.
2. If you'd like her to tell her friends, "[Your name here] is amazing in bed."
3. If you'd like your wife or long-term partner to feel like she has a satisfying sex life with you.
4. Because a woman having an orgasm is really hot. Even more so if you helped.

do you and porn need to see less of each other?

MORE AND MORE guys are telling us that after watching tons of porn—with its "hot lesbian action," enhanced body parts, and loud, easily-obtained female orgasms—the sight of one normal, naked human female in their bed is practically disappointing.

After watching porn, partner sex became different to me. Unless my girlfriend became the porn image, my penis stopped responding and I got turned off. Fantasies of the porn chicks dominated my head.

As a connoisseur of "perfect" porn, it's sometimes a problem in that I prefer to think about the women I see online rather than my girlfriend. It generates a lot of guilt and tension.

Some of these guys have gone on a self-imposed cold-turkey porn hiatus. If you find that porn is interfering with your ability to enjoy your *real* sex life, you might consider a similar "trial separation." To do so, set a number of months for which you'll allow yourself no porn access at all. Then pay attention to how it affects your thoughts and reactions to real partners, and decide at the end of that time what role you want porn to play in your life. Men who've tried it tell us they've been pleased with the results!

emotionless pseudo-sex in XXX downloads, this book is about the real thing. If you're a guy who hasn't already checked out these sections, we recommend you read up on:

- ○ the clitoris, page 16
- ○ the G-spot, page 150
- ○ oral sex, page 90

I ♥ FEMALE ORGASM

how to make her very, very happy
(eight tips on being a great lover)

We've talked to thousands of women about what makes a great lover, and what a partner can do to increase the odds that she'll have an orgasm. Besides the tips covered in the sections listed above, here's the best of their collective wisdom. These are the things that women talk about when there are no guys around to hear, the things they wish guys knew and bemoan that not enough do.

1. **A great lover is showered and shaven** (we're talking facial hair). Beards and mustaches are usually soft, but a day or two's growth of prickly facial hair can be particularly unpleasant. Sandpaper against one's face or between one's thighs isn't much of a turn-on.

2. **A great lover masters the art of foreplay.** Technically, foreplay includes all the touching, kissing, stroking, caressing, nibbling, licking, whispering, and grinding that happens before intercourse. We believe foreplay *is* sex—many women, and men, too, say this "foreplay" stuff is the best, sexiest part of all. Calling it foreplay suggests that it's like the opening act, the musician you listen to politely before the headliner (intercourse) comes on. Countless sexually experienced people have told us that some of the most thrilling, turned-on sex of their lives was as a teenager making out (foreplay!), months or years before they ever had intercourse. Some scientists believe human females need foreplay because they don't go into "heat" like most other mammals. Mammals with heat cycles are only sexually active certain times of the month (or year), but female humans are lucky to be able to be aroused any day of the month. Foreplay is what gets their blood flowing.

   Whether intercourse is in the cards or not for a given sexual interlude, good foreplay boosts the chance a woman will have an orgasm, because if she's enjoying it, her arousal level sails up, up, up. Female orgasms take place only at the highest arousal levels—and foreplay is what moves a woman's body and mind up the path.

3. **A great lover asks (and listens).** There's a stereotype that men don't ask for directions. When it comes to sex, the stereotype is true too often, since guys are raised to believe that when they're in a sexual situation, they're supposed to know what they're doing. Even if they don't know, they often figure they should pretend. This issue of asking—and listening to verbal and nonverbal cues from his partner—is just as relevant for a man who's never had sex as for one who's bedded a hundred partners. Any man who has slept with more than one woman quickly realizes that what women like in bed, and how they respond sexually, varies so tremendously that it's not safe to assume that a new girlfriend likes to be touched (or licked or penetrated) the same way the old one did. So asking questions and checking in are not, as some guys fear, a sign of sexual cluelessness; to many women, they're a sign of a man who knows what it takes truly to please a woman.

> *My last partner was the best. He asked me what I wanted, made it no secret that he enjoyed making me feel good, looked at my genitals, explored all my parts, took his time. He would keep things fresh by mixing up techniques.*

> *Listening is probably the most important thing a partner can do. Someone who listens to what I like is the best at helping me have an orgasm.*

In real life, women prefer guys who communicate and ask questions. Women appreciate when guys check in as they move to start some new thing (and respect the answer), give extra points to a boyfriend who says, "I love feedback—tell me how I can make this even better for you," and adore a man who tries out a few different techniques (flicking their nipples with his tongue versus sucking on them versus gently biting them, a few different depths and angles of penetration during intercourse, etc.) to ask which they most enjoy.

Communication during sex definitely does *not* have to mean long, clinical conversations. Lots of communication happens nonverbally, with moans and sighs, breathing that picks up, one partner moving another partner's hand to where he or she wants that hand to be. But a certain degree of verbal communication is key, too: A low, sultry "Is this okay?" as a man's finger moves into his partner's underwear, or as his head arrives between her thighs, can be answered with an appreciative, "Mmm-hmm." Not only does this *not* break the mood, it helps the woman relax and enjoy, knowing that her partner actually cares. And if the answer is, "Not yet" or "Let's try this first," a great lover wants to know that—and may (or may not) get farther in the end if his partner knows he'll respect her limits and her pace each step of the way.

Ease your way down my pants. The longer you take to get there the better. I feel the sexiest and most turned on the more I'm caressed. It's all about desire. I need to feel comfortable, so always ask if it's okay. And then take your time.

By the way, men aren't the only ones who should be getting consent and checking in as things proceed; women can and should be asking the same questions, requesting feedback, and trying out techniques to find out what their partners like.

eavesdropping on girl-talk

DORIAN REPORTS THAT when women talk privately with other women, it's almost unheard of for a woman to complain about a partner who spends too much time on foreplay. The reverse problem, partners who are in too much of a rush, comes up all the time as a source of frustration. If a partner isn't sure, most women say it's better to err on the side of too much rather than too little.

My body is very sensitive and men tend to think they can take things so much faster than my body wants to go. My most amazing orgasms result from a very slow buildup that finally becomes completely overwhelming.

Help get me really aroused before you even think about touching my vulva. Wait until I crave that stimulation so much I feel as though I'm going to explode without it.

4. **A great lover knows what to do with a clitoris.** First, he knows where to find it (for some pointers, see page 70). Second, he knows not to rush for the clit too early. Some guys would be thrilled if their partner started rubbing their penis within the first minute of making out. Most women don't want the same kind of immediate attention to their clit. In order for clitoral touching to feel good, most women need to be aroused already. (The same way men are often surprised to realize women don't want a hand to go between their legs right away, women are often surprised to learn how early in a sexual interlude guys would enjoy attention to their privates. Of course people's preferences vary widely; it can be a fun, and fascinating, conversation to have with a partner.)

My boyfriend asks me what I like and don't like, so I tell him and show him exactly how I want to be touched. His techniques I like best are when he uses lots of lube and massages my clitoris with his middle finger. He asks me how I want it, so I tell him faster, slower, harder, in circles.

Third, he checks in with his partner to find out how her clit likes to be touched, realizing that this likely changes as her arousal climbs. Watching her masturbate (and being willing to let her watch him do the same) can offer fantastic insights, if she's comfortable with the idea. And finally, he knows that for most women, clitoral stimulation is the primary route to female orgasm. If one partner or the other doesn't spend some time making sure this gold nugget gets its share of attention, female orgasms will probably be hard to come by. (For more specific suggestions on what to do when you've got a clit at your fingertips—or at your lips—and how to work with common clitoral challenges, see page 22.)

5. **A great lover knows his penis is merely one tool among many.** Penises are pretty remarkable inventions, no question about it. Yet women privately complain that many men's love for their own body's favorite part distracts them from the wonders of all the other parts that also have a lot to offer. It's up to each male lover to prove he knows how to use the whole toolbox. (For more on this, see "Advanced Penisology," page 204.)

6. **A great lover masters the art of patience.** One of the greatest gifts a man can give his female partner—especially one who worries that she's taking too long to have an orgasm—is to tell her honestly, "Let's keep doing this as long as it feels good to you. I'm not in a rush. I'm enjoying this, too." In fact, if the "this" being discussed is some sexual activity other than intercourse, she probably won't believe him without several more reassurances. After making these reassurances, he'd be wise to set up a futon on the floor next to the bed to cushion her in case she falls out of bed in shock. (Of course, don't say things like this unless you mean them.)

Patience is unquestionably a trait to cultivate if you're working toward an I ♥ Female Orgasm merit badge. (If you're not clear on how long female orgasms can take, see page 20.)

Case in point: Lots of women enjoy receiving oral sex. Lots of guys are willing to do it, but don't spend enough time down there to have it lead to orgasm. One solution: Test your sense of time against the bedside clock. In your head, come up with a minimum amount of time that you're going to perform oral sex; let's say thirty minutes. Sneak a peek at the bedside clock as you start, and then don't look at the clock again until you *think* thirty minutes has passed. When you sneak your second peek, you may be surprised at how little time has actually passed. It's easy to lose track of time in bed! So get back to it!

> *I want to feel that however long it takes me to reach orgasm is fine, and that it's okay if I want to have more than one, and that if I need to have them after your orgasm that you won't roll over and neglect me. I won't want to get very aroused if I don't think you'll stick around through it.*

7. A great lover knows that women come first (at least some of the time). Although many couples see simultaneous orgasms as the prize to strive for, connoisseurs of female orgasm know that they often work better when they come before the male one. Reverse the order so his orgasm is first, and you risk ending up with a guy who's bored or even falls asleep. But if the woman's pleasure is the first focus, he's likely to stay awake and interested for the whole process, right through to his own orgasm. Plus, given how female arousal works, there's a good chance she'll be happy to continue until he comes. She might even go on to have another orgasm or two. "Ladies first" doesn't have to be the motto every time you're in bed together, but realizing how well this approach works is a breakthrough for many couples.

> *The fact that my boyfriend wanted me to orgasm before he did was so sweet. He had such determination to make me happy that it helped me.*

> *My last boyfriend almost always was able to make me climax and probably was the best person I've ever had sex with. He was very giving and would almost always go down on me prior to us having intercourse. This would help in that I'd be wet enough for him to enter me without too much discomfort.*

great lovers are sure she consents

A TRULY EXCELLENT lover wants to be having sex with someone who wants to be having sex with him. Anyone can be a victim of sexual assault or abuse, and anyone can perpetrate sexual assault or abuse: women, men, straight, gay, lesbian, bisexual, transgender. Statistically speaking, in about 90 percent of sexual assault cases women are the victims, and in about 10 percent of cases men are the victims.

When it comes to sexual assault, we've all heard of cases where somebody attacks a woman after breaking into her apartment, or a date rape occurs where a woman said, "No," and a man refused to listen. What's more challenging for a lot of guys are situations where it's not 100 percent clear: She didn't say no, but she didn't exactly say yes, either. Mainstream culture encourages guys to have sex whenever they have the chance. As a result, a lot of men take pride in "scoring"—the more sex partners, the better. When they see an opportunity to have sex, they go for it, even if they're not fully certain their partner wants the experience or is enjoying it.

Here's one way to think about it: If given the choice, would you rather be known for how much sex you've had, or how great a lover you are? The fact is, the only person who knows exactly how much sex you've had is you. Guys who brag in the locker room about all the action they're getting can make up numbers as easily as women can fake orgasms. Being a great lover is a status you earn by what you do—and don't do—in bed. That's your true reputation.

The finest kind of lover takes pride not just in the sex that he has, but also the sex he turns down. When a great lover finds himself in a situation where he'd love to have sex but isn't sure how his partner feels about it, or how she'll feel about it the next day, he pauses and checks in. Maybe she's had too much to drink; maybe he's not sure if she really wants to do this; maybe she said yes, she wants to have sex, but he notices she's crying. Certainly, she could be crying for reasons that have nothing to do with him: Sex can be an emotional experience. But he can't know that unless he stops and makes sure she wants to go forward.

In some cases sex just wasn't meant to be that night. It can definitely be a letdown to miss out on a sexual experience that seemed to be within your reach. But it's far better to let it go than to create a situation where either of you has serious regrets, or even worse, feels the sex wasn't consensual. If there's still a spark between you, there will be plenty of other opportunities.

Is your partner a sexual abuse or assault survivor? See page 38 for information and resources about how you can be supportive of her healing process.

8. A great lover lets a woman know that he's enjoying himself. Just as most guys prefer a partner who makes it easy to see and hear when she's enjoying herself, women prefer men whose words and sounds let them know just how good it feels. Countless women have asked us why guys are so silent during sex. Too many early sexual experiences in the rec room with mom and dad upstairs, or in a dorm where sound travels far too easily, perhaps? Once you're an adult having sex in a place where silence isn't required, remember that many women find men's sighs and moans of pleasure to be a huge turn-on.

> *I wish men would vocalize their own pleasure more. Knowing that my partner is enjoying the experience is perhaps the best part of a sexual encounter and allows me to get more aroused and more likely to reach orgasm.*

Advanced Penisology

Here's another subject that's not covered in high school sex ed class: How to convince your penis to do what you want it to.

Most guys have encountered one or more of these challenges at some point:

○ *They can't get an erection, or can't keep one.*
○ *They come sooner than they want to.*
○ *It takes longer than they want to come, or they can't come at all.*

Each of these situations is unique, but they all have one thing in common: The man's penis isn't working the way he wants it to. Many guys grow up with the idea that they should always be able to perform, even if they're not in the mood or feeling ambivalent. This view is reinforced in porn, where men are always rock hard and ready to go. In reality, before Viagra, and even since, many hours were spent during which the director, film crew, and female cast lolled around waiting for the male star to get an erection or were forced to do retakes (or fancy editing) because the guy came too early, too late, or not at all.

Most guys' first experiences of orgasm and ejaculation are through masturbation. Now, masturbation is one of America's favorite pastimes, and it's perfectly healthy. But all that "hands-on training"—often using the same technique that reliably brings a fast orgasm each time—sometimes doesn't translate perfectly to sex with another human being. While intercourse isn't what happens in every instance of sex, let's look at it for the sake of comparison.

KEY DIFFERENCES:
SEX WITH YOUR HAND VERSUS INTERCOURSE WITH A WOMAN

	YOUR HAND	WITH A WOMAN
Naked woman	Usually no naked woman involved, unless you count imaginary friends or the images you downloaded onto your computer.	She's hot, she's naked, and she wants you! The sheer thrill of it can lead to premature ejaculation. Or, stage fright can make it difficult to get hard or come.
Time	As fast as possible, please, before your roommate comes home. Many guys find they can come in two to five minutes or less if they want to.	If you get hard as soon as you get turned on, and have a long sex session with tons of foreplay, you may want to stay hard but not come for a *long* time. Or, you may not be able to come at all, even when you want to.
Arousal roller coaster	Ready, aim, fire! A smooth climb to the top.	Your mission looks something like this: Build up enough sexual excitement fast to get hard and stay hard throughout foreplay; definitely be hard enough to put on a condom. Then you start having intercourse, possibly the most exciting part of all, and your little guy is enveloped by

	YOUR HAND	**WITH A WOMAN**
Arousal roller coaster		all the pleasurable sensations of being inside her—but, uh oh, now you have to change gears so you don't come too fast. When you're having sex, arousal can involve a lot of loop-de-loops.
On the mind	A desire to come and maybe a fantasy to help.	"Woo-hoo! I'm actually doing it!" That *whataluckybastardIam* feeling can lead to lightning-fast ejaculation. But at the same time, you may be thinking, "What if she gets pregnant?" "What if I catch something from her, or she from me?" "Am I hurting her?" "Is she enjoying this?" or any of a trillion variations of "Where is this relationship going?" or "Was having sex with her the right decision?" All those kinds of (perfectly reasonable) conflicting thoughts can work against staying hard and coming when you want to.
Technique	You've had plenty of time to perfect your skills, and you can stick with the same basic technique—as fast as you want—from beginning to end.	Sexual technique is definitely not taught as part of the classroom curriculum, and porn is a misleading instructor at best. Rushing straight through intercourse, with constant jackhammer thrusting, risks being a recipe for a frustrated partner and/or a wet spot earlier than you intended.

I ♥ FEMALE ORGASM

With all this in mind, of course penises don't always do exactly what you want them to, particularly when intercourse, not masturbation, is on the agenda. It's totally normal for perfectly healthy, young guys to sometimes come sooner than they want to or not be able to get it up or get off; more than two-thirds of the guys who filled out our survey said they ran into these challenges at least once in a while. If this stuff happens occasionally, don't worry about it. If there's a partner in your bed at the time, there are plenty of other ways to pleasure her, including using fingers or a phallic object for penetration if that's what she was looking forward to. If one or more of these challenges is becoming a regular occurrence, and that's bothering you, check out the tips below.

Advanced Penisology Troubleshooting Guide for Guys

Challenge: You can't get an erection, or you can't keep one as long as you'd like.

The causes of "erectile dysfunction" can be either physical or psychological. For most guys with occasional problems in this arena, the sexual episode in question involved one or more of these factors that make it more difficult for a guy to get an erection:

○ He was drunk.
○ She was intimidatingly hot.
○ He had already ejaculated once or more earlier that day.
○ It was a casual hook-up, and he was nervous or uncomfortable since he didn't know her very well.
○ There weren't any condoms available.
○ He was exhausted, stressed out, or just plain nervous.
○ He was in a rush.
○ He was on a medication that affects his arousal or erections (common for many antidepressants, as well as other medications).

Or it could have been nothing at all—sometimes an erection will play hard to get (or should that be soft to get?) for no reason.

The last thing to do when you can't get hard is to freak out, because that creates even more performance anxiety the next time you have the opportunity to have sex. If you can see that some of the factors on the list above may have been the culprit, that'll help you change your strategy (or at least better understand your body's responses) next time. You can also try relaxing and enjoying the sensations that feel good without worrying about whether or not you get hard. Sometimes the erection shows up when you're just enjoying yourself and not trying to make it happen.

Don't obsess about it. Relax. Don't force it and don't get nervous about it. Usually if I just lie down, put my arms around my girl and gently kiss and touch her, I can get my dink back in the ring.

Typically, this happens when I've been drinking: "whiskey dick." I've found the best way to solve it is just not to drink as much.

Foreplay is the best solution to this for me. I used to go in once my erection was good enough to go in, or had just reached its peak, and I'd rush things. Most guys don't want foreplay because they have no self-control and can't wait to start intercourse. However, I find the longer I wait, the better it is for both of us.

For men with difficulties getting erections, Viagra can seem like an easy solution. But Viagra and its competitors (Cialis, Levitra, and the rest) bring with them serious health risks. We'd far rather see men—particularly young guys—find and confront the root of their sexual challenges, rather than become dependent on pharmaceuticals. If getting an erection is a consistent problem for you—during partnered sex and alone—then it's worth asking a doctor to rule out possible physical causes. These can be wide-ranging, including hormonal imbalances, thyroid problems, medications you're taking, sexually transmitted infections, or chronic illnesses like diabetes. Also, check out "Need More Detailed Troubleshooting Help?" on page 212.

Even Shakespeare knew that, as the *Macbeth* quote at the bottom of this image reads, "[Drink] provokes the desire but takes away the performance."

Challenge: You come sooner than you want to.

For all the talk about Viagra, many more men struggle with a very different problem: coming sooner than they want to when they're with a partner. A few ideas on how to troubleshoot this one:

○ If you come faster with a new partner because you find her really hot, tell her! She'll probably be flattered to hear how much she turns you on. This kind of problem may resolve itself as the newness of the relationship wears off.

○ Remember the power of the tongue. Yes, it can be a point of pride to last a long time. But there's a difference between your ego and her orgasm. For most women, clitoral stimulation is what it's all about, and that has little, if anything, to do with how long you last. If she has her orgasm before intercourse begins, as often works so well, then you don't have to worry about "lasting" at all; you can come at whatever point is most pleasurable for you.

Cunnilingus gives me a chance to relax and focus the sex act on my partner for a while. Once she's satisfied, it doesn't matter if I finish in ten seconds or forty-five minutes. The pressure to "perform" just goes away.

○ Come earlier in the day. Many guys have figured out that if they masturbate before a date, that'll slow them down that night.

○ Wear a condom. Sometimes that small decrease in sensation is exactly what you need.

○ Try an encore. Some guys find if they come too fast the first time, they're ready to go again fifteen minutes later—with a lot more stamina in Round Two.

○ Take a break from whatever activity (intercourse, oral sex, etc.) is so physically pleasurable for you, and do something else for a while (maybe pleasure her) before returning to it.

It helps me to try a less animalistic position. The thrill of doggy style makes for quick coming, whereas many sitting positions are pleasurable but less hormonally thrilling.

○ Relax and actually tune in to the sensations in your penis, rather than tensing up or trying to avoid thinking about how it feels.

This sounds cliché, but being really relaxed allows me to perform longer. I've found that when I'm really anxious about things (personal life, work, etc.) I can't concentrate on the sensations, and I'll come before I realize I'm coming. It seems like the times I'm most stressed out are when I end up being a ten-minute wonder.

○ Know your "point of no return." Because intercourse can be an incredibly stimulating experience physically, visually, and emotionally, guys sometimes rush headlong toward orgasm. They race up the mountain—only to tumble head over heels down the other side.

Some men try to stave off their orgasm by concentrating on something completely non-erotic, like doing math problems in their head or thinking about sports. As a college student, Marshall used to bite his tongue, theorizing that pain was the best distraction of all. Many guys find that while that works for a while, they're ultimately fighting a lost cause. Rather than sidestep the problem with these techniques, it's better to address it head on.

The key is to learn to identify the point when you've neared the top of the orgasmic mountain, the moment when you're on the brink of having an orgasm, without actually having one. Here's how to train yourself:

First, practice when you're masturbating. Most guys speed through masturbation, eager to have an orgasm. Instead, take your time. Sex researchers and therapists William Hartman and Marilyn Fithian found that if a man perfects the skills to be able to masturbate for fifteen to twenty minutes before he has an orgasm, he'll be able to last as long as he wants to during intercourse.

During this period of twenty minutes, there may be times when you feel like you're really close to having an orgasm. Don't stop stimulating yourself entirely, but back off just slightly, easing up on the intensity of your touch. When the moment passes, continue the stimulation again. Repeat this process, always paying close attention to the experience of

I ♥ FEMALE ORGASM

being close to coming, but figure out how to move through that with a lesser degree of stimulation until the "I'm gonna come" feeling subsides.

Once you've mastered this technique during masturbation, you can apply what you've learned to intercourse. If you feel yourself approaching the point of no return, slow down or stop moving inside your partner. Remember, only in porn videos does the man thrust constantly—that's for the viewer's entertainment. So, pause your action. Consciously slow your breathing. Relax all the muscles in your body, particularly those in your legs and butt. Doing so can work wonders for your ability to last longer. Strengthening your PC muscles with Kegel exercises, described on page 26, and then squeezing when you want to slow yourself down, can also help.

I just take it slow now and don't try to "go for broke" quickly. As my girlfriend puts it, "It's a marathon, not a sprint." She also is more accepting of the fact that sometimes I just need to stop thrusting to regain control.

The easiest way to slow yourself down when you're on top is to give her a long passionate kiss and stop moving altogether for a second.

Challenge: It takes too long to come, or you can't come at all.

We get a lot of questions from younger guys who have trouble having an orgasm at all. This needn't be a crisis; men, like women, can have a great time without always having an orgasm.

If I can't or don't feel like coming, it's okay, because sex is about the entirety of the experience to me. Now, sometimes this doesn't work for my partners so I have to reassure them that this isn't an all-the-time thing, and that there will be other days—trust me!

Many guys in this situation have already tried everything they can think of to make themselves come: receiving oral sex, fantasy, positions they find particularly sexy, dirty talk, and more. Sometimes those are just the ticket, sometimes not. As with any sexual problem that's bothering you, if this is a regular experience you're not able to resolve on your own, you might see a doctor to rule out any physical

need more detailed troubleshooting help?

THE BEST BOOK out there on male sexuality for men who have sex with women is *Great Sex: A Man's Guide to the Secret Principles of Total-Body Sex*, by Michael Castleman. It's full of fantastic advice on how to be a great lover, and how to deal with specific challenges.

For information about how to find a sex therapist, see page 89.

causes. Some prescription medications can be the source of the problem, as can drugs like alcohol, ecstasy, or speed. Over and over, men who filled out our survey said the thing they'd discovered that helped them most was not to drink before sex.

When it comes to psychological causes of not being able to come, one major factor is what author Michael Castleman calls the "delivery boy mentality." A man with a delivery boy mentality takes great pride in his ability to please his partner; he wants to be thought of as an excellent lover, a man who has the skills to "deliver" the female orgasm.

If this sounds like you, you have every right to be proud. You've probably rightfully received praise on your lovemaking skills, and as fans of the female orgasm, we shake your hand! The problem is, the delivery boy mentality can trip you up when it comes to your own orgasm. By conditioning yourself to be a long-lasting sex machine, ready and willing to provide the pleasure your woman wants, you may be neglecting your own pleasure. Let go of the myth that the ideal man is focused only on giving his partner an ideal sexual experience. It's okay to be human, to enjoy sex simply for the sake of your own pleasure. It's okay to be vulnerable in front of her and let yourself go.

If I'm doing something other than focusing on being pleasured, like fondling her breasts or stimulating her clitoris, it's very hard for me to come.

I put all kinds of pressure on myself. I have to remind myself it's not all about her—I'm supposed to have a good time, too. If I'm not enjoying myself eventually it's going to screw up the vibe.

If you're having trouble coming, it's also possible that your penis isn't getting the stimulation it's used to from your self-loving technique. If you grip your penis with your own hand harder than any vagina ever could, try experimenting with using a lighter, slower touch. If you first discovered how to masturbate in an unusual or unique position, you might want to increase your versatility by experimenting with other positions that are more similar to the experience of having your penis inside your partner's vagina, even if they're less pleasurable initially. It's fully possible to "train" yourself to respond to and enjoy a variety of kinds of physical stimulation using techniques similar to those described for women in "Changing Your Self-Love Technique," page 54.

for women:
secrets of male sexuality

A WELL-KNOWN cartoon portrays female sexuality as a complex machine, full of dials, switches, gauges, lights, and whistles. The other half of the cartoon represents male sexuality: a simple on-off switch.

Despite its reputation, male sexuality—including erection, orgasm, and ejaculation—is definitely *not* a simple switch, but is as wonderful, mysterious, and sometimes complicated as its female equivalent.

Our advice to women who encounter men whose penises aren't working exactly the way they had hoped: Don't worry about it. Just as you wouldn't want him to have a crisis if your orgasm just is nowhere to be found on a given day, he doesn't want you to have a crisis over a noncooperative penis. In fact, if he suspects that you're upset about it (based on your desperate measures, questions, accusations, or tears), that'll increase his own anxiety, creating the risk that the problem will grow because now you're both stressed out about it. Especially if it's something that happens only occasionally, your best bet is to let him know that as far as you're concerned, it's not a big deal. Don't make the mistake of believing a man's erection is a good barometer for how he feels about you.

a few inches (of text) on penis size

IF YOU BELIEVE the spam in your e-mail inbox, you'd think the primary way to please a woman is to be really, really well-endowed. You'll be glad to know that we can tell you the answer to the age-old question "Does size matter?"

During our educational programs, while the men are out of the room discussing manly issues with Marshall, the women sometimes get to talking about penis size. Dorian has now had the chance to poll thousands upon thousands of women on this question, and without the men in the room, the women don't have to worry about hurting anyone's feelings. Dorian's unscientific poll (of women who have had enough male partners to have developed an opinion on the matter) has three possible answers:

1. Bigger is better. I find a big penis more pleasurable.
2. Small is beautiful. I find big penises uncomfortable or painful.
3. Penis size really isn't a significant factor in my pleasure. It's not the size of the boat, it's the motion of the ocean.

The responses Dorian gets from female audience members are close to identical regardless of where we go:

○ About 10 percent of women choose category one: "I like it big!"
○ About 5 to 10 percent of women say they prefer a smaller penis because big can be uncomfortable.
○ Eighty to 85 percent of women say it really, truly, honestly does not matter to them. When Dorian asks, "So are you saying that what your partner does with his hands, fingers, lips, tongue, and words matter more to you?" the room is full of nodding and applause.

Guys, what does this mean for you? If you have a big penis, hopefully you can find a woman who will be thrilled to discover you. Remember that for most women, it requires far, far more than your penis to get off. Women roll their eyes about well-hung guys with the attitude that their third leg, swinging between the other two, is everything a woman could ever need or want.

If your joystick is on the smaller side, know that there are plenty of women in the world who would be downright relieved to find you. Be reassured, too, that nearly all women would choose an excellent lover with any size penis over a clueless guy with a big dick. There's plenty throughout this book to help you become the kind of partner women brag to their friends about.

And if you're kind of average, well, so are most guys! Don't waste your time and money on pills, pumps, lotions, surgeries, weights, or exercises to make you bigger; none of them have been proven to make any permanent difference, and many risk damaging your ding-a-ling. Remind yourself that men tend to care more about penis size than most women do, and choose to spend your time focusing on the things that really do turn women on.

i'll take the tongue, please

TWO-THIRDS OF our female survey respondents said that if forced to choose, they would prefer to spend the rest of their lives with a partner with a skilled tongue rather than a big penis. (Only women who had tried both were allowed to vote.)

faking

A FEMALE ORGASM is a beautiful thing. Most people would like to see more of them in their lifetime. But is seeing believing? A lot of folks start squirming uncomfortably in their seats when the issue of faking comes up. You have questions on the subject? We've got answers.

First things first: *Is there any way to tell for sure if a woman is faking or not?*

Some partners have heard that you can recognize a real orgasm by physical signs like the red flush on a woman's face or neck, vaginal contractions, spasms or tremors throughout her body, curled toes, hard nipples, dilated pupils, elevated heart rate, or quivering lower lip. Indeed, each of those things *can* be present when a woman has an orgasm—but they would more accurately be considered signs of arousal (or, in the case of hard nipples and dilated pupils, they could be an indicator that your bedroom is cold and dark). Many women experience some combination of those physical effects when they're aroused—whether they have an orgasm or not. Nearly all can easily be faked.

But surely there must be some way to spot a fake?

There is: Through the use of a positron emission tomographic (PET) scanner. This useful device, which costs a mere $3 million, can measure the activity of her cerebral cortex. But without a PET scanner, no, there's absolutely no way to accurately distinguish an orgasmic woman from a talented actress.

But here's the deal: Rather than agonizing over the authenticity of her orgasms, focus instead on the root cause of faking by not pressuring her to have an orgasm. Some partners couldn't care less about female pleasure and orgasm. If you're reading this book, you're probably not one of them—you *do* want her to have a good time. But women say there's another kind of partner, too: the ones who care too much.

Some partners get into their heads that because of their lovemaking prowess, female orgasm is a gift they bestow upon their lovers. They see it as a personal challenge to make the woman come. Whether it's spoken aloud or not, women quickly catch on to the fact that it would make their sweetie really happy if they had an orgasm. But, as we've discussed throughout this book, there are any number of reasons why they might not be able to have one, reasons that have nothing to do with the partner's lovemaking skills.

If a partner is trying really hard—with tongue, fingers, or penis—to help a woman have an orgasm, and she suspects (or knows) it's just not going to happen, she may start to get nervous, tired, or sore. Those states make it even harder to come, and she feels the orgasmic brass ring slipping out of reach.

I had a boyfriend who I had to fake it with for a long time. No matter how much I tried to help, he didn't want to listen to my advice, but he wouldn't stop until I supposedly "had one."

For some women, faking provides an easy solution. Her partner thinks she had an orgasm, so he or she is happy. The woman's happy because her partner's happy. All is well and good—until the next time they're in bed together, when the partner repeats the same techniques thinking they worked last time, and the woman is faced with the same dilemma. The cycle repeats itself, until she either fesses up and the two of them have a heartfelt conversation about it, or she delivers the news over the breakup: "Oh yeah, and one other thing: I've never had an orgasm with you! I was FAKING every time!" Those are words nobody ever wants to hear.

If that's the case, what's the use in trying?

Somebody smart once said, "Live for the journey, not the destination." Women say that sex is about more than achieving orgasm. It's also about intimacy, love, the thrill of skin against skin, human connection. Just because a woman doesn't have an orgasm doesn't mean that she didn't have a great time. Most women say that at least some of the time, they can be perfectly satisfied without coming.

If I tell you I don't think I can have an orgasm—and sometimes I can tell it just isn't going to happen—don't belabor the point. Enjoy yourself, come, and don't feel bummed that I didn't come, because I really DID enjoy being with you!

Here's the bottom line of what women want from their partners: Do things that focus on the woman's pleasure, be really, really patient, and let go of the end goal of an orgasm. By "focus on the woman's pleasure," they usually mean oral sex or stimulation of her clit with your or her fingers or a vibrator, not just intercourse. By "really, really patient," they mean allow twenty to forty minutes or more, if she's enjoying herself and says she'd like to continue. Be happy if she's happy, whether or not there are fireworks in the end.

Faking Dos and Don'ts (for Partners)

1. **DON'T announce, "I'm gonna make you come."** That is, unless you want to guarantee she'll fake an orgasm for you. When a woman hears words like these, she feels incredible pressure to make you happy. Her orgasm becomes something that's for your pleasure rather than her own. And if it's for your pleasure, she figures, she might as well put on a good (fake) show for you to enjoy.

2. **DON'T ask, "Did you come?"** As much as you might be tempted to inquire, keep your curiosity to yourself. It's too difficult for her to answer: If she says no, she'll worry you'll be disappointed. If she says yes, you'll have no way of knowing if she's lying or telling the truth. Also, if she did have an orgasm, she doesn't need a reminder that her real orgasms don't involve the artificial moans and screams one sees in Hollywood and porn movies. The last thing she should have to worry about at the moment of her peak pleasure is whether or not she's being expressive enough to let you know she's having an orgasm!

   That said, after you've been together at least a few times, it's okay to say, "Sometimes it's hard for me to tell if you have orgasms." Let her answer and listen. Follow up with, "Are there things I could do differently to help you?" Communicate with your words and reactions that you're okay if she has an orgasm or not, as long as you're doing what you can to make sure she's enjoying herself.

3. **DON'T fake orgasm yourself.** Given that men usually ejaculate when they have an orgasm, it's obviously harder for guys to fake. But it's certainly not impossible, as this guy points out:

> *If we're having intercourse for a second time in a short period of time, I usually keep going until she's had another orgasm, and then I fake an ejaculation. Yeah, it can be done with a bit of acting, as well as flexing the muscle down there. Women aren't the only ones who can fake it.*

The Golden Rule is apropos here: Do yourself and your partner a favor, and don't fake. It's perfectly normal for a man occasionally to lose his erection during sex, and women need to understand this. Men are not infallible machines, but human beings with body parts that have minds of their own.

4. **DO be wary of female orgasms that are too good to be true.** If your girlfriend always has a simultaneous orgasm with you after two minutes of intercourse, know while such a feat is physically possible, it's quite rare. Of course, don't make the mistake of accusing her of faking, lest you offend one of the few lucky women on earth who can come that quickly and easily. But don't be lax about following all the other suggestions in this chapter, like giving her ample opportunity to get off in other ways.

5. **DO accept a woman's faking confession graciously.** If a woman ever admits to you that she faked an orgasm, stay calm and thank her for her honesty. This news can be frustrating to hear, but no one wants to be stuck having dishonest sex forever. She's just given you the gift of truth. Now it's your turn to use this newfound knowledge as an opportunity to get back on track and figure out how to work

together (it's her responsibility as well as yours) to help her come.

Faking Dos and Don'ts (for Women)

1. **DON'T fake, ever.** Pledge to yourself that you're going to be a girl who doesn't fake it. If you make this promise, it pretty much guarantees there will be some sexual situations in your life when you don't have an orgasm, and your partner will know it. Get okay with that. Realize that in the long run, some orgasm-free sex episodes are far better than "training" your partner to repeat an ineffective technique on you and every future woman he or she sleeps with. As one of our friends said, "Every faked female orgasm moves humanity further from achieving a real one."

   My first girlfriend faked it—quite poorly—and it had negative effects on our relationship. My last girlfriend never faked. We talked about my performance. When it wasn't good, I wanted to know so I could improve.

   If your partner knows you're honest when you don't come, he or she can also begin to trust that when you do scream his name or grab onto her shoulders, that orgasm was for real. That kind of trust and honesty builds great relationships inside the bedroom and out.

2. **DO break the cycle if you've been faking.** Your pseudo-gasms may not matter if it's a short-term fling or if you're about to end things anyway. But if this is a long-term love, you owe it to yourself to help your partner help you have real orgasms.

   Obviously, if you like this person, you don't want to hurt his or her feelings. Let's say you've been faking orgasms after five minutes of oral sex, and you suspect you could come for real if the stimulation continued longer. Here's one approach that's only half-honest, but may do the trick to get you back on track without causing a major crisis: "Honey, I've been reading this book about female orgasm. There was a section about how orgasms can feel, and how long it can take women to get there. It got me wondering if I could have bigger orgasms if we did stuff for longer—sometimes it feels really, really good, but the more I read, the more I'm not sure if I'm having orgasms all the time or not. Would you be up for trying some different things, or just going for longer, to see how it feels for me?"

If you have real orgasms sometimes but fake when you can tell it's not happening (so your partner *thinks* you come every time), try gradually cutting back on your faking. Sometime when you can tell an orgasm just isn't meant to be, don't fake—let your partner know you had a good time but you're not going to come tonight. Gently introduce the idea that sometimes you come and sometimes you don't, reassuring your partner that an orgasm isn't the only thing that determines whether you enjoyed yourself. (It takes some partners months or years of reassurances to become comfortable with the idea that many women can enjoy sex whether or not they have an orgasm every time.) Intersperse real, fake, and non-orgasms, gradually providing fewer fakes and allowing sex without orgasm to happen from time to time. As your partner adjusts to the idea that you don't always come—and that you're okay with that—phase out your faking entirely.

3. DO be firm and honest if you're being pressured. If you get the sense your partner's pride hinges on whether or not you come, you may begin to dread what's ahead. Rather than just enjoying each other, the interlude has been transformed into a test of performance, your partner's and yours. When a partner tells you your orgasm is his or her goal, or keeps asking if you came, be kind but clear: "Sometimes I have orgasms, sometimes I don't. That's not really the point. I love being with you; it feels really good." Give him or her positive feedback for the things he or she is doing that

you like ("I love how long you go down on me" or "You feel so good inside me"). If you have ideas for what could help you come, share them. In the end, be honest about how long you want the pleasuring to continue, and, if you're asked, whether or not you had an orgasm. Your significant other may need to be reassured many times that you don't need to have an orgasm every time in order to consider it great sex and be totally satisfied—many guys, in particular, can't imagine this could be true. Over time, your partner will come to respect your honesty and be less invested in your orgasm as the only sign that he or she did a good job. You may be rewarded with a more relaxed partner. Without the pressure, you might be able to breathe easier, too—which, ironically, could lead to more female orgasms.

BIG O on the big screen:
When Harry Met Sally

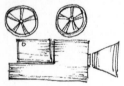

THE MOST FAMOUS "female orgasm" in cinematic history is a fake. Over lunch at a diner in New York City, Sally (Meg Ryan) and Harry (Billy Crystal), argue about whether a man can tell if a woman is faking an orgasm. To prove her point, Sally puts down her fork and proceeds (fully-clothed) to fake an orgasm, starting with gentle moaning and building up to a loud head-tossing, fists-banging-on-table orgasm that captures the attention of everyone in the diner. When finished, Sally returns to her lunch while another customer places her order with the waitress with the now-classic line, "I'll have what she's having."

9

Coming with Pride:
lesbian, bisexual, transgender, queer, and straight-but-adventurous orgasms

One of the cool things about a subject like female orgasm is that it's about a woman's body, not her sexual orientation. For the most part, an orgasm is an orgasm—it's one experience the straightest married woman probably has in common with the radical queer grrrl next door. As a result, this book is for lesbian, bisexual, transgender, and queer women—as well as for heterosexual ones (of course, not every section applies to every individual). The same basic concepts about oral sex work regardless of the gender of the person whose tongue it is. Women of all sexual orientations can enjoy the hum of a vibrator on just the right spot. Some lesbians find it challenging to have orgasms, just like some straight women. Information about how most women like to have their clits touched doesn't vary depending on whether her background music is Barry White or Ani DiFranco.

That said, there *are* some differences when women have sex with other women. The woman on top, for instance, can push her knee hard up against the other's crotch for the bottom woman to grind against, a move that would elicit howls of pain if the bottom partner were male. Two women can compare their orgasms— and each other's "performance" at the identical activities—more directly than a woman sleeping with a man. And without a penis in the bedroom, there's no

a note on the word "queer"

QUEER CAN BE a controversial word in the lesbian, gay, bisexual, transgender (GLBT) community, because of its ugly history of being used as an epithet to hurt people. In recent decades, some younger GLBT activists began to use the word to describe themselves, "reclaiming" queer as their own to reduce its power to be used against them. More recently, the community's "alphabet soup" has stretched with its inclusivity: It's not uncommon to see strings of letters like GLBTTQQAI for gay, lesbian, bisexual, transgender, transsexual, queer, questioning, ally, intersex, sometimes with more letters added for genderqueer, two-spirited, and asexual. As a result, growing numbers of people now use "queer" as a blissfully short umbrella term that stands for all these identities and more. Many like that the term acknowledges and allows for difference, rather than claiming that gay people are just like straight ones. Others within the community still find the word offensive.

We use the word queer in this book because we find it's the shorthand most young GLBT adults use for themselves—and also because we both identify as bisexual and find queer to be a comfortable and inclusive way to name the GLBT communities we're part of. We don't deny that it's still being used in hateful ways, including in schoolyards across the country. As with all words, its meaning depends on who's saying it, how it's said, and what that person means when he or she uses it.

assumption that the night will end with intercourse, tab A in slot B. This chapter takes a look at some of the differences between sex with male and female partners. That's not because they have to be *very* different—in fact, a lot of people who've tried both say sex is a similar experience regardless of the gender of the person you're getting it on with.

Women who have sex with women are a diverse bunch. Many describe themselves as lesbians, primarily or exclusively sexually attracted to women. Others are attracted to people of all genders, and may call themselves bisexual, pansexual, or prefer another identity label or no label at all. Some say things like, "I fall in love with the person, not the gender." (In our survey, after "heterosexual," "bisexual" was the most common sexual orientation women used to describe themselves.)

Growing numbers of young women "experiment" sexually with other women—or hope to—in part because it's more socially acceptable than it used to be, allowing bi-curious and lesbian-questioning women to test the waters earlier in their lives. Sometimes women are encouraged by a male partner who thinks it's "hot" to see two women together and wants to watch (not, we think, a great reason for a woman to start kissing women if she's not interested in them herself). The word "heteroflexible" entered the vocabulary in recent years: people who generally consider themselves heterosexual, but could be "flexible" with the right person, in the right situation, perhaps with the right amount of tequila. In our survey, one in five women who described themselves as heterosexual said they'd had sexual experiences with another woman, and that's not just making out on the dance floor: 30 percent of women who checked the "heterosexual" box and said they'd been sexual with other women reported having performed oral sex on another woman.

As the transgender, genderqueer, and intersex movements gain strength and visibility, growing numbers of people are speaking up about not fitting neatly into either "male" or "female" boxes, or about having partners who don't. For instance, a woman may not know how to describe her relationship and her own sexual orientation if her partner has a female body but thinks of himself as genderqueer and uses male pronouns. Is the woman lesbian because her partner has a female body? Bisexual because she's attracted to the female, male, and gender-fluid aspects of her partner? Heterosexual because her partner considers himself a guy? Sexual orientation labels can be limiting when viewed against the complexity of gender. In fact, to say gender is complex is an understatement. This chapter isn't about untangling the subject, or saying some kinds of girl-girl sex are more valid or more important than others. Our vision is a broad one—hopefully broad enough to fit the many, many women who sometimes or only have sex with other women, those who hope to someday, and also those who are blowtorching the very concept of "woman" and "gender" into new realities.

who says it ain't natural?

THE ANIMAL KINGDOM has abundant examples of female-female sexual love. In some species a certain percentage of animals in a population behave as "lesbians," having sex with other females and, in some cases, forming long-term bonds and even parenting together. More commonly, some or all of the females of a species "mate" with both males and females. (We're focusing on female animals here, but just so you don't get the wrong idea, animal homosexuality is just as common, if not more so, among males.) A few examples, from the book *Biological Exuberance*:

- Bonobo (pygmy chimpanzee) females rub their genitals together, gazing into each other's eyes while they do so and making sounds and expressions believed to indicate that they're having orgasms.
- Female squirrel monkeys not only have sex and kiss each other on the mouth, but pairs with close relationships often "co-mother" each other's children, with infants developing strong bonds with both females.
- Some eastern gray kangaroo females form pair-bonds with other females but not with males. These female kangaroo couples "mount" each other sexually and affectionately groom, lick, and nibble each other.
- Pairs of dolphin females caress and stroke each other's bodies with their fins and snouts, and take turns rubbing each other's clitorises. Two females sometimes swim together with one's dorsal fin in the other's vulva.

Other species where females commonly have sex with each other include chimpanzees, baboons, whales, seals, deer, caribou, buffalo, giraffes, antelopes, warthogs, lions, cheetahs, hyenas, koalas, squirrels, bats, ducks, and other birds.

I ♥ FEMALE ORGASM

the best parts of girl-girl sex

WHEN PEOPLE ASK how lesbians have sex (and they do ask, over and over), what they're really trying to figure out, of course, is how it's possible to have sex without a penis. The question reveals the flawed but widespread assumption that sex equals a penis in a vagina—which makes it impossible for many to imagine sex with, say, two vaginas and no penis. As readers of this book know, the best sex is about *way* more than just a penis in a vagina; it involves hands and fingers, lips and tongues, breasts and nipples, labia and clitorises—not to mention the more than fifty other body parts women named on our survey when asked to tell us their favorite erogenous zones (page 24). Lesbian, bi, and queer women are just as likely to have every one of those body parts as anyone else, and it's not difficult to combine them in ways that feel fantastic. For women who love penetration (some queer women do, some don't), fingers do a great job. You can vary the thickness by changing the number of fingers, and fingers can curl and place pressure in ways that penises can't. Dildos—worn as strap-ons (see page 232) or used by hand—are always an option, too.

There isn't anything unenjoyable about being sexual with a woman. I love everything. Rubbing, tasting, stimulating her breasts, kissing her whole body, oral sex, fingering. I love it all. Sex with women is slow, patient, and exciting. The payoff for all the work and energy is the intimacy and moaning.

I like them because women's bodies are soft and beautiful and curvy and sexy and work like mine. Also, I understand the way women's minds work better than I understand men's, making the emotional connection and trust a little easier.

I love exploring someone's body and taking my time. I love breasts. I love my own breasts as well as other women's. Kissing another woman is one of the most sensual experiences of my life.

I LOVE being with women! It's like a sexual awakening for me. I love kissing all over her body. I love touching her for hours. I love using my hands and mouth, or a toy, whatever. It's about the emotion involved. Even when we're being rough and dirty, it's still about the love underneath it all.

Some women also remarked on how hot it can be to touch your partner's body and be able to imagine *exactly* how it feels to be touched there. Some said the "forbiddenness" of same-sex sex can make it feel extra sexy, or that being with a woman can make it feel safer to "lose control" during sex.

and the challenges

THAT SAID, SEX with another woman isn't all sunsets, roses, and orgasmic perfection.

I think the biggest challenge is that not all women are the same. Just because you're turned on by rough penetration doesn't mean your partner is. You have to really communicate about it. Also, there's always the fear that she might be better than you at something. Like what if my partner really turns me on when she's using her tongue to stimulate my clitoris, and I do the same to her and she doesn't react?

I'm used to boys, I don't know so much what to do to girls.

Even though I have all the same parts, I didn't know what she liked or disliked, and was afraid of doing something wrong. I wanted to be good, but I ended up being scared.

When I first kissed a girl, I wasn't sure what to do with her boobs. Mine are pretty compact and hers were the real deal and I had no idea how she might want to be touched or even what you DO with them.

Others added:

○ Flirting with, asking out, or otherwise finding a female partner can be tough since there's less of a social script about how to do it—and because you sometimes have to guess if a given woman would be flattered or offended to be asked out by another woman.

○ Some women find it challenging to be sexually assertive, or to find a female partner who is. Relationships between women sometimes lack a sexual initiator, a role that men are often expected to assume.

○ Compared with pleasuring a male partner, it can be harder to help a woman have an orgasm, to know if she came, and to climax simultaneously (that's probably why simultaneous orgasm is less often a goal among lesbian couples).

○ Some women feel guilty about having sex with other women, because we live in a homophobic society that's uncomfortable with and sometimes hostile toward same-sex sex and relationships.

Lesbians and bisexual women also have to deal with the reality of homophobia in their lives. One nineteen-year-old woman commented on our survey, "I am constantly worried my family or someone from my hometown will find out and I will be disowned or killed because of it." It's not uncommon for GLBT people to fear being the victim of antigay violence. For more resources and support about this kind of violence, as well as same-sex sexual assault and domestic violence, contact the National Coalition of Anti-Violence Programs at www.ncavp.org, or call 212-714-1141.

Thanks to the work of many GLBT activists and straight allies, the United States is a much safer place for queer people than it was fifty or even twenty years ago. Activists have worked hard to pass antidiscrimination laws and other protections, and to help people become more understanding and accepting of the diversity of sexual orientations and gender identities. Unfortunately, while great progress has been made, there is still much work to be done as violence and discrimination against GLBT people continue across the country.

While the political work is being done, people continue to fall in love and have sex with partners of the same sex, as they have throughout history.

lesbian sex secrets

If you're going to be rock and rolling with another woman, you'd be wise to take to heart these tips from women who have gone before you:

1. **Cut your nails.** While there are exceptions to every rule, most women who have sex with women want their partner to have smooth, trimmed fingernails. Fingers and hands can be at the heart of the action when women sleep together, and being stabbed by a daggerlike fingernail between your legs isn't pleasant. Some say the fastest way to distinguish between "lesbian" porn featuring women *pretending* to be lesbians, and porn featuring the real thing, is to check out the length of the women's fingernails.

   I enjoy using my hands to have sex with a woman. I enjoy most any sexual act with a woman, but using my hands I'm the most comfortable and have had the best results.

2. **The journey may be the destination.** The process of enjoying each other's bodies, touching and being touched (or licked, sucked, stroked, fingered) is the main point. Breast play or oral sex isn't just "getting ready for the real part," it *is* the real part. (Of course, this can be true for couples of any gender combination.) That means it can go on as long as you want. If you're both enjoying it, be creative and get lost in the pleasure.

3. **Rediscover the joy of grinding.** Many women find that rubbing their body against another woman's body is a pleasure all its own. Rubbing your clits together can hit both of your most sensitive parts at once. Your breasts can rub against each other at the same time. There's even a special word for woman-woman grinding, tribadism, but a lot of women just call it delicious.

   I love being humped by a woman (though I HATE that word—it makes me think of dogs humping the legs of strangers). I think I really enjoy it because of the pressure on my pubic bone, and the feeling of moving together with someone in a kind of rhythm.

There's something really amazing about grinding with a woman. It's just pure, unhampered, skin-to-skin, sensual fun.

4. **Call your own shots on penetration.** Whether or not you like the sensation of having something in your vagina is about as personal a preference as whether you sleep on your side or your stomach. Among queer women, penetration is totally optional. (It's optional for straight women, too, but they often face way more pressure to have penetrative sex.) Your female partner's never liked penetration? No problem! You can make her clit sing. You love the feeling of something inside you, the bigger, the better? The two of you can have a good ol' time shopping for the biggest purple silicone schlong you can find. Of course, fingers and hands can work great for this, too. A woman may enjoy a finger or two inside her, unmoving, to give her something to squeeze against, but may not like the feeling of in-and-out thrusting. It's totally up to you; your Queerness Quotient doesn't hinge on your opinion about having anything in your vagina.

We use sex toys quite frequently and have dreams of building our own sex palace/dungeon! My partner has a transgendered identity and, thus, we do a lot of acts that could be interpreted as heterosexual (blow jobs, penile-vaginal/anal intercourse). Of course, we do these all with the aid of a harness and dildo. A strap-on is almost necessary for us to have a normal sex life.

5. **Be smart about safer sex.** It's a myth that lesbians aren't at risk for HIV and STIs. It's true that HIV risk is lower for women having sex with other women than for those sleeping with men, but it's not zero. Plus, there's no shortage of nasty STIs that women can inadvertently share with their partners through skin-to-skin contact (like grinding, described above), vaginal fluids, menstrual blood, or sharing sex toys. You're not off the hook in the safer sex department just because the one between your

sexy strap-ons

SOME FEMALE COUPLES have great fun having sex with a strap-on, a dildo worn in a harness. (Lots of straight couples play with a strap-on, too, using them for vaginal penetration, or for anal penetration of either partner.) Harnesses come in leather, vinyl, and rubber, with different designs depending on whether you want a center strap running between your legs or not. Most strap-on harnesses are designed for pelvic thrusting, but some women prefer thigh harnesses. Some harness designs give the wearer more clitoral pressure than others; some even have a pouch where the wearer can insert an egg vibrator. You can strap on a dildo of any size or style, as long as it has a base wide enough to keep it in the harness. For more on dildos, see page 176.

My girlfriend and I bought a blue silicone unrealistic six inch dildo and a nylon fabric harness from an Internet site. The dildo's name is Ernie. We enjoy sex together very much, but she considers herself mostly straight and prefers the feeling of penetration. I also tried it out and it's growing on me.

I love my cock—it's huge and camouflage-colored. I use it with a leather harness. I got it shortly before I turned twenty. I wanted a cock that I could identify with, that would feel like an extension of my own body, not a toy.

It usually takes a while to get good at wearing and using a strap-on. There's a reason why teenage boys tend to be awkward at intercourse at first. And guys don't have to worry about adjusting straps just so, having their tool flop away from their pelvis, or not being able to feel where they're thrusting! Like all things, practice helps, and it doesn't have to be a perfect performance for both women to have fun. The woman wearing the strap-on may want to penetrate her partner with fingers first, and then gently insert the dildo. The woman being penetrated is always in charge, because she has nerve endings and the dildo doesn't.

Strap-ons definitely aren't a requirement for woman-on-woman sex; some find it easier to use a dildo by hand, or aren't interested in penetration at all. But couples who love them think they're a pretty sweet invention.

I ♥ FEMALE ORGASM

sheets is female, so read up on the relevant sections of the Preventing Bugs and Babies chapter (page 250). You can skip the parts about accidentally getting pregnant—that's one thing you don't have to worry about if there are no sperm being released in the vicinity of your vagina!

6. Most aspects of sex between women are in every other chapter of this book. Lesbian, bi, and queer sex is about the clitoris and all the great things you can do with it (chapter 1), masturbation (chapter 2), oral sex (chapter 4), G-spots and female ejaculation (chapter 6), sex toys (chapter 7), and anal play (chapter 10). Enjoy!

for more on lesbian sex

The Whole Lesbian Sex Book, by Felice Newman

We're endlessly impressed with this book, the best we've found on the subject. It's fun to read, covers everything under the sun, and is as accepting and nonjudgmental as a good friend. Inclusive of bi women and trans people, as well as lesbians.

orgasms and queer sex

WE SAID AT the start of this chapter that an orgasm is an orgasm. And yet, the dynamics of female orgasm change when women sleep with women. If intercourse is the presumed focus when women sleep with men, orgasms sometimes take on the same role for female couples. The goal becomes for both women to have an orgasm, which signifies that it's time to get up and figure out what's for dinner. (Maybe you've heard the old joke: "Why do people have orgasms?" "How else would we know when to stop?") Of course, sex doesn't have to lead to an orgasm every time for each partner, and sexual or sensual pleasure doesn't have to end after the orgasms, unless you want it to. While some women lament how few sexual activities allow both partners to come at the same moment, most enjoy the fact that queer sex typically involves alternating and taking turns. That allows each partner to devote all her energy and focus at a given moment to either giving or receiving sexual pleasure, without trying to do both at once.

We find that lesbian and bisexual women who haven't had an orgasm, or who find it difficult to do so, are often particularly troubled by this fact, as if "belonging to the lesbian club" should automatically make orgasms flow freely. The reality is that having a female partner is no guarantee of having an orgasm—and not being able to "give" your female partner an orgasm doesn't give you an F in Lesbianism. Some women having sex with women—like women having sex with men—need to touch their own clit or use a vibrator during partnered sex to be able to get off. That's the reality of how some bodies work, not a sign of some shortcoming on the partner's part.

Likewise, some women of all sexual orientations have bodies that just haven't made the orgasm connection yet, for a myriad of reasons or no reason at all, as we explored in more detail in chapter 3. A small percentage of queer women who are able to come say doing so isn't important to them. Some say that for them, the thrill of sex is pleasuring their female partner. Their sexual high point is the other woman's big O.

One dynamic is nearly impossible to avoid when women have sex with each other: orgasm comparison, and sometimes orgasm competition. Given the orgasmic diversity in the universe, it's unlikely that both women's orgasms will be the same in any given relationship or interlude. More likely, one woman's climaxes will be faster and the other's slower, one's will feel stronger and the other's weaker, one's will go on and on while the other's slip by in the blink of an eye.

The solution? Well, it's unlikely two women are going to become orgasmic twins, no matter how hard they try. (Of course, male-female couples also frequently have gaping differences between their orgasms, but they typically write these off as "men and women are different" and don't expect otherwise.) Two women may feel compelled to experiment to see if new approaches could help the "lesser" orgasms get stronger, longer, or more likely to go from zero to sixty in 3.9 minutes. But rather than stressing too much, it's probably best to acknowledge and embrace the fact that their sexual responses are different—not better or worse.

transgender experiences

WHEN WE TALK about "female orgasm" in a book like this, in most cases we're talking about people for whom the doctor or midwife said, "It's a girl!" when they were born. They have XX chromosomes, a vagina, and a clitoris, and when they reached puberty, they developed breasts and started menstruating. They grew up in a culture that socialized them as girls and women. But there are also people who've had a different path to womanhood.

Some people, for example, were born with male genitalia and XY chromosomes. At birth, the doctor or midwife said they were male, and they were socialized to be boys and men, but as they grew up they felt they were female. Transgender is one word to describe people whose gender identity—who they feel they are inside—is different than the gender they were assigned at birth. In this case, the person might consider herself to be a transwoman, or MTF (for male to female). A transwoman may choose to take hormones like estrogen, and have surgery to make her body look more like the gender she feels she is. This could include surgery to enhance her breasts and to transform her penis into a clitoris and a vagina. Some transwomen don't take hormones or have surgery, but still identify as female.

Many transwomen say their experience of sexuality changed when they began to take hormones. Some say they began to feel a broader range of emotions, and some that their libido decreased. Many found they began to feel more sexual, as their body changed to match their gender identity.

Research on orgasms after sex reassignment surgery is limited, but the existing studies and anecdotal reports say that yes, most (but not all) MTFs are able to have orgasms with their "new" genitalia. A clitoris is created using skin and nerves from the head of the penis, and an effort is made to preserve nerves and arousal tissue. It takes a while, of course, to heal from such a significant surgery, and for sensation to return. Transwomen who choose to have intercourse usually find it's most comfortable if they add lube, because their new vaginal walls were constructed from the shaft of the penis and may produce limited lubrication on their own.

Many transwomen report that they had to relearn how to masturbate and have an orgasm—similar to the way many women born with female genitalia have to explore their body's responses. Transwomen often say female arousal feels quite different from what they experienced previously, and there's no erection to tell you you're aroused. Some transwomen say they have better orgasms after their surgeries, because they're finally enjoying a body that feels more "right" for them.

After the surgery I was looking forward to making love the way I'd always imagined in my own head. The first time it mostly hurt—it was really validating

emotionally, but it was like, "Oh, be careful! Go slow! Use some more lube!"
It was nice that it got better every time. Gradually I got more familiar with it
and my body healed, so now it's a lot of fun. I don't have a lot of sensation
from vaginal intercourse, because most of the nerves are around the clitoris.
They use the glans of the penis to form the clitoris. But if he shifts up so his
pelvis pushes on my clitoris and he does a little grinding, then it hits just the
right spot. If he does that and he sucks on my nipples a little bit, it doesn't take
me long at all.

For two years before surgery I was on hormones, but I never had orgasms
because I wouldn't let anyone touch me below the waist. Then after I healed
from my surgery, I thought it was broken. Nothing down there seemed to work
right. But I practiced a little bit on my own, and then it was like, "Woah!"
Once I got the "Woah!" down, everything else fell into place. I get very excited
very easily by guys. I'm dating a man now—I can have an orgasm just by him
touching me on the underside of my breasts, or touching my clitoris. The
orgasms are different than anything I experienced as a non-female. They're
earth-shattering. They're more centered around me—before they were cen-
tered around a part of my body.

Transgender also describes the experience of people born with female genitalia
and socialized to be women, but who feel male deep down inside. Like male-to-
female transpeople, FTM (female to male) transpeople can choose to take hormones (testosterone) and have surgery to make their body match their gender
identity. Their experience is one of male sexuality, beyond the scope of a book about
female orgasm.

Some people who use the word transgender to describe themselves don't feel
that they're either 100 percent male or female, but are somewhere in between male
and female, a bit of both, another gender entirely (a "third gender"), or none of the
above. These people may call themselves genderqueer, FTX, or have some other
way of describing their gender.

I'm a biological woman but have a masculine identity and a discomfort with
my own body. I often identify with queer or transgender. A label I often use for

I ♥ **FEMALE ORGASM**

myself is boi. This term accurately describes my identity as a transgendered individual with the body of a female and the soul of a male. The play on words indicates a male pronoun but the spelling indicates that I'm not the normative boy.

I identify as transgender, because it's the least restrictive gender word I can find. I'm not a man, but I'm not a woman either. I don't feel gendered in any way. I simply don't have the innate feeling of "man" or "woman." It makes sense to me for my body to reflect that, so I am in the process of making it neither a male nor a female body.

I find that when I'm having sex with someone who does not see me as a woman, I'm much more comfortable having vaginal intercourse. I'm also a lot more open about my love of anal sex, as it's less gendered in general. Anal sex remains a safe activity, because everyone has an anus to play with, regardless of gender and assigned sex.

Transgender people's orgasms depend on their genitals, hormones, gender socialization, identity, the relationship they're in, their mood, how turned on they are, and countless other factors—just like everyone else's orgasms! For more on transgender sexuality issues, see www.ifge.org (the International Foundation for Gender Education).

intersex experiences

WE'VE BEEN WRITING about gender identity—whether or not someone *feels* like who he or she is inside is a man, woman, or some other identity. There are also people who *biologically* don't fit neatly into categories of male and female. For example, most people are born with either XX or XY chromosomes, and a vagina or penis to match. But that's not the case for everyone. Some people are born with only an X chromosome (called XO), or get an extra sex chromosome, like XXY. Other people are born with "ambiguous genitalia" that isn't clearly male or female; they might have characteristics of both. Sometimes people use the word "hermaphrodite" to describe this condition. However, those in the community prefer the terms intersex or DSD (disorders of sex development), which are more accurate, less stigmatizing descriptions. These days, intersex or DSD describes the full range of conditions that can indicate a person doesn't fit squarely into the male or female checkboxes.

> *I was born without external genitalia—I didn't have a clitoris, vagina, or penis. Due to my confusion about my sexuality and gender identity, and my self-consciousness about my body, when I was growing up I declared that I wouldn't date or marry. But in the last year, I've realized that sex is something I can enjoy, after all, despite my background. I'll need more surgery at some point to have "normal" vaginal intercourse, but my boyfriend and I make it work. When he stimulates the area where the entrance to my vagina will be with his fingers or penis, I usually climax fairly quickly. Being in this relationship has been good for me—it's given me hope that I can be sexually satisfied, and I can provide satisfaction for someone else, even with my physical differences.*

One of the biggest factors affecting some intersex people's orgasms is whether they had medical interventions like genital surgery as an infant or small child. Some doctors perform medically unnecessary surgeries to make a child's genitals look more "normal," with no regard for what effect this might have on the person's future sexual pleasure. For example, a doctor could cut off part of a baby girl's clitoris if it's believed to be "too long—too much like a penis." While the girl's genitals may look more "average" after the surgery, she just lost some of the most sensitive nerve endings in her body. How could that *not* have an impact on her sexual pleasure and orgasms?

> *I've had two, maybe three, experiences that resemble the descriptions of spontaneous orgasm. This has been the only pleasure available to me so far. I was born almost a hermaphrodite, with a full female reproductive system and genitals, but also an ambiguous organ that might have been either a large clitoris or a micro-penis, and half a male system. The doctors never checked for female organs, and at the age of three they closed my labia and covered my possible clitoris in a skin graft. They imagined I should be a boy. Puberty arrived in my mid-twenties, primarily female with some extra androgens. I have a vagina*

if your partner is trans or intersex

IN OUR MANY conversations with transgender and intersex people and their partners over the years, a few themes emerge consistently about being a respectful sex partner of a trans or intersex person:

- Ask, ask, ask. . . There's no way to know what your partner likes and is comfortable with without talking about it.
- . . . But don't turn every sexual encounter into Transgender or Intersex 101. There's a time and place for partner education, but sometimes it's time simply to play or snuggle.
- Use the trans or intersex person's preferred gender pronouns and words for his or her genitals. Follow his or her lead.
- Realize that some people may not want certain parts of their bodies touched sexually. For instance, an FTM who hasn't had surgery may not want a partner to caress his breasts, because he identifies as a man. These preferences may change over time.
- Be willing to let go of some of what you already know about how to please a partner, and be open to finding creative ideas together.
- Once you figure out what sexual activities you and your partner enjoy, have fun! Don't worry about what identity labels you need or how these might change. You'll figure that out over time.

with lots of sensation, which would be almost normal except that its opening is the width of a straw. I have almost no clitoral sensation. I do have desires, and I wish there were a way to indulge them. But no doctor anywhere is willing to touch my case because I'm not a child anymore. There is a hell—it's located at a hospital in Baltimore. Don't do this to your kids.

The intersex movement's message is clear: Unless there's a medical emergency, keep doctors' scalpels away from children's genitals. Parents and doctors can make an educated guess, based on genitals, hormones, and chromosomes, whether a child is likely to feel he or she is male or female as an adult, and raise the child to be that gender. Once the person is an adult, he or she is free to choose to have surgery to change the appearance of his or her genitals, or not.

Intersex people lucky enough to have escaped childhood genital surgery are often the ones who say their sex lives are the most satisfying, because their genitals work just fine for purposes of pleasure.

There are entire books and websites devoted to intersex and DSD issues; if you're interested in reading more, check out www.isna.org (Intersex Society of North America) and www.ipdx.org (Intersex Initiative).

10

Knocking at the Back Door: advice for the anally-curious

Anal sex: It's the titillating taboo of the decade. Just the inclusion of this chapter in a book on female orgasm has some people thinking, "All right!," while others are shaking their heads, "Oh, really?"

We believe it's important to address anal sex because we're asked *so* many questions about it. In fact, in terms of the sheer number of questions about all sex topics, it ranks second, only after female orgasm itself. In our online survey, 35 percent of women said they'd had anal sex as the receiving partner (with a penis or a dildo). How you approach anal sex can make a huge difference as to whether it's pleasurable or painful. If it's something you're considering, definitely read these pages so you don't have to learn the hard way.

While anal sex was once stereotyped as "something gay men do" (in reality, some gay men do, some don't), it's an increasingly common activity among straight, bi, and lesbian people. According to interviews with over 12,000 people conducted by the Centers for Disease Control and Prevention, among 20-to-24-year-olds, 33 percent of men and 30 percent of women reported having had anal sex with a different-sex partner. By ages 35 to 39, that figure climbs to 42 percent of men and 34 percent of women. (The CDC also found that about 4 percent of men have had anal sex with another man, but didn't collect data on anal play among

anal sex around the world

THE UNITED STATES ranks seventh in terms of the percentage of adults who say they've had anal sex, according to the Durex Global Sex Survey. (These percentages are probably somewhat higher than the actual numbers since people who volunteer to fill out Durex's survey may not be representative.) Last on the list? Taiwan, where only 1 percent of people list it among their experiences. Here's the top ten list:

1. Chile 55%
2. Greece 55%
3. Italy 50%
4. Croatia 49%
5. Finland 49%
6. Norway 48%
7. United States 47%
8. France 46%
9. Bulgaria 45%
10. Sweden 45%

women having sex with women.) All the percentages are higher than they've been in the past, perhaps a sign of the increased popularity of butt sex, an increased willingness to admit to it in a research interview, or both.

many ways to play

THE ANUS IS dense with nerve endings, and lots of women say it can be an erogenous zone for them. Anal stimulation can be provided by a woman's own or a partner's fingers (touching around the opening or putting a finger inside), with a tongue (see "What's Rimming?", page 245), or with sex toys. Some women who like the sensations of having their anuses touched also enjoy anal intercourse, while others find most penises too big to be comfortable.

I find anal sex to be pleasurable, but with fingers or a small dildo. This is because when it comes to anal sex you have to work up to something larger. There are a lot of nerves just dying to be touched.

I prefer anal sex with fingers and we do that all the time, but anal sex with a penis hurts so much.

One of my very favorite things is to have vaginal intercourse with my husband with me on top, and with a butt plug inserted in my anus. The feeling of the butt plug and his penis stimulating my G-spot provides me with hands-down, unequivocally, the most intense orgasms that I have ever, ever had.

Why Do People Like It?

WOMEN MAY ENJOY anal sex for lots of different reasons:

○ Some love the way it feels. In our survey, 25 percent of women who've had anal sex described their best experience with it as "very pleasurable," and another 38 percent said it was "somewhat pleasurable." The rest didn't care for the experience at all. While the percentage of women who can have orgasms through anal sex alone is pretty small, more are able to come through a combination of anal and clitoral stimulation. Some guys also reported that they enjoyed the sensation; a partner's anus feels different than a vagina around their penis (many who've tried it say not necessarily better, but different).
○ Some women are turned on by the excitement of breaking a taboo, the idea that anal sex is "naughtier" than other kinds of sex, similar to the way many people say they're turned on by having sex in a place where they could be caught.

All the nerves there make it feel good, and because it seems like such a naughty thing, it turns me on more.

○ Other women don't particularly enjoy the physical sensation of anal sex, but their partner enjoys the act so much that the women like doing it occasionally as a "special treat" for their partner. Some women feel a special emotional connection during anal sex because the act seems particularly intimate to them.

I enjoy anal sex because I know my partner is turned on by it, and having him turned on makes me very turned on. It's always a little uncomfortable, sometimes quite painful, but I still enjoy it, just not too often.

I like anal sex because it's different. It feels good, and I love knowing that it's so tight and pleasurable for my partner. I don't do it very often, which also makes it fun. With my first boyfriend, it was a special something we did when I had my period.

Some men with female partners enjoy being on the receiving end of anal sex (being penetrated with fingers or a sex toy) for all the reasons above, plus the additional bonus of prostate stimulation. In fact, some guys can have orgasms this way, because the prostate, the gland that produces the fluid for male ejaculate, is about two inches inside the rectum, toward the front of a man's body. Many men find prostate stimulation feels great, and some can ejaculate from the attention their prostate gets during anal penetration.

essential tips for good anal sex

NO MATTER WHO'S on the receiving end, anal sex can be a positive experience, whether or not it's an orgasmic one. It can also be downright painful and unpleasant if it's not done carefully and respectfully.

1. **Make sure both partners are willing and interested.** We'll say it again: Everyone has the right to decide what they will and won't do sexually. It's perfectly okay to "just say no" to any sexual activity that doesn't appeal to you, including this one. The partner who's been told "no" doesn't have the right to badger or coerce the one who's not interested. It's equally wrong for a partner to pretend he or she "accidentally went in the wrong hole" or to "slip it in" sometime when his or her partner is drunk, high, sleeping, or otherwise unaware—that's rape. Talk about it first, make sure you're both in agreement, and if so, proceed to step #2.

2. **Get relaxed and in the mood.** Like vaginal penetration, anal sex works best when you've spent some time kissing and caressing to get in the mood. Most people unconsciously condition themselves to keep the muscles around their anus tight, perhaps providing inspiration for terms like "tight ass" and "anal retentive." You can use the Kegel exercises described on page 26 to get acquainted with the muscles in that part of your body, and learn how to squeeze and relax them fully. (Kegel exercises squeeze and relax both vaginal and anal muscles together; they're all connected.) Figuring out how to relax one's anal muscles can make penetration much easier, and it works better if anal play is something the receiving partner actually desires. If she's honestly not interested, the anus knows and may not relax, making for painful or uncomfortable anal sex.

3. **Start small.** If you're ready to experiment with what it feels like to have something inside your anus, start with fingers before you try a penis or

what's rimming?

"RIMMING" REFERS TO sexual contact between one person's mouth or tongue, and another person's anus (also known as analingus or "a rim job"). Many people who've tried rimming find it pleasurable because of the combination of the tongue's abilities (which oral sex aficionados know well) and because the anus is sensitive. Others say to each her own, but they're going to steer clear of putting their tongue down there. Rimming does carry a risk of transmitting bacteria and STIs such as hepatitis A. Plastic wrap or dental dams are effective barrier methods (for more on using this lowly kitchen supply for safer sex, see page 267). Considerate recipients of rimming always wash or shower beforehand.

what about the shocker?

ONE OF ONLY a handful of sexual acts with the honor of having its own hand gesture, "the shocker" is the act of insert-ing two fingers (usually the middle and index fingers) into a woman's vagina and another (usually the pinkie) into her anus at the same time. The "shock" is presumably that the woman wasn't expecting the finger in her anus. Known by many other names, including "two in the pink, one in the stink" and "two in the goo, one in the poo," the shocker name and gesture are recent inventions (though we don't expect to see them listed alongside the light bulb and the zipper anytime soon). Part of the shocker's thrill seems to be the fact that most members of older generations don't know what the gesture means, allowing for a crude in-joke among younger generations. Parents and school administrators are catching on fast, though, as the gesture has been mak-ing widespread appearances on Facebook.com and MySpace.com, and even popping up in high school yearbook photos.

Do women like being on the receiving end of the shocker? Most women say they'd rather not be "shocked" by any kind of penetration. Even if they enjoy the pinky-in-the-anus sensation—some do, some definitely do not—they'd prefer their partner to ask, "Is this okay?" before plunging inside. (Most guys prefer the same respect before a partner inserts a finger in his anus!)

Despite the dirty humor of the gesture, the shocker is missing something important: a finger dedicated to clitoral stimulation. If you're looking for a combo-move, clitoral plus vaginal or clitoral plus anal is more likely to impress.

dildo. You can use either your finger or your partner's. The person insert-ing the finger should trim his or her nails; some people like to wear a latex glove to make the surface of their hand even smoother. Put plenty of water-based lube on the finger you're going to insert to make insertion more comfortable and safer.

It took me a long time before I worked my way up to fully enjoying anal sex. It's really hard to relax those muscles enough that you don't feel discomfort. The best thing is to slowly work your way up. For instance, on the first experience try one finger for a little while. Next time try a little longer. Maybe add another finger once that's comfortable, and so on.

4. **Use lots of lube and a condom.** Unlike the vagina, which gets wet as a woman gets turned on, the anus doesn't produce its own natural lubricant. Therefore, using water-based lube for anal penetration isn't optional—it's essential. Lube helps make anal sex comfortable and reduces friction that could result in small tears in the tissue of the rectum. There's more info about lube on page 133. There's no such thing as too much lube when it comes to back door action. A condom is important (unless you're both fully tested and trust each other to have unprotected sex only with each other), because unprotected anal sex is higher risk for HIV and STI transmission than unprotected vaginal sex. Hint: The smoother the condom the better; this is not the time to pull out your prized collection of ribbed and textured condoms.

Because the rectum can contain bacteria that aren't healthy for a vagina, anything that's been inside the anus should get washed (or get a fresh glove or condom) before going into a vagina.

Can you get pregnant by having anal sex without a condom? It's nearly impossible, because sperm would have to make their way out the anus to the opening of the vagina, and then swim up the vagina. Sperm are ambitious little guys, but it's highly unlikely they'd make it that far. Do be careful about getting ejaculate near the entrance to the vagina, though—the closer sperm get, the greater the pregnancy risk.

5. **Go slow, slow, slow.** Porn is a huge source of misinformation about women's sexuality in general, as you've read throughout this book. This couldn't be truer than with anal sex. If you've seen hard, pounding anal sex with no warm-up in porn, and expect to replicate the performance and have both partners enjoy it, you've been greatly misled. Whether

receiving fingers, a sex toy, or a penis, the anus needs a slow, gentle approach. Start with lots of foreplay, whether it's a massage, touching the outside with a finger, or rimming. Some people find it more comfortable if the sphincter is approached at a slight angle. Once penetration begins, the person being penetrated always chooses the speed and depth of penetration, as well as when she wants her partner to stop moving or pull out. The penetrating partner should be closely tuned in to whether the angle is comfortable for his or her partner. Because the walls of the rectum can be more sensitive than the walls of the vagina, it can take creativity and patience to figure out which position feels best. Pulling out should be just as slow and careful a process as inserting.

the scoop on anal-ease

STAY AWAY FROM the product called Anal-Ease (also spelled Anal-Eze), and other numbing agents or lubricants that contain benzocaine. Benzocaine is a local anesthetic typically used for topical pain relief. With anal sex, pain is your body's way of telling you that something's not right, that you could be being hurt or harmed. It's one thing to use a local anesthetic after you've been stung by a bee: You know what happened, the bee is now gone, and you're left coping with the pain. But with anal sex, if something hurts, you should stop and figure out what's wrong, not numb yourself up and push forward, potentially damaging your body in the process. Anal sex done right doesn't hurt. Plus, being numb reduces the possibility that you might actually enjoy it!

Start slowly and communicate with your partner. Tell your partner when it's okay to go in a little further, when to stop for a moment to let you get accustomed to it. Once you're all the way in, wait a minute and just hold me and comfort me and make sure I'm ready before you start moving again. Talk to me and kiss me on the cheek or shoulder (in a sweet way, not a sexy way). Once I'm ready, start slowly and ask me before going faster or harder.

As with any sexual activity, some women have powerful orgasms as a result of anal sex, some strongly dislike the sensations, some aren't interested at all, and everywhere in between. Adding clitoral or G-spot stimulation at the same time can make it easier for a woman to have an orgasm during anal sex. So can figuring out a position that works well for the bodies of the people involved.

I've had orgasms from anal sex alone sometimes, but they're much stronger and more likely when my clitoris is being stimulated, too.

I'm very particular about anal sex. I only find anal sex pleasurable if there's clitoral stimulation involved and if my partner doesn't expect anything more than slight penetration. There's no "in and out" and no full penetration, just slight entry by the head of the penis.

I love anal sex, but only in a face-to-face position, not doggy-style. I lie on my back and hook my legs around my partner's waist, so we're basically in missionary position, except we're having anal instead of vaginal sex. For me, the sensations are really pleasurable and even more intense than vaginal sex. I can have orgasms in this position because his pubic bone hits my clit, plus I think I get some G-spot action internally. I'm a lot more relaxed in this position than from the rear, and I think the angle is better.

going deeper

INTERESTED IN EXPLORING anal sex further? Here are two books to check out:

- *The Ultimate Guide to Anal Sex for Women,* by Tristan Taormino
  A slim, friendly volume by anal sex's most enthusiastic female proponent, addressing myths, positions, toys, and more. Inclusive of heterosexual, lesbian, and bi readers. An equivalent guide for men was written by Bill Brent.

- *Anal Pleasure and Health,* by Jack Morin
  The classic book on the subject, Morin's approach is more serious and detailed, but still quite accessible for the anal sex curious or the connoisseur. Inclusive of heterosexual, lesbian, gay, and bi readers.

11

Preventing Bugs and Babies:
safer sex and birth control

Most of life's pleasures have downsides. Ice cream tastes great and is rich in calcium, but it's also full of sugar and cholesterol. Swimming is incredible on a hot day—as long as you don't drown. Orgasms can be ecstasy, but some of the activities that lead to orgasms also open the door to sexually transmitted infections (STIs, also called STDs for sexually transmitted diseases) and unplanned pregnancies. This chapter is your handy reference guide to preventing these things from slipping into your life when what you were really after was an orgasm. It's also about how not to pass along HIV or another STI to your partner. Obviously, for women having sex only with other women or men with men, accidental babies aren't a risk, but STIs are.

preventing babies

IF YOU WANT one, a baby is a lovely thing (2 AM shrieking and endless diaper changes aside). If you weren't planning on having one, an unexpected pregnancy can turn your life upside down. You may already know that:

○ A woman can get pregnant the very first time she has intercourse.

○ There's no such thing as a "safe time" to have intercourse during a woman's menstrual cycle (unless you're an experienced user of the fertility awareness method—more on this later). Women can ovulate at any point in their cycle.

○ Douching with Coke doesn't prevent pregnancy. Neither does Pepsi. (We've been asked the question!)

That said, there are some highly effective ways to prevent conception if you're planning to have sex that could involve sperm and egg meeting each other and you're hoping not to get pregnant. On the pages that follow is a handy-dandy reference chart.

Birth control statistics on effectiveness can be confusing, so here's a quick note on how to understand the numbers. A 98 percent effectiveness rate means that if 100 couples used the method for a year, on average two of them would get pregnant. "Perfect use" means they used the method correctly and consistently, every single time they had intercourse. "Typical use" is usually a lower number because humans being human, we mess up: People forget to take their pill, or neglect to take a condom with them but have intercourse anyway. You can do better. Aim for perfection!

the latest on birth control

BIRTH CONTROL OPTIONS continue to expand and change. For updates and more detailed information, check www.plannedparenthood.org and www.fwhc.org.

One other thing: The chart below doesn't list the various possible reasons why a given person shouldn't use a given method. Contraception you can buy in a store without a prescription is usually safe and appropriate for anyone to use (of course, read the information inside the package to be sure). For hormonal methods and devices (like diaphragms and IUDs) that require a visit to a doctor or clinic, you'll want to discuss your health history with the practitioner to be sure the method that appeals is a good match for you. He or she may also be a good person to help you weigh the pros and cons of a few methods you're considering.

HANDY-DANDY BIRTH CONTROL QUICK REFERENCE CHART

BIRTH CONTROL TYPE	WHAT IT IS	HOW EFFECTIVE? (PERFECT USE)
Non-Hormonal Methods		
Abstinence	Defined in different ways by different people. If the goal is to avoid pregnancy, at the very least abstinence means not having penile-vaginal intercourse, and not doing anything else that could get semen in or near the vagina.	100%
Condom (male)	Thin sheath of latex or plastic worn over an erect penis. Traps sperm so it can't enter vagina.	98%
Female condom	Loose, thin plastic pouch with two flexible plastic rings, worn inside vagina. Traps sperm so it can't enter vagina.	95%

HOW EFFECTIVE? (TYPICAL USE)	A FEW PROS AND CONS

No one knows

- Unquestionably the most effective way to avoid getting pregnant (or getting someone else pregnant).
- Dramatically reduces HIV and STI risk (this depends on whether you're engaging in behaviors other than intercourse that could transmit HIV or STIs).
- Free and always available.
- No health risks.
- Can still experience sexual pleasure and orgasm (depending on how you define abstinence).
- Not realistic or desirable for some people at some points in their lives.

85%

- Widely available in drug and grocery stores.
- Inexpensive.
- Effective for both pregnancy prevention and HIV/STI risk reduction.
- Can reduce spontaneity.
- Must remember to use it.
- Can decrease sensation for condom wearer (can be an advantage for a guy who wants to slow himself down!).

79%

- Available without a prescription. Sold in some drug stores, sex stores, and online.
- More sensation for men than male condom.
- Effective for both pregnancy prevention and HIV/STI risk reduction.
- Not made of latex, so appropriate for those with latex allergies, and can be used with oil-based lubes.
- Does not have to interrupt sex: can be inserted up to 8 hours before intercourse. Can reduce spontaneity if not inserted in advance.
- Must remember to use it.
- Requires woman to be comfortable inserting lubricated female condom inside herself. Can be awkward to do, especially at first.
- Costs more than male condoms.

Sources for birth control chart information: "Contraceptive Efficacy" by James Trussell in Contraceptive Technology (2007), Planned Parenthood, and the Feminist Women's Health Center.

BIRTH CONTROL TYPE	WHAT IT IS	HOW EFFECTIVE? (PERFECT USE)
Non-Hormonal Methods, continued		
IUD (ParaGard, copper IUD)	Doctor or practitioner inserts a small T-shaped plastic device in uterus. Has tiny copper wire wrapped around stem. No one knows for certain why IUDs work.	99.4%
Diaphragm	Doctor or practitioner fits woman with a shallow rubber cup that goes over cervix. The woman fills it with spermicide and inserts each time before intercourse, to create a physical and chemical barrier.	94%
Sponge	Round piece of spongy foam containing spermicide, with ribbon loop attached to remove it. Inserted deep in vagina to trap and kill sperm.	91% (lower for women who have given birth)
Spermicides (foams, creams, gel, film, suppositories)	Inserted deep into vagina. Film and suppositories melt into liquid inside the body. All methods kill sperm inside vagina.	82%

Sources for birth control chart information: "Contraceptive Efficacy" by James Trussell in Contraceptive Technology (2007), Planned Parenthood, and the Feminist Women's Health Center.

HOW EFFECTIVE? (TYPICAL USE)	A FEW PROS AND CONS
99.2%	■ Highly effective for long period of time (10 years). ■ Allows for spontaneity. ■ Must be inserted by doctor or practitioner. ■ Can cause heavier periods with increased cramps. ■ Rarely, could cause infection or wall of uterus could be punctured during insertion. ■ Does not prevent transmission of HIV or STIs.
84%	■ Generally cannot be felt by either partner during intercourse. ■ Must be fitted by doctor or practitioner. ■ Must remember to use it. ■ Does not have to interrupt sex: can be inserted up to six hours before intercourse. Can reduce spontaneity if not inserted in advance. ■ Some women have reactions to spermicide. ■ Can increase the risk of bladder infections. ■ Some women find them uncomfortable. ■ Can be messy. ■ Does not prevent transmission of HIV or STIs.
84% (lower for women who have given birth)	■ Available in drug stores without a prescription. ■ Generally cannot be felt by either partner. ■ Does not have to interrupt sex: can be inserted up to 24 hours in advance. Can reduce spontaneity if not inserted in advance. ■ Must remember to use it. ■ Irritating to some women's vaginas. ■ Can't use it during a woman's period. ■ Does not prevent transmission of HIV or STIs.
71%	■ Widely available at grocery and drug stores. ■ Relatively inexpensive. ■ Generally cannot be felt by either partner. ■ Lubrication can increase pleasure. ■ Good for "doubling up" for extra protection while using another method. ■ Must remember to use it. ■ Can reduce spontaneity. ■ Can be messy.

BIRTH CONTROL TYPE	WHAT IT IS	HOW EFFECTIVE? (PERFECT USE)
Non-Hormonal Methods, continued		
Spermicides		
Fertility awareness method	Woman tracks her body's signs throughout menstrual cycle to determine when she is fertile and infertile. On fertile days, couple either doesn't have intercourse or uses another birth control method. This is *not* the same as the rhythm method, which is based on when an *average* woman is fertile rather than tracking an individual woman's fertility indicators.	97%
Hormonal Methods		
The Pill (oral contraceptives)	Woman swallows pill each day to prevent ovulation.	99.7%
The Ring (NuvaRing)	Flexible, transparent plastic ring inserted into vagina once a month, releases hormones to prevent ovulation.	99.7%

HOW EFFECTIVE? (TYPICAL USE)	A FEW PROS AND CONS
	■ Some people have reactions or allergies to some spermicides. ■ Taste limits oral sex after use. ■ Can irritate the vagina, which can increase risk of HIV or STIs.
75%	■ Very inexpensive. ■ No health risks. ■ Results in increased knowledge and awareness of woman's body ■ Requires detailed knowledge to use effectively (classes and/or the book *Taking Charge of Your Fertility*). ■ Requires daily, accurate information gathering and recordkeeping. ■ Requires commitment to abstain from intercourse or use other methods on potentially fertile days, which can be 10 days per month or more. ■ Does not prevent HIV or STIs.
92%	■ Allows for spontaneity. ■ Usually decreases length of period and cramps, regulates menstrual cycle. ■ Have to remember to take it at the same time every day. ■ Prescription needed. ■ Does not prevent transmission of HIV or STIs. * See list of side effects at end.
92%	■ Allows for spontaneity. ■ Usually decreases length of period and cramps, regulates menstrual cycle. ■ Prescription needed. ■ Must be replaced each month. ■ Can irritate the vagina. ■ Does not prevent transmission of HIV or STIs. * See list of side effects at end.

Sources for birth control chart information: "Contraceptive Efficacy" by James Trussell in *Contraceptive Technology* (2007), Planned Parenthood, and the Feminist Women's Health Center.

BIRTH CONTROL TYPE	WHAT IT IS	HOW EFFECTIVE? (PERFECT USE)
Hormonal Methods, continued		
The Patch (Ortho Evra)	Beige plastic patch sticks to skin (a bit like a Band-Aid) on woman's stomach, arm, butt, or torso. Releases hormones to prevent ovulation.	99.7%
The Shot (Depo Provera)	Doctor or practitioner gives woman an injection of hormones every 3 months to prevent ovulation.	99.7%
IUD (Mirena, hormone IUD)	Doctor or practitioner inserts a small T-shaped plastic device in uterus, releases hormones. No one knows for certain why IUDs work.	99.8%

* Hormonal methods of birth control sometimes have other side effects, which vary from woman to woman. Not every method has every potential side effect, so ask your health practitioner, check the websites in The Latest on Birth Control on page 251, or read the product insert to find out risks for each specific method. Some side effects may be temporary and wear off after a few weeks or months of using the method. Side effects for hormonal methods can include changes in appetite, blood clots (rare), changes in sex drive, depression, dizziness, hair loss, increased blood pressure (rare), increased hair on face or body, headache, irregular bleeding patterns, mood swings, nausea, nervousness, skin rash, sore breasts, weight gain, and weight loss.

HOW EFFECTIVE? (TYPICAL USE)	A FEW PROS AND CONS

Sources for birth control chart information: "Contraceptive Efficacy" by James Trussell in Contraceptive Technology (2007), Planned Parenthood, and the Feminist Women's Health Center.

92%
- Allows for spontaneity.
- Usually decreases length of period and cramps, regulates menstrual cycle.
- Prescription needed.
- Must be replaced each week.
- Can irritate skin near the patch.
- May be visible (at least when you're undressed).
- Does not prevent transmission of HIV or STIs.
* See list of side effects at end.

97%
- Allows for spontaneity.
- Possibly lighter or no menstruation.
- Must see a practitioner every 3 months.
- Cannot stop taking medication immediately if side effects are problematic.
- Risk of bone thinning.
- Does not prevent transmission of HIV or STIs.
* See list of common side effects at end.

99.8%
- Highly effective for long period of time (up to 5 years).
- Allows for spontaneity.
- Possibly lighter or no menstruation.
- Must see a practitioner for insertion.
- Rarely, could cause infection or wall of uterus could be punctured during insertion.
- Does not prevent transmission of HIV or STIs.
* See list of side effects at end.

Some hormonal methods of birth control may slightly reduce the risk of certain cancers, such as ovarian or endometrial cancers. Research on current hormonal birth control methods is conflicting on the subject of breast cancer: Some studies find no increased risk, while others find slightly higher rates of breast cancer among women who've used hormonal contraception. Because all of these hormonal methods are relatively new (even today's oral contraceptives are quite different from the pills prescribed a decade or two ago), it will be decades until there is concrete evidence either way in people, not rats.

Smokers who use hormonal birth control have significantly higher rates of side effects, including some of the most dangerous ones.

emergency contraception

EMERGENCY CONTRACEPTION (EC), also known as Plan B or the "morning after pill," prevents pregnancy *after* you've had sex. While it's not a good regular method of birth control, it's quite effective for a woman whose birth control failed (for example, a condom broke), who didn't use birth control (bad plan!), or who was forced to have sex. As soon as possible after having intercourse, the woman takes pills that contain the same hormones that are in birth control pills, or has an IUD inserted, and these prevent ovulation or fertilization. If a woman has unprotected sex and takes emergency contraception pills within three days, the odds are 96 percent to 99.5 percent that she won't get pregnant. If she has a copper IUD inserted after unprotected sex, the odds are 99.9 percent that she won't get pregnant. EC works better the sooner you use it: within three days is ideal, but it can be used up to five days after intercourse. You can get EC pills in drugstores without a prescription if you're over 18; younger teens need a prescription. For more information about getting emergency contraception, call 1-888-NOT-2-LATE or go to http://ec.princeton.edu/.

It's great that EC exists for emergency situations, but don't rely on it as your primary method of birth control. Used on an ongoing basis, EC pills are far less effective than other birth control methods (only about 60 to 80 percent with perfect use). Plus, they can cause nausea, vomiting, breast tenderness, irregular bleeding, dizziness, and headaches. These side effects may be well worth it in a time of crisis, but they'd sure take the fun out of sex if you had to experience them every time.

preventing bugs (hiv and stis)

WHEN WE SAY "bugs," we mean everything from literal insects (creepy little crabs that crawl around your pubic hair) to figurative ones: bacteria and viruses

I ♥ FEMALE ORGASM

you can catch from sexual contact. Some STIs are easily curable (like gonorrhea), while others (like HIV) can't be cured, only managed. Other STIs are life-threatening, particularly without treatment. In general, there are two primary ways bugs get from one person to another during sex:

○ Bodily fluids: HIV, chlamydia, gonorrhea, and hepatitis B are primarily spread when blood, semen, pre-cum, or vaginal secretions come into contact with mucous membranes (the lining of the mouth, vagina, rectum, or urethra).
○ Skin-to-skin contact: Herpes, HPV (genital warts), syphilis, trichomoniasis, and crabs spread primarily when skin touches skin, such as when genitals touch other genitals or a person's mouth.

If you're trying to avoid bug infections and infestations, or trying to protect your partner from catching something from you, here's your menu of options:

1. You can choose to abstain from all partnered sex. If you never have any sexual contact with anyone else, you can't catch whatever they might have. Some people choosing not to have partnered sex still have orgasms from masturbation.

2. You can avoid all sexual activities that create contact between bodily fluids and mucous membranes, such as vaginal, oral, or anal sex. You'd still have the option of having "outercourse," all the sexual activities that involve hands, fingers, or rubbing against each other's bodies (frottage). Many people can have orgasms this way. While this approach eliminates the risk of catching or transmitting the STIs that travel through bodily fluids, you're still at risk for other STIs if there's genital area skin-to-skin contact.

3. You can use barrier methods like condoms and dental dams. Used correctly and consistently, these are highly effective at reducing (but not eliminating) the risk of HIV and STIs, especially the ones transmitted through bodily fluids. Barriers reduce the risk of STIs transmitted through skin-to-skin

contact, too, but they're not as effective at this since you can be infected from skin that's not covered by the barrier (like pubic area skin where a condom doesn't cover). This is the option most sexually active adults choose, especially if they're not in a committed, long-term, monogamous relationship, or if they know one partner has HIV or an STI.

4. You and your partner can become "fluid-bonded." Let's say that two people:

○ have both been tested (it can take up to six weeks after a possible exposure for HIV antibodies to show up in a test), or they've never had any other sex partners or reasons they could be at risk
○ know that they're both HIV negative and have no other STIs
○ are in a monogamous relationship and completely trust each other not to cheat (more on this below) and
○ have made responsible non-condom-based birth control plans if they're a male-female couple that doesn't want to get pregnant (or one of them is infertile or has had a vasectomy or tubal ligation, or she's past menopause).

If all of the above are true, then this couple can't catch HIV or STIs from each other, and they might choose to have sex without condoms or other barrier methods. People using this approach must agree to tell each other if they "slip up" in some way (like having unprotected sex with someone else) before they put their partner at risk. If that happens, they return to using safer sex supplies until they're retested. Warning: This approach relies *very heavily* on trust. It works best in a relationship where the partners have gotten to know each other well over time.

Some people in open or polyamorous (honestly nonmonogamous) relationships don't use safer sex supplies with their long-term, trustworthy primary partner(s) once they've been tested, but agree that they'll always use barrier methods for sex with any other partner.

super-snappy guide to condoms

WANT TO BE transformed from a typical condom user (85 percent effectiveness against pregnancy) to a perfect one (98 percent effectiveness)? Read on. While even perfect condom use can't provide a 100 percent protection guarantee, a study in the journal *Sexually Transmitted Diseases* found that using a condom is 10,000 times more effective for HIV prevention than using nothing at all.

1. **Test-drive condom brands.** You wouldn't buy a car you hadn't test-driven! While you can't try out a condom *before* you buy it, condom wearers benefit from the same kind of comparison shopping since different brands and styles fit different bodies better. You're more likely to use the thing if you or your partner find it comfortable. Condomania.com even sells tailor-made condoms, custom designed for each man's intimate measurements.

   Here's the inside scoop on "ribbed for her pleasure" and other textured condoms: Most women who've tried them tell us they prefer the smooth ride of the regular kind. Some do like them, though, so there's no harm trying one out. Just make sure you have a standard condom close by in case she gives the ribbed version a thumbs-down.

2. **Check the expiration date.** You're a well-prepared Boy Scout or Girl Scout, always carrying a condom because "you never know"? Not a bad idea—but when the time comes to use your trusty prophylactic, check the date on the package. Sometimes it takes longer than anticipated for the "you never know" opportunity to arise.

3. **Be careful how you open the wrapper.** You're in a hurry. You may be in the dark. You have other, more exciting things on your mind (like what you're about to do once you've, um, wrapped his package). But in your rush, don't succumb to the temptation to open the condom wrapper with your teeth or scissors. This risks nicking the condom, creating tiny tears or weak points that can lead it to break once your passionate action puts it under stress.

4. Put a drop or two of lube *inside* the condom. This is optional, but many guys find it gives them more sensation. Don't overdo it—you don't want the condom to slide right off the penis.

5. Leave space at the tip. As you unroll the condom over the penis, pinch the air out of the tip so the explosive jet of semen (okay, we're being dramatic) will have somewhere to go.

6. Don't flip it over. You're unrolling the condom to the base of the penis. If you suddenly realize you've got it upside down (hint: it won't unroll that way), don't just flip it over—the place the condom touched the tip of the penis could now contain pre-cum or STIs, and when you flip it over, that side will now face inside the woman's body. Throw it away and start again with a fresh condom. (You bought the 12-pack, right?)

7. Hold on as you pull out. You defeat the whole purpose of wearing a condom if you complete the act, withdraw the penis, but accidentally leave the condom inside her with semen seeping out of it. Most guys' hard-ons soften quickly after they ejaculate, making it easier for the condom to slip off. To prevent that, he should withdraw promptly after he comes, holding onto the base of the condom while he does.

bonus condom tips

○ Stick with latex or polyurethane condoms. Most condoms are made of latex rubber. Some people are allergic to latex, so polyurethane condoms are available as a good alternative. (You can buy them online if you can't find them in stores.) Lambskin condoms and "natural condoms" can protect against pregnancy, but not HIV and STIs.

○ Lube makes sex safer. For vaginal or anal penetration, condoms and lube go together like popcorn with butter. Not only does adding lubricant make penetration feel better, it reduces the chance the condom will break. This is true even if the condom comes prelubricated—we recommend you add more. With latex condoms, use only water-based lubricants, not massage oil or hand lotion. (And not butter—that's for popcorn.) There's more about lube on page 133.

○ Flavored condoms and nonlubricated condoms are perfect for oral sex on a man. While oral sex can't get a woman preggo, and is lower risk for most STIs, it doesn't eliminate all STI risk. Genital herpes on your mouth or gonorrhea in your throat are not charming. Using condoms for oral sex is a smart move, especially for a partner whose health status you don't know. Just stick with the nonlubricated kind, since lube probably isn't one of your favorite flavors.

○ Don't believe the lies about condoms. Some people have been told that condoms are full of microscopic holes big enough to allow HIV and sperm to pass through them. This is misinformation, plain and simple, taught by people who think scaring teenagers out of using condoms will also scare them out of having sex. The problem is, the strategy backfires: We've met lots of young adults who've decided to have intercourse without condoms, because they've been taught condoms are useless.

The United States has high safety standards for condoms, which are regulated by the FDA. In order to be sold in this country, manufacturers must electronically test every condom for holes, and perform extra tests on some condoms from every batch. In a two-year study of HIV discordant couples (one HIV

top ten safest condoms

WHILE ALL CONDOMS sold in the United States pass excellent safety standards, independent testing by *Consumer Reports* found these to be the top ten safest brands, based on strength and reliability testing. The first seven all received the same high rating and are listed alphabetically:

1. Durex Extra Sensitive Lubricated Latex: safest condom on the market (of those tested)

2. Durex Performax Lubricated

3. LifeStyles Classic Collection Ultra Sensitive Lubricated

4. TheyFit Lubricated

5. Trojan Extended Pleasure Climax Control Lubricant

6. Trojan Non-Lubricated

7. Trojan Ultra Pleasure Spermicidal Lubricant

8. LifeStyles Classic Collection Dual Pleasure Lubricated

9. Beyond Seven Lubricated

10. Class Act Ultra Thin & Sensitive (while these are the last on this list, they did quite well, out-performing more than half of the other condoms tested. We're not listing the losers, but you can read the complete ranking at www.consumerreports.org/cro/health-fitness/health-care [click on condoms and contraception]) positive person, one HIV negative person) who used condoms correctly every time they had vaginal or anal intercourse, no HIV negative partner became HIV positive. The results are almost as good for pregnancy prevention: If 100 male-female couples have intercourse *without* condoms for a year, eighty-five of them will wind up with a bun in the oven; if they use condoms correctly every time, only two will. Condoms aren't perfect, but they're very, very effective.

female condoms

FEMALE CONDOMS ARE a welcome addition to the safer sex scene. We think it's a shame so few people have ever seen or tried one because there's a lot that makes them worth considering! Unlike a regular condom, which is unrolled over the penis, a female condom is a transparent plastic pouch that's inserted into the vagina or anus. It stays in place all by itself, thanks to two soft, flexible plastic rings, and the magic of its simple design. They do a look a little funny if you're not used to them—but a male condom would look like a pretty odd contraption if you'd never seen one before.

There are a few things that make female condoms particularly nifty. First, because they're loose, not tight around the penis, many guys find they get more sensation compared to a regular condom. Most women find them just as comfortable as any other condom. Some women like using female-controlled birth control, and not having to rely on (or convince) a partner to wear a condom. Also, because female condoms can be inserted up to eight hours before intercourse, you can insert one at the very beginning of a sexual interlude, eliminating the need to interrupt the action to put on a male condom. Theoretically, you could insert one before you go out on a date—you know, put on the earrings, put on the bra, insert the female condom.

female condom tips

○ **Practice makes perfect.** Female condoms can be a little awkward to insert at first, but it gets easier the more you do it. We recommend a woman try inserting one first when she's *not* in a sexual situation, because until you've done it a few times, the distraction of a partner nibbling on

266

your shoulder or kissing your ear can make it tricky to insert the slippery, prelubricated pouch.

○ **Figure out where to find them.** Female condoms aren't as easy to come by as male ones, but they're sold in some drugstores, and also available at some Planned Parenthood offices, health clinics, college health services, condom and sex stores, and online. They cost more per condom than a regular condom. Word from the company is that once the newest version of the female condom gets FDA approval (within the next few years, they hope), the price will drop to be about the same as a male condom.

○ **Consider a backup method.** Since female condoms are a few percentage points less effective than male condoms (you can compare the numbers on the birth control chart earlier in this chapter), many couples use them with a secondary method, like hormonal birth control or one of the spermicide options.

○ **Don't double up.** Using a female condom and a male one at the same time is a no-no. It doesn't offer double protection—but it just might double the risk that both condoms will tear from the friction, leaving you with no protection at all.

dental dams

DENTAL DAMS ARE thin squares of latex that can be placed over a vulva for oral sex on a woman, or over an anus for analingus on anyone. While oral sex on either a male or female partner is lower risk than intercourse for transmission of HIV and most STIs, there's still some risk involved. STIs that are transmitted through skin-to-skin contact, like herpes, can easily be transmitted from mouth to genitals or vice versa (yes, a partner with oral herpes on his or her mouth can kiss it right onto your genitals, and you can also inadvertently infect a loved one's mouth with your genital herpes sore).

QUESTION: What's worse than having your doctor tell you that you have an STI? ANSWER: Having your dentist tell you.

That's the reason dental dams were invented. While the first dental dams came from dental suppliers (dentists still use them to keep individual teeth clean and dry during dental surgery), now there are many brands of larger, thinner, silkier dams designed specifically for sex. Some store-bought dams come scented or flavored like ice cream: vanilla, chocolate, strawberry. Despite many requests from cunnilingus fans, we've yet to hear of a company producing vagina-scented dams.

There's a popular and easily-accessible alternative to buying dams: plastic wrap. Found in nearly every kitchen and grocery store in America, plastic wrap is cheap and plentiful. You can wrap your partner's entire pubic area for hands-free oral sex. Plus, because it's clear, it allows the licker to see where he or she is licking, an advantage in most people's books.

There's a commonly-held belief that you shouldn't use microwavable plastic wrap for this purpose, but as far as we can tell somebody made that up. We've come up empty-handed in our extensive quest to find the research that suggested this. The pores in microwavable plastic wrap don't open up until it's reached the boiling point, and while you may have some really hot sex, it's probably not *that* hot. If you're standing in a store choosing which plastic wrap to buy for sex, sure, play it safe and stick with the non microwavable kind. But if you're in a pinch and all that's in the kitchen drawer is the microwavable stuff, using that is certainly safer than using nothing at all.

do-it-yourself dental dams

IN A PINCH? You can make your own dam out of a condom by cutting off the tip and cutting a straight line down one side. If you've got a latex glove, cut off the fingers but not the thumb, then cut straight through one side. You can even stick your tongue in the thumb!

We've taught about safer sex enough to realize that most people simply aren't going to use dental dams or plastic wrap when they have oral sex. For many people, just using a condom consistently requires a lot of effort and dedication, and we agree this is the highest priority for people with male partners. But dams are a great option for people committed to lowering their risk, people in high-risk situations, those with partners they don't know well, and those working hard not to share their HIV virus or STI with a partner.

Eight safer sex secrets for the real world

IT'S ONE THING to learn about safer sex in theory. It can be something else entirely to try to implement those theories in real-life situations and relationships. We've talked with thousands of people about safer sex, including what works—and what doesn't—in their sex lives, and these are the tips people tell us helped them the most:

1. **Don't make assumptions based on looks—ask.** There's absolutely no way to know if someone has HIV or another STI by looking at them. Attractive, healthy, sexy, intelligent, charming, *good* people get STIs and HIV. They may or may not know they're infected. Given that you can't know a new partner's health status, using safer sex supplies every single time is the safest way to go. Getting tested gives you some additional information to go on. Talking about it helps, too, although there's no guarantee your partner knows his or her status or will tell you the truth. If you can't figure out how to possibly bring up the subject, try, "Okay, this is really awkward, but I know we're supposed to be asking each other if we know if we have any STIs or HIV." People who've been bold enough to say those words report that unless their partner is a total jerk, the other person is inevitably relieved they brought it up. Some studies find that half of people who know they're HIV positive don't volunteer the information unless their partner asks them, because they figure if their partner cares to know, he or she will ask. Once you have the information, you can plan accordingly.

2. **Keep your safer sex supplies close to your heart—or at least, close to where you might have sex.** You'd be surprised at how many people plan to have safer sex, but don't because at the key moment, a condom wasn't readily available, or because they figured their partner would have one. Having safer sex supplies is the responsibility of both partners—it's not just the guy's job. Make a habit of having supplies within arm's reach of anywhere you might end up having sex, both at your place and your partner's. Having a condom in your bag doesn't mean you're planning on

having sex that day any more than carrying Advil means you're planning to get a headache. Smart ladies and gents are always prepared; safe is far better than sorry.

3. **Double up on methods.** Using condoms *plus* another method works great for birth control. For instance, if the pill is typically 92 percent effective, and condoms are typically 85 percent effective, used together the odds that a woman would accidentally get pregnant drop to a stunningly tiny number (we'll leave that calculation to the statisticians among you). Plus, you get STI and HIV protection. Male and female condoms can be combined with any other method of birth control except each other. (Don't use a male and a female condom at the same time.)

4. **Consider vaccination.** Hepatitis A, hepatitis B, and HPV can all be transmitted through sexual contact, and all now have vaccines to help prevent their spread. Some of these vaccines have been around a while, and you might have been routinely vaccinated as a kid. The HPV vaccine first became available in 2006.

5. **Know the pros and cons of nonoxynol-9.** Nonoxynol-9 is a spermicide that's used in some kinds of birth control (like the ones in the "spermicide" row in our chart earlier in this chapter), and is sometimes found in lube or on condoms that advertise "with spermicide." It's a popular ingredient because it's effective at the job it's designed for: killing sperm. The problem is, in addition to killing sperm, N-9 can irritate the lining of the vagina or rectum. The irritated lining, in turn, is more vulnerable to HIV and STIs. If the primary reason you're using condoms is to protect yourself from HIV or STIs, avoid anything containing nonoxynol-9. If you and your partner know you don't have STIs or HIV and your primary goal is to prevent pregnancy, then it's a viable option. Also, some people are allergic to the spermicide, so before you diagnose yourself with a latex allergy, be sure to try out some latex that isn't coated in nonoxynol-9.

I ♥ FEMALE ORGASM

6. **If you've taken risks in the past, make a plan for the future.** Like dieting or exercising, safer sex is more likely to happen if you plan for it than if you hope it'll just fall into place by itself. If you have regrets about unsafe sex you've had in the past, get tested, get the treatment you need, and make a plan for the future so you can move on. If you find you're putting yourself at risk repeatedly, ask yourself why. Is there a common thread that ties together the times you took unnecessary risks? For example, alcohol and other drugs can make it more challenging to have safer sex. If you see that your biggest "mess-ups" typically happen after a night of partying that ends with a hookup and unprotected sex, you may realize that alcohol is a major source of the problem. Perhaps you'd decide to limit your number of drinks in the future, or ask friends to keep an eye on you so that if you drink too much, you end up in your own bed alone, not in someone else's.

7. **Know your PEP (post-exposure prophylaxis).** If you think you may have been exposed to HIV through very recent unprotected sex, PEP can prevent you from being infected. PEP involves taking the same medications given to HIV positive people to fight the virus. In this case, the goal is to prevent infection in the first place. In order for PEP to be effective, a person needs to start treatment within seventy-two hours of being exposed (the earlier the better). To get PEP, call your doctor or local emergency room right away and find someone who is knowledgeable about PEP or "HIV prophylaxis." While PEP is sometimes mistakenly called the "morning after pill," taking it isn't so simple. The side effects can be nasty—diarrhea, nausea, and vomiting, to name a few—and you have to take the drugs for thirty days.

8. **If it doesn't look or feel right down there, see your doctor.** Some high school sex ed teachers show students photo after gory photo of severe cases of STIs, leaving their students gagging and shielding their eyes from the images. The teachers' goal is to scare students into always practicing safer sex—or possibly to scare them away from ever having sex at all. The problem with these kinds of pictures is that by showing only the extreme cases, they leave viewers with a misleading impression of what an STI looks like. People think as long as their own and their partner's genitals aren't lesion-covered and pus-infested, they must be okay.

In reality, most STI symptoms are much more subtle, and many women have no symptoms at all, especially in an STI's early stages. If you notice potentially mild symptoms but ignore them hoping they'll go away, it's possible you'll end up with much more severe symptoms as the STI moves from the infection site to the entire body.

Most doctors and health clinic practitioners have treated so many people for STIs that it's not a big deal to them; there are over 15 million new cases reported in the United States every year. Don't let your embarrassment at seeing your doctor for an STI (or at confronting the reality that you got infected with one) keep you from getting testing and treatment.

if you get infected

YOU'VE BEEN DIAGNOSED with an STI or HIV? That's not news most people want to hear. But don't despair:

○ Most STIs are completely curable, usually with antibiotics. If yours is, get it treated promptly.

○ If you've been diagnosed with HIV or an STI that doesn't currently have a cure (like herpes or HPV), talk to your doctor about what treatments are available. Even infections and viruses that can't be cured can be managed to keep you as safe and healthy as possible. Medications can enable people who are HIV positive to live long lives. Make responsible decisions so you won't infect future partners. Seek out others with the same diagnosis (there are support groups, online message boards, and listservs) as a source of hope and support for the challenges ahead. People who are HIV positive or have an STI *can* have sex, relationships, and rich, fulfilling lives.

○ Plan for the future so you won't be reinfected or catch something new.

I ♥ FEMALE ORGASM

postscript

When the doctor told Dorian she had cancer, she didn't know if she'd live to see her thirtieth birthday. The possibility of her dying young terrified us both beyond words.

The truth is, none of us know if we're going to live to be thirty, or fifty, or one hundred. But we do know that our lives will be better if we surround ourselves with people we love and respect, who love and respect us in return—and if we care for and respect our bodies, because they're what we've got, as long as we're here. It's incredible, really, the things that bodies can do, and orgasms have got to be among the sweetest.

Orgasms reduce stress, relieve menstrual cramps and headaches, burn calories, reduce junk food cravings, help you sleep better, and are perfect to share with someone you love. Wherever your life's journey takes you, we wish you good health, long life, and plenty of orgasms!

acknowledgments

Little did our friends, relatives, and professional contacts know that when we signed a book contract, they were signing up, too. We don't exaggerate when we say that every page in this book is better thanks to these people's willingness to give us feedback on draft chapters, fill in stray details, and answer our endless questions. At times during the revision process we wondered if we'd solicited too much advice. It wasn't always easy to incorporate the tremendously diverse perspectives and sometimes contradictory recommendations of so many different people. Yet in the end, the input of all these people—college students to Baby Boomers, sexuality experts and regular folks, people of all genders and sexual orientations—coalesced to make this book a thousand times smarter and richer than it would be if we hadn't sought out so much help.

We are deeply indebted to Ashton Applewhite, Miriam Axel-Lute, Laura Gates-Lupton, Buck Miller, Suzanne Miller, Honey Nichols, Aly Mifa Solot, and Kathryn Turner, each of whom spent countless hours reading, suggesting, correcting, questioning, massaging, and revising chapter after chapter. Josh Albertson, Janie Fronek, Jonathan Glover, Julie Kersey, Theodore Nickles, and Liz Salomon also contributed significantly and repeatedly throughout our writing process. As in our last experience working with him, editor and publisher Matthew Lore "got it" immediately, and his infectious enthusiasm and supportive patience kept us going.

Research assistants Alexandra Buerkle and Lindsay Laczak doggedly tracked down the research findings that inform every chapter of this book. Our office assistant, Oona Edmands, tabulated survey findings and kept our business's details rolling smoothly along while we wrote and revised chapters. Illustrator Shirley Chiang's drawings provided the perfect light-hearted touch to bring the book to life.

Throughout the writing process we turned to people with specific expertise to confirm, clarify, or explain the nuance of specific topics we wanted to be sure we got just right. We appreciate the insightful assistance we received from Virginia Braun, Dan Cohen, Betty Dodson, Chris Fariello, David Ferguson, Bill Finger, Eric Garrison, Paul Joannides, Denise Leclair, Thomas Kelson Lewis, Lih-Mei Liao, Erika Pluhar, Gina Rourke, Judy Seifer, Bill Taverner, James Trussell, Paula Vincent, James Weber, and Rhetta Wiley.

We owe enormous thanks to the many people who reviewed chapters, brainstormed subtitles, improved slang, filled in gaps, prescreened movies, translated sex terms from other languages, and helped in a zillion other important ways small and large: Matt Alinger, Bri Beecher, Jillian Borden, Denton Cairnes, Jennifer de Coste, Hannah Durocher, Rebecca Durocher, Julie Ebin, Carol Anne Germain, Jane Gottlieb, Ken Heskestad, Peter Hill, Heidi Kelly, Gail Leondar-Wright, Meika Loe, Sharon Maccini, Caitlin McDiarmid, Luke Mechem, Gwynn Miller, Leslie Morrell, Julia Nickles, Marjorie Nickles, Michael Oates Palmer, Lily Pike, Emma Potik, Karin Potik, Jeff Root, Alex Shkolyar, Alison Singer, Tricia Realbuto, KaeLyn Rich, Kelly Siebe, Barbara Solot, Evan Solot, Goldie Solot, Miki Solot, Ryan Solot, Vicki Solot, Lockhart Steele, Rebecca Tell, Robin Tell, Marnie Tumolo and the University of California San Diego Women's Center, Tristan Turk, Nancy Vineberg, Walter vom Saal, and the vulva-loving superstars at vaginapagina.com.

This book would probably not exist had it not been for the early inspiration provided by Toby Simon and the encouragement of Laura Briggs. Additional shoutouts to Kersplebedeb, Brandon Maccherone, Jeff Sonnabend, Dan Winchester, Larry Winchester, and the staff of the Cambridge Center for Adult Education and Fenway Community Health.

Last but certainly not least, we thank the tens of thousands of people who have attended our educational programs and the nearly 2,000 who filled out our online survey. Your generosity in sharing extraordinarily private experiences, joys, fears, questions, and insights ground our work in the real world. You have taught us more than we could have ever imagined.

I ♥ FEMALE ORGASM

index

birth control pills, 83, 256–57
bisexual, defining, 225
Blank, Hanne, 81
Blank, Joani, 72
blended fantasies, 33
bodily fluids and STIs, 261–62
body image issues, 80–82, 88–89, 96–98
Body Image Workbook, The (Cash), 81
bondage, discipline/domination, and sado-
    masochism (BDSM), 182–83
boys, 4, 5, 43–45, 51–53
brainstorming sex play options, 189–92
breast cancer, early discovery of, 2–4
Brinkley, David, 52
Brown University, 4–5, 6–7
buildup to orgasm, 23, 26, 55–56, 173, 199
butt plugs, 181, 243
butt sex. *See* anal sex

C
Cash, Thomas, 81
Castleman, Michael, 212
Centers for Disease Control and Preven-
    tion, 241–42
cervix, 117
childhood, learning about masturbation
    during, 4, 5, 43–45, 51–53
chlamydia, 261–62
circulatory conditions affecting orgasm,
    82–83
cleaning sex toys, 183
Clinton, Bill, 95
clitoris
    coital alignment position and, 120–21,
        131
    glans and shaft of, 70, 72
    great lovers and, 200–201
    humming over, 111
    overview, 16–18
    piercing the, 184–85
    sensitivity of, 22–23, 25
    size of clitoris and intensity of orgasm,
        18

stimulating during intercourse,
    126–27, 141
tips for partners, 34–38
vibrators and, 173
cock rings, 183
coital alignment technique, 120–21, 131
coming, female orgasm as, 15
communication
    on clitoral sensitivity, 23
    on faking orgasm, 219–21
    during oral sex, 104, 106–9, 110
    on oral sex, 98–99, 114
    overview, 36–37
    saying no, 98
    sighs and moans as, 204
    on STIs and HIV, 269
    on what feels good, 24, 34–35, 140,
        198–200
    with women who fail to orgasm,
        218–19
    See also troubleshooting
condoms
    for anal sex, 247
    for birth control, 252–53
    female condoms, 252–53, 266–67
    guide to, 263–66
    latex condoms and oil-based lubri-
        cants, 135, 136, 264–65
    making dental dams from, 268
    practicing masturbation with, 142
    on vegetable sex toys, 180
Consumer Reports, 265
Cornog, Martha, 62
Courage to Heal (Bass and Davis), 39
cowgirl position, 117–18
crabs, 261–62
crisscross position, 119–20
cunnilingus. *See* oral sex on women

D
Davis, Laura, 39, 40
Dear Abby, 4
delivery boy mentality, 212

befriending your, 69–72
female genital mutilation, 67, 238–39
masturbation and condition of, 46–47
stimulation to, 35–36
vulva, 18, 19, 69–72, 73, 184–87
See also clitoris; vagina
genital surgery, 238–40
genital warts (HPV), 261–62
Gillette Venus Vibrance, 172
girls
age at first orgasm, 5, 64
masturbation and, 60, 62
social conditioning of, 42–43
See also women
glans of the clitoris, 70
GLBT (gay, lesbian, bisexual, transgender) issues, 224, 229
Goldstein, Richard, 52
gonorrhea, 261–62, 265
Gräfenberg, Ernst, 154
grinding, 121, 131–32, 230–31
G-spot
female ejaculation and, 150–51, 163
location of, 152–56
toys for, 176, 178–79, 180
G Spot, The (Perry, Whipple, and Ladas), 154
Guide to Getting It On, The (Joannides), 20

H
Haines, Staci, 39
Harry Potter's broom, 185
Heiman, Julia, 89
hepatitis, 261–62, 270
hermaphrodites, 237–40
herpes, 261–62, 265, 267
heteroflexible, 225
Hippocrates, 136–37
Hitachi Magic Wand massager, 169
Hite Report, The (Hite), 54
HIV
asking potential partners about, 269
fear of, 82

preventing with condoms, 265–66
transmission of, 231, 233, 261–62
treatment for, 272
HIV prophylaxis, 271
homophobia, effect of, 229
homosexuality among animals, 226
hormonal birth control, 256–59
HPV (genital warts), 261–62
humor, 149

I
intercourse
female self-touching during, 126–30
lubricant with, 135
men's masturbation versus, 205–6, 210
in movies versus real life, 115–16
orgasms during, 85–89, 124–27, 131–33
positions for, 116–19, 119–23, 128, 132, 141, 249
tips for guys, 139–42
intersex community, 9, 225, 237–40
IUDs, 254–55, 258–59

J
Janus Report, The, 51
Japanese nipple clamps, 183
Japanese on masturbation, 25
Joannides, Paul, 20
Johanson, Sue, 164
Journal of Sex Research, 148, 161, 175

K
Karras, Nick, 72
Kaufman, Miriam, 81
Kegel, Arnold, 26
Kegel exercises
for anal muscles, 245
for PC muscles, 26–29, 85, 163, 211
Kinsey, Alfred, 152

L
labia majora and minora, 70
Ladas, Alice Kahn, 154

troubleshooting guide, 207–13
vagina equated to, 18
PEP (post-exposure prophylaxis), 271
performance anxiety, male, 8
perineum, 72
Perry, John, 154
Petals (Karras), 72
phone sex, 33–34
physical aspects of female orgasm
    arousal and, 20, 21
    G-spot, 152–54, 155
    intercourse position and, 116
    muscle contractions, 14
    sensitivity to pain decreases, 16
    vaginal lubrication, 22, 23, 35
physical causes for erectile dysfunction,
    208
physical disabilities and body image, 80
piercings, 184–87
pituitary function test, 84
Planned Parenthood, 97
planning for first time sex, 144
planning for safer sex, 271
plastic wrap
    for oral sex, 95–96, 135, 245, 261–62,
      267–68
    for sex toys, 180
plateau phase of arousal, 20, 21, 79
Pleasantville (movie), 49
polyurethane condoms, 264
pornography
    anal sex in, 247–48
    boys/men learning about sex from,
      193–95
    concepts of sex from, 71
    female ejaculation on, 157
    as spoiler to open sexuality, 168
    taking a break from, 196
    waiting for erections before filming, 204
positions
    experimenting with, 122–23
    for intercourse, 116–23, 128, 132, 141,
      249

for oral sex, 100–103
post-exposure prophylaxis (PEP), 271
pregnancy
    from anal sex, 247
    body's desire for, 137
    fear of, 82
    intercourse during, 142
    preventing, 250–51
    sexual desire during, 26
    See also birth control
premature ejaculation, 209–11
pre-orgasmic women, 67
Presidential Physical Fitness Program, 60
pressure of clitoral touching, 35
pressure of vibrators, 173
prolactin level test, 84
prostaglandins, 142

Q
Queendom.com, 80
queer, defining, 224

R
rape, effect of, 38–40, 79, 203
rape scenarios, 31–32, 33
religion and masturbation, 48
resolution phase after orgasm, 20, 21
reverse cowgirl position, 117–18
rimming, 245
ring birth control, 256–57

S
sadomasochism, 182–83
safepiercing.org, 187
safer sex secrets, 269–72
safewords, 182
Sears, Roebuck and Company, 168
Seifer, Judith, 84
self-consciousness about oral sex, 92–94,
    96–97
self-touch
    advantages of, 2–4, 68–69
    experimental, 72–74

woman on top position, 117–19, 223
women
  anal stimulation of, 243–49
  asking for directions, 199
  body image issues, 80–82, 88–89, 96–98
  duration of time before orgasm, 20–21
  erogenous zones of, 24
  faking orgasms, 216–22
  on large penis versus oral sex, 215
  making your first time a great time, 143–49

personal responsibility for orgasm, 82, 86, 124–25
responding to man's ED, 213
sensations felt during orgasm, 14–15
sexual issues of, 8–9
uncertainty about having an orgasm, 64–67
See also girls; lesbian sex

Y
yeast infections, 97, 111, 135

The authors of this
book are pleased to donate 10
percent of their royalties to Breast
Cancer Action, one of the smartest, savviest
organizations confronting the cancer epidemic
and working toward true cancer prevention. To
join their national grassroots movement, get
involved at www.bcaction.org.

BREAST
CANCER
ACTION

Do you
♥ female orgasm?
Get a T-shirt or button and
tell the world! Men's and women's shirts
available at www.ilovefemaleorgasm.com.